LAST
CHANCE
TO SAVE
AMERICAN
DEMOCRACY

For a
country &
world,

Scott

LAST CHANCE TO SAVE AMERICAN DEMOCRACY

*Republicans Will Permanently Take Power in the
2022-2024 Elections Unless Democrats Follow This Plan*

HAVEN SCOTT McVARISH

5Journeys
—MEDIA—

5Journeys
—M E D I A—

10736 Jefferson Blvd #947
Culver City, CA 90230
media@5Journeys.media
www.5Journeys.media

Last Chance to Save American Democracy
© 2020 by Haven Scott McVarish

Development editing by: Ann Maynard of Command + Z Content

Other editing by: Linda Havens

Line editing, proofreading, and interior book design provided by Indigo: Editing, Design, and More:
- Line editor: Kristen Hall-Geisler
- Proofreaders: Cooper Lee Bombardier and Laura Garwood
- Interior book designer: Vinnie Kinsella
www.indigoediting.com

Cover design: P. KARTIK REDDY

Paperback ISBN: 978-1-7358191-0-5
Hardback ISBN: 978-1-7358191-2-9
Ebook ISBN: 978-1-7358191-1-2

You can put party first, country first, or democracy first.
I dedicate this book with gratitude for and solidarity with those who
put democracy before party or country.
And especially to Betsy, who is my favorite one of those people.

CONTENTS

PART 1

All Patriotism Is Fake Unless a Love of Democracy Is at Its Center 1

PROLOGUE 3

INTRODUCTION 5

CHAPTER 1
Understand That the 2016 Trump Victory Was an Unintended Result of
the GOP's Seven-Year Attack on Democracy 13

CHAPTER 2
Understand That Elections ≠ Democracy 23

CHAPTER 3
Understand Why the GOP Has Almost Ended American Democracy 41

PART 2

Your Warning: Democracy Won't End with Tanks Rolling Down
DC Streets 65

CHAPTER 4
Understand the GOP's Four Weapons Used to Almost End American
Democracy 67

CHAPTER 5
Understand How Democrats Will Not Save American Democracy on
Their Own 117

CHAPTER 6
We Just Want a Better World; Is That So Difficult? 135

PART 3

Democrats Won't Save Democracy Unless You—the Reader—Organize
for It 141

CHAPTER 7
#DemRevPlan Solutions 1-7: Let the Majority Govern.............................. 143

CHAPTER 8
#DemRevPlan Solutions 8-9: Fulfilling Democracy's Promise to Those Hurt
in the GOP Attacks Against Democracy 193

CHAPTER 9
#DemRevPlan Solutions 10–12: Democracy Needs Truth 203

CHAPTER 10
Plan B: Balance of Power Party 217

CHAPTER 11
Understand What You Must Do in 2020–2021 Since It's Up to You to Save
Democracy 221

APPENDICES

APPENDIX 1
Teams and Assets Tips 239

APPENDIX 2
Allies Programs Tips 245

APPENDIX 3
Scripts Tips 247

APPENDIX 4
Meeting Congressional Democrats Tips 253

APPENDIX 5
Democracy Revival Camp January 18–22, 2021, Tips 261

APPENDIX 6
Hosting DemRev Parties Tips 263

APPENDIX 7
Last Chance to Save American Democracy One-Pager 265

APPENDIX 8
#DemRevPlan One-Pager 267

APPENDIX 9
Republicans Will Fight a Democracy Revival in 2021 Using These Three
Tactics 269

APPENDIX 10
Republicans Brand Democrats Like a Cowboy Brands a Heifer;
Democrats, Not So Much 275

ABOUT THE AUTHOR 279

PART 1

All Patriotism Is Fake Unless a Love of Democracy Is at Its Center

PROLOGUE

Obama was playing by rules that the other side was not. That has been a dilemma for the Democrats for a while now. The Democrats are still playing by normal standards and the Republicans have only one thing in mind, and that is to wield and hold onto power, period.

—David Maraniss, Pulitzer Prize-winning journalist[1]

Grateful to Be Lucky

I was born in the United States, but my American citizenship is just luck. I could have been born in the crowded streets of Mumbai or the killing plains of South Sudan. I could have been raised under an authoritarian government in Beijing, Moscow, or Havana. I could have had my family and career under the watchful theocratic governments of Saudi Arabia or Iran, or fifteenth-century Spain for that matter. My US citizenship beginning in 1969 was random luck.

For that I am so grateful.

Do you understand how lucky you are as well? You can read this book, which attacks our government, post videos about it on YouTube, or tweet about it with no negative consequences other than Russian trolls and your reactionary cousin perhaps.

You did nothing to deserve being born in a democracy, nor did I. Maybe you think it was karma, earned reincarnation, or God's will that gave us this opportunity. But don't fall for that trap. That's how some of the richest and most powerful in our society justify saying that there was a plan for them to be born into the top 1% of the world in wealth and comfort. Accordingly, under this view, they are justified in not being concerned about the other 99% who deserve their lower caste in society.

Other than Native Americans and descendants of enslaved peoples, most of us were born in the United States due to the risks and sacrifices taken by immigrants—either our parents or generations before them. But when our democracy is threatened, it is *our* freedom and opportunities that are threatened. The important question is, are you doing anything to protect the democratic system and all of the freedoms and opportunities that are given to us?

I tried. I failed. And that's where our story starts.

Note

1.   Chauncey DeVega, "Biographer and Journalist David Maraniss on Trump, Obama and History Turned 'Upside down.'" Salon, 3 Jan. 2020, www.salon.com/2020/01/03/biographer-and-journalist-david-maraniss-on-trump-obama-and-history-turned-upside-down/.

INTRODUCTION

They actually intentionally give you those lists of people that have something to do with your committees, because they know that they're the ones that are most likely to say yes…. It makes prostitutes out of our elected officials. When the leadership says, if you want to advance, you have to demean yourself and go over there at taxpayer time and make phone calls to people that don't even want to talk to you, asking them for money for your party so that you can somehow advance the cause of "good government."

—Representative Zach Wamp (R-TN)[1]

I had just finished my third debate during the 2018 Democratic primary for Congress. Excuse the brag, but I had won the debate hands down yet again. Incredibly, I was the only candidate talking about the need to impeach Trump while the others were parroting Democratic Party talking points on health care. But on the ride back home, I turned to my wife and said, "I don't want to go to Congress. I'm done."

That afternoon before the debate, I had had a come-to-Jesus moment with the head of my fundraising staff. He was tired of my moaning about the cold calls I was making to raise money. So he laid it all out for me. What he told me made me sick to my stomach. And though I had managed successful campaigns for a dozen local candidates, his words led me to understand how naive I was about American politics. At that moment, I decided that getting elected to Congress was a hell of a lot worse than quitting the campaign.

What currently passes for campaigning in American democracy will give you a view into the larger problem facing our country. To win, almost all candidates must spend their entire campaign begging rich people and their political action committees (PACs) for money. The candidates who attract the most rich donors or supporters have the greatest shot at winning. The candidates who are then elected are expected to follow their party's approach to advance the interests—whether financial or ideological—of those rich donors. This is the focus of chapter 3.

Any viable congressional candidate in a competitive media market must raise at least $750,000 by the time of the primary. They do this by making calls to people seven or eight hours per day, five or six days per week, and asking for money. They have a call manager at their side to speed up the process. The candidate operates from a tight script; there's no real discussion with these potential donors because there are too many calls to make. The vast majority of these people are strangers to the candidate and often do not even live in their district. The minimum the candidate seeks is $500, but the aim is $2,700, or $5,400 if they are married.

That's pretty much the entire campaign until sixty days before the vote. There are some public events, but they take up no more than five to ten hours per week, compared to the forty-plus hours per week of calls. Practically no time is spent connecting with voters, hearing their concerns, or discussing issues with them.

All candidates for Congress are telemarketing fundraisers. All of this is caused by the Republicans' first Weapon Against Democracy, covered in chapter 4. For those of us who don't like the act of telemarketing, it's pretty demoralizing. My chief fundraiser had previously run the fundraising operation for the Democrats' House of Representatives' members. This was his come-to-Jesus talk:

If you win the race, the real fundraising begins. The amount of money you can raise as a newly elected congressman in the first three months after your election will determine which committees you get appointed to. How much money you raise each quarter will define your level of influence within your party's caucus. So on most days when Congress is in session, you will join with the other members of Congress from your party in a room across from the capitol. You will sit in a cubicle with your call manager. And you make calls all day asking for money. At the end of the week, you will fly back to your district and hold multiple fundraisers unless you have one scheduled in some hotel lobby in DC. At night during the week, you will often go to fundraisers, usually thrown by corporate lobbyists. That's what you do as a congressman. The more you do, the more you get ahead in the party. Are you ready for that?

I was not.

I complained to my fundraiser that members of Congress were basically cash cows for their parties. He told me I had to win in order to change the system. I then asked him, "How many of your candidates have you told that to?" He replied, "All of them." I asked, "And how many try to change the system once elected?" And he just smiled and said, "Well, that's really a leadership issue."

There's the rub.

The buying of politicians will be difficult to stop because the ones who have received the most money—that is, the leaders of each party—have no incentive to stop it.

Powerful politicians owe their power to being star fundraisers. Why would they change the system that has enabled them to get ahead? How else do you think the most uncharismatic American in public office—Mitch McConnell—is the second most powerful politician in the country? Or how do Senator Chuck Schumer of New York and Speaker Nancy Pelosi of California stay the leaders of the Democratic Party despite leading their party to defeat in the 2010, 2012, 2014, and 2016 congressional elections? Chapter 5 goes into greater detail on these types of political challenges Democrats face internally as they struggle to save democracy.

This is the part of running for Congress that keeps most good people from running. You have to be a special type of person who is comfortable with constantly begging rich people for money. Congress now is in session only two days per week, and they fundraise the other five.[2] As Colorado congressman Ken Buck has stated, as a member of the House Committee on Rules, he is expected to "pay" $450,000 in dues to his party: "So you pay dues to a private, partisan organization to serve in government…$450,000 means that a member has to hold receptions in Washington, DC. Who comes to those receptions with checks? Lobbyists [and] special interests that want something in return."

I guess I missed how this all works when I watched Schoolhouse Rock's "I'm Just a Bill."

Congress has become a financial club whose membership fees are extremely high and paid for by others.

There been few candidates for Congress as reluctant as me. My law firm had been growing and was rated in the top three for immigration law firms in Los Angeles. My wife and I were planning to have another child (we ended up having twins), and I had worked on enough campaigns to know the sacrifice a family makes during elections. But I saw what Trump was doing to the country. I felt like Democratic leaders were passively normalizing Trump by not seeking his impeachment. Waiting for Mueller was their terrible plan, as I noted on the campaign trail to applause, because it was not Mueller's job to defend democracy. It is all of our jobs. This is the focus of chapter 2.

Besides my decade-long involvement in community organizing and leading political campaigns, I ran one of the biggest unions in California and have spent my life as a part-time political activist. I've been a Democratic delegate to the California convention, written a previous book on political movements, and run a nonprofit dedicated to saving democracy. I have an MA and a JD from the UCLA's Department of Public Policy and its School of Law. I've spent many sleepless nights over the current political state of our country, determined to find solutions. But I have to tell you, I was ignorant when it came to the actual job of a member of Congress—namely, to be a full-time fundraiser. Don't feel bad if this is as surprising—and demoralizing—to you as it was to me.

After selling my law firm and getting quarantined during a pandemic, I had the space to focus on cutting through the smog that is obscuring what happened to our elections—and to our democracy. More importantly, I had the time to figure out a way to fix it. That's why I wrote this book.

Everybody else seems focused on the travesty that is the Trump presidency right now. I get it. His narcissism is unbelievable. There's a never-ending parade of scandals and failed appointees. The Trump family and members of his administration are more interested in leveraging the government for their personal financial gain than actual governance.[3] Despite his insistence that he has complete authority over our country, he repeatedly claims he has no responsibility for his administration's failed response to COVID-19. And as the November 2020 election draws closer, his fear of losing is accelerating his drive toward authoritarianism.

I hope you enjoyed that previous paragraph, because the rest of the book is free of Trump bashing (relatively speaking). Yes, he is the epitome of all that is wrong in politics, our country, and the world. But he rode into power because of the GOP's attacks on democracy during the first half of the 2010 decade. He did not orchestrate those attacks—notwithstanding his racist birtherism aiming to delegitimize President Obama. And even if his unhealthy lifestyle and refusal to wear a mask result in his death from COVID-19 before this book is published, the GOP's 4 Weapons Against Democracy (unlimited dark money, extreme partisan gerrymandering, voter suppression, and diversionary propaganda) would remain as powerful as ever.

If Trump is no longer in the White House come January 2021, the GOP's 4 Weapons Against Democracy will still blow up and destroy the Democratic Party on November 8, 2022, around eight p.m. Pacific Standard Time. That is when we will learn the outcome of the first midterm election when Trump is no longer on the ballot. That will be the moment when Democrats are thrown out of government yet again. But this time it won't just be for one decade; it will be forever. Yes, we will continue to have elections, but as explored in chapter 2, elections do not mean we have a democracy.

The window to prevent this 2022 wipeout is extremely small. On November 8, 2022, the dismantling of democracy will be complete, regardless of who is in the White House. From that point on, we will be forever ruled by Republicans despite the popular will. Simply put, the Democrats will never govern again. As the November 2020 election shapes up to be another blue wave, Democrats can't imagine losing it all so quickly as I am predicting. Democrats could not have imagined that they would have lost all their gains made from the Obama landslide in 2008. But they were summarily tossed out of power just twenty-four months later.

Given Trump's actions during the summer of 2020, it is important to distinguish his particular drive to become the authoritarian leader of the US from the Republican elites' effort to keep Republicans in power despite the popular will. They are two separate efforts. Even if Trump is ejected from the White House, the efforts of the Republican elites continue. If Trump manages to steal the election, then the efforts of the Republican elites will just be subsumed under the new Trump regime. Either way, democracy will end in the United States after the 2022 mid-term election.

It's our duty as citizens of a democracy to come to grips with this. In fact, if we consider democracy to be more important than country or party, it is our number-one priority. We must understand what the heck happened in the 2010 decade. Then we must act on the opportunity afforded by the repulsion to Trump that the majority of America feels and fix our democracy in 2021. Otherwise, mark 11/8/2022 on your calendar now as the death knell for democracy.

The plan to save our democracy is laid out in chapters 7–10 of this book. I call it the #DemRevPlan. If *we* force Democrats in Congress to follow it, American democracy will be strengthened in powerful, yet common sense ways. Furthermore, Democrats would consistently hold a six- to ten-member majority in the Senate, continually win 60% of the House, and control the White House and Supreme Court at least 80% of the time (unless, of course, their policies are rejected by Americans and Republicans begin to offer actual alternatives).

If you are thinking, "Surely if the stakes were as high as this book suggests, we'd be warned," consider this book your warning. We either save democracy in 2021, or we lose it based on our inaction.

Who Is This Book For?

1. If you're tired of Democrats losing elections or not having power, this will show you how Democrats can be in power for the next decade or two.
2. If you feel like all of your activism has gained very little for the cause, you will now have the solutions to revive our democracy, which will finally enable your advocacy efforts to be successful.
3. If you're just absolutely done with people like Trump and McConnell being the leaders of our country, this is for you. Without the solutions in part 3, McConnell will retake the Senate in 2022 and Donald Trump Jr. will take the White House in 2024.

4. If you want a more progressive country—fans of dear Bernie Sanders and Alexandria Ocasio-Cortez—this book will show you what must be done first. Once we have these significant Democratic majorities, Democrats won't have to govern from the center-right.

5. If you would like a return to bipartisanship—allies of future president Biden—this book will show you what must be done first. Because until we disarm the GOP of its 4 Weapons Against Democracy, Republicans will have zero incentive to cooperate in governing the country.

6. If you do not know what to do or how to get involved, we give you the detailed, step-by-step action plan. You can be part of this historic moment in saving democracy for this generation and the next. We cannot wait to see what you do.

So let's start this book at the point when 53.9% of the country got a rude awakening. A night in 2016 that no one will ever forget.

Notes

1. Sharyl Attkisson, Sinclair Broadcast Group. "'Full Measure: The Price of Power." KTUL, 29 May 2017, ktul.com/news/connect-to-congress/full-measure-the-price-of-power.

2. Derek Willis et al., "How Congress Stopped Working." *ProPublica*, www.propublica.org/article/how-congress-stopped-working.

3. Bob Brigham, "Trump Knows He Going to Lose and He's Scooping up as Much Cash as He Can before He's Ousted: Ex-White House Official." Raw Story, 25 July 2020, www.rawstory.com/2020/07/trumps-knows-he-going-to-lose-and-hes-scooping-up-as-much-cash-as-he-can-before-hes-ousted-ex-white-house-official/.

CHAPTER 1

Understand That the 2016 Trump Victory Was an Unintended Result of the GOP's Seven-Year Attack on Democracy

I am quite sure I will never forget Election Night 2016. We were in a room full of a thousand Culinary Workers Union members and activists in Vegas, ready to celebrate the election of the first woman president in the United States. The night ended in catastrophic disappointment. My wife and I then made the long drive back to Los Angeles with a carload of Clinton volunteers as Trump's victory became official. We were in disbelief. And in tears.

Our country—our neighbors—had elected a sexual predator whose campaign to the White House was based on the racist demonization of hardworking immigrants. As the months painfully went by and his policies began to hurt more and more people, I alternated between anger and disbelief.

- Anger that Trump had welcomed Russian interference into our election and was not held accountable
- Anger at his defense of racists and Nazis
- Anger that he pushed tax breaks that will let his family save almost a billion dollars[1] while it's harder to get or stay in the middle class for the rest of us
- Anger that while the planet burns, Trump's golfing at his resort has already cost taxpayers over $133,000,000[2] while he fools his supporters by constantly bragging that he's forsaking his $400,000 presidential salary
- Frustration at Democrats in the 2016 election—and the media—who kept focusing on health care but stayed virtually silent regarding how Republicans have crippled majority-rules democracy and the people's power of voting

- Anger that Trump was assassinating leaders in other countries to invite a war against Iran simply to distract us from his own impeachment
- Fear that so many more people will die as Trump first denied the importance of COVID-19, then focused more on the blame game than actually fighting the virus
- Outrage as Trump seemed to oppose the media, protestors, and Democratic Party leaders more than he opposed brutal dictators such as North Korea's Kim Jong-un or Russia's Vladimir Putin

A lot of this is personal for me. I have spent my entire career working on issues of immigrants' and union rights and improving public schools, and my wife has worked on health care, disability, and employment rights. My anger, though, isn't just at Trump.

I am angry at Democrats for failing again. I realized that night in Las Vegas that Democratic leaders will not save us. They do not have a plan, at least one that will work against the Republican's 4 Weapons Against Democracy detailed in chapter 4. It will be up to us—the cliched "we the people"—to save ourselves. Since that election, I have dedicated myself to understanding how Republicans could keep winning elections after embroiling us in two fruitless and horrific wars and the Great Recession in the 2000s, then doing nothing but obstruct Obama, vote to repeal Obamacare, and investigate Hillary Clinton's emails in the 2010s.

How could Republicans have gone from forty senators to controlling the Senate and House for eight years? How could the Democrats have lost the White House running against Trump, the most unfit person to ever be a party nominee?

Republicans won the House elections in 2010, 2012, 2014, and 2016 and the Senate elections (or at least gained seats) in 2010, 2012, 2014, 2016, and 2018. Were they really more popular than Democrats during this time?

This book is a result of my deep dive into understanding the answers to these questions. And the answers are even more disturbing than the prospect of Trump's re-election in 2020. Things are far worse than our Democratic leaders are talking about publicly.

Before we go any further, let's look at what happened in the 2010 decade. The rest of the book expands on some of these points at greater length. But I want you to get up to speed as fast as possible to understand just how *unusual* the Republicans' reversal of fortune was after they got wiped out in 2008.

What Happened to Democracy in the 2010 Decade

In 2008, the United States felt like a democracy full of opportunities and freedoms. So many of us were fighting to expand those opportunities and freedoms for all. After eight years of President George W. Bush and recession and wars, our country demanded change. We elected Barack Obama as president. The coalition that elected him was growing demographically and was set to prevent the party of Bush and recessions from governing for a generation or more.

Fearing that outcome, Republican billionaire funders understood they needed to change state and national laws so that their party could stay in power even though a shrinking minority of Americans supported them.[3] They used three weapons to attack free and fair elections: First, they financially supported lawsuits that led to a Republican-dominated Supreme Court changing how elections could be funded. Thus, beginning in 2010, giant corporations and billionaires started dumping unprecedented sums of money into state and national elections with no transparency. Republicans were able to massively outspend Democrats in key battleground elections, sometimes 20 to 1.

Because of this—not because of Obamacare, as I show below—the GOP swept into power in state and federal government in 2010 throughout the United States. Second, once the *Citizens United* decision enabled them to buy majorities in states where they only had minority support, they had to take further measures to keep those majorities. Accordingly, they changed election maps in 2011 by concentrating Democratic voters into fewer districts. This made it almost impossible for Democrats to win majorities in many states or in Congress as a whole. Third, once they had voter-proof majorities, they then began targeting Democratic Party supporters in Republican-controlled states by purging voter rolls and making it difficult for groups in the Obama coalition to both register to vote and cast a vote. Fourth, they used a sophisticated scheme to hide those three Weapons Against Democracy. They ran what amounts to a counterintelligence program aimed at keeping the media, the public, and even the Democratic Party focused on anything but the GOP's 4 Weapons Against Democracy.

Because of those 4 Weapons Against Democracy, the Republicans maintained majorities in state and federal governments starting in 2010, despite having fewer voters supporting them than Democrats.[4, 5, 6]

Because of those Republican majorities, bad things began happening. Our country went backward in many ways in the 2010s: It became harder to buy a home, harder to find a steady job, harder to pay for college. For most of the country, income, wealth, and life expectancy stagnated during this decade.

Politically, President Obama's agenda was stalled for the last six years of his presidency. Republicans then constantly criticized him for being slow to clean up the wars and recession he inherited from Bush. He accomplished almost nothing that was on the wish list of Democrats or progressives, despite being re-elected with massive support from the electorate. Republican senate majority leader Mitch McConnell of Kentucky was even able to stop him from appointing federal judges, including to the Supreme Court during his second term.

Meanwhile, Republican candidate Donald Trump was able to solicit Russian help with his own election to succeed Obama, and later—with Republicans safely in the majority—get away with it. White supremacist movements began growing again. Mass slaughter due to gun violence continued unabated in our schools and communities, yet Congress did not pass a single piece of gun-control legislation. Tax breaks were targeted to help super-rich Americans—the vast majority of whom are Republicans or Republican donors[7]—gain more of the nation's wealth than at any time in history. And no progress was made on major social and economic issues such as global climate change, racism, immigration, health care, homelessness, or so many others.

Then came COVID-19. The incompetence and corruption of Republicans unnecessarily cost America 150,000 lives in its first five months. Add in ongoing deaths of Black Americans at the hands of the police and Trump's repression of peaceful protestors, and now, at the dawn of the 2020s, people are pissed. And awake.

On the political right and on the left, it's clear to all that we have a dysfunctional government. Our investments in critical infrastructure, such as education, science, and even bridges, have decreased. Storms and fires rage out of control due to climate change, and our government does nothing. There's more intolerance and attacks on "the other." Our country is in decline both domestically and internationally. Our response to the pandemic of COVID-19 has been piecemeal at best and months too late. Trump has accelerated the decline of America so quickly that his red hats saying "Make America Great Again" are best read as mocking irony.

This decline is a direct result of the power shift away from Democrats in 2008. People forget, though, just how huge that power shift was.

Think back to 2008. That election was bigger than one Democratic president. President Obama won the Electoral College 365–173 and won the popular vote by 9.5 million votes. Democrats held a supermajority in the Senate (60–40 advantage), a significant House of Representatives majority, and twice as many blue-governed states than red.

Reread that paragraph. It's vital to understand how big the Democratic majority was in order to understand what happened in 2010 that reversed all of that. It's also important because if the Democrats win big in 2020, they will likely fall into the same trap of a lazy triumphalism. They imagine that they will stay in power for the foreseeable future and forget the lesson of 2010.

It seemed that after 2008, we—just like the abolitionists of the late nineteenth believed—would see the arc of history bending toward justice.[8] It hasn't. This is because justice is only present in a democracy. Since 2008 there has been a sustained attack on American democracy that very few people seem to understand and upon which almost no elected Democrat stays publicly focused.

In 2008 it was clear that the Democrats were secure in their role as our country's governing party. The believed it would be lasting like President Franklin Roosevelt's majorities seventy years earlier. Political experts were looking at the demographic changes ahead and noting that the Democratic Party's advantage would continue to grow steadily.

But instead, Republicans clawed back starting in 2010. (See Figure 1.)

In 2008 the Democrats held more than 4,000 state legislative seats, while the Republicans held 3,200. In sixteen states Democrats held the governor's mansion and both state houses, while Republicans held only nine

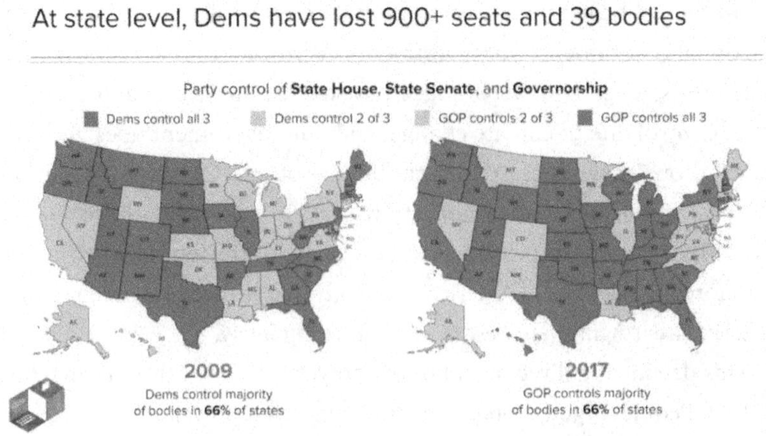

At state level, Dems have lost 900+ seats and 39 bodies

Figure 1. Source: Tech for Campaigns www.techforcampaigns.org; Heilweil, Rebecca. "This Silicon Valley Organization Aims To Flip Red States Blue." *Forbes*, Forbes Magazine, 8 June 2017, www.forbes.com/sites/rebeccaheilweil1/2017/06/07/this-silicon-valley-organization-is-working -to-flip-red-states-blue/#67ce3ab8206c

trifectas. After the Republicans unleashed Weapon #2—the gerrymandering of 2011—Democrats lost almost 1,000 state legislative seats (on top of seats lost in 2010). By 2017, Republicans had twenty-six trifectas and Democrats only six—a swing of twenty-five state trifectas in seven years. Yet during this same time Obama was re-elected and Hillary Clinton received three million more votes than Trump—beating him by more than 2%. In this same period, the Republicans had not a single legislative accomplishment other than shutting down the government, thanks to Senator Ted Cruz of Texas.

The "enduring majority" of the Democrats only lasted for two years. Why? Was it that Obama's policies turned out to be unpopular? He was re-elected in 2012 against his well-funded and highly respected opponent Massachusetts governor Mitt Romney. The false narrative that voters rejected Democrats for Obamacare or because Democrats overreached is easily dispelled by looking at the polling on the congressional generic ballots just months before those elections in 2010, 2012, 2014, and 2016. (See Figure 2.)

Despite the polling showing that the Democrats were well positioned to win those elections, they ended up losing all of those elections. The polling shows there was not a sustained upwelling of anti-Democratic-Party sentiment throughout these years. In fact, it shows the opposite. On the whole, the majority of Americans wanted Democrats to govern from 2008 to 2020. Yet the Democrats lost seats or their majority, or remained in the

2010

FOX News	6/8-6/9	900 RV	38	41	Democrats +3
PPP (D)	6/4-6/7	650 RV	41	43	Democrats +2
ABC News/Wash Post	6/3-6/6	RV	44	47	Democrats +3
Gallup	5/31-6/6	1600 RV	46	46	Tie

2012

Bloomberg	6/15-6/18	734 LV	41	48	Democrats +7
Rasmussen Reports	6/11-6/17	3500 LV	45	38	Republicans +7
Pew Research	6/7-6/17	1563 RV	43	47	Democrats +4
Reuters/Ipsos	6/7-6/11	848 RV	44	47	Democrats +3

2014

FOX News	7/20-7/22	1057 RV	41	43	Democrats +2
Rasmussen Reports	7/21-7/27	3500 LV	39	41	Democrats +2
CNN/Opinion Research	7/18-7/20	899 RV	44	48	Democrats +4
Pew Research	7/8-7/14	1420 RV	45	47	Democrats +2
Rasmussen Reports	7/14-7/20	3500 LV	39	39	Tie
Rasmussen Reports	7/7-7/13	3500 LV	38	39	Democrats +1
Quinnipiac	6/24-6/30	1446 RV	39	41	Democrats +2
Rasmussen Reports	6/30-7/6	3500 LV	38	41	Democrats +3
Rasmussen Reports	6/23-6/29	3500 LV	38	40	Democrats +2
FOX News	6/21-6/23	1018 RV	42	42	Tie
CBS News/NY Times	6/20-6/22	RV	39	42	Democrats +3
Rasmussen Reports	6/16-6/22	3500 LV	38	40	Democrats +2
Rasmussen Reports	6/9-6/15	3500 LV	37	39	Democrats +2
Bloomberg	6/6-6/9	763 LV	43	43	Tie
Rasmussen Reports	6/2-6/8	3500 LV	37	41	Democrats +4
FOX News	6/1-6/3	1006 RV	43	39	Republicans +4
ABC News/Wash Post	5/29-6/1	RV	45	47	Democrats +2
Rasmussen Reports	5/26-6/1	3500 LV	38	41	Democrats +3
Rasmussen Reports	5/19-5/25	3500 LV	38	42	Democrats +4
CBS News	5/16-5/19	RV	39	40	Democrats +1
Rasmussen Reports	5/12-5/18	3500 LV	37	41	Democrats +4
FOX News	5/10-5/13	1025 RV	40	43	Democrats +3
Rasmussen Reports	5/5-5/11	3500 LV	38	40	Democrats +2
CNN/Opinion Research	5/2-5/4	911 RV	46	45	Republicans +1
Rasmussen Reports	4/28-5/4	3500 LV	37	41	Democrats +4
Gallup	4/24-4/30	RV	44	49	Democrats +5
ABC News/Wash Post	4/24-4/27	855 RV	44	45	Democrats +1

Figure 2. Source: Real Clear Politics (RealClearPolitics.com).

2016

NBC News/Wall St. Jrnl	11/3-11/5	1282 LV	47	44	Democrats +3
McClatchy/Marist	11/1-11/3	940 LV	48	47	Democrats +1
Economist/YouGov	10/30-11/1	1228 LV	46	41	Democrats +5
Reuters/Ipsos	10/29-11/2	1858 LV	42	41	Democrats +1
CBS News/NY Times	10/28-11/1	1333 RV	49	46	Democrats +3
Economist/YouGov	10/22-10/26	1209 LV	45	40	Democrats +5
FOX News	10/22-10/25	1221 LV	47	45	Democrats +2
ABC News	10/22-10/24	828 LV	47	46	Democrats +1
Associated Press-GfK	10/20-10/24	1212 LV	46	41	Democrats +5
CNN/ORC	10/20-10/23	779 LV	50	47	Democrats +3
Reuters/Ipsos	10/20-10/24	1170 LV	44	39	Democrats +5
Economist/YouGov	10/15-10/18	925 RV	43	38	Democrats +5
Bloomberg	10/14-10/17	1006 LV	47	43	Democrats +4
Reuters/Ipsos	10/13-10/17	1190 LV	43	39	Democrats +4
CBS News	10/12-10/16	1189 LV	50	45	Democrats +5
NBC News/Wall St. Jrnl	10/10-10/13	905 LV	47	44	Democrats +3
ABC News/Wash Post	10/10-10/13	740 LV	47	44	Democrats +3
FOX News	10/10-10/12	917 LV	48	42	Democrats +6
GWU/Battleground	10/8-10/13	1000 LV	47	42	Democrats +5
NBC News/Wall St. Jrnl	10/8-10/10	900 RV	48	42	Democrats +6
Reuters/Ipsos	10/6-10/10	2363 A	46	36	Democrats +10
NBC News/Wall St. Jrnl	10/8-10/9	500 RV	49	42	Democrats +7
Economist/YouGov	10/7-10/8	971 RV	42	39	Democrats +3
Economist/YouGov	10/1-10/3	911 RV	43	37	Democrats +6
Reuters/Ipsos	9/29-10/3	1669 RV	42	38	Democrats +4
FOX News	9/27-9/29	911 LV	44	43	Democrats +1
Reuters/Ipsos	9/22-9/26	1041 LV	42	36	Democrats +6
Bloomberg	9/21-9/24	1002 LV	46	44	Democrats +2
Economist/YouGov	9/22-9/24	948 RV	43	38	Democrats +5
NBC News/Wall St. Jrnl	9/16-9/19	1000 RV	48	45	Democrats +3
McClatchy/Marist	9/15-9/20	758 LV	49	45	Democrats +4
Economist/YouGov	9/18-9/19	936 RV	43	36	Democrats +7
Reuters/Ipsos	9/15-9/19	1111 LV	39	40	Republicans +1
Economist/YouGov	9/10-9/13	926 RV	44	38	Democrats +6
Reuters/Ipsos	9/8-9/12	1752 A	40	38	Democrats +2
Economist/YouGov	9/4-9/6	955 RV	41	38	Democrats +3
Reuters/Ipsos	9/1-9/5	1084 LV	40	39	Democrats +1
CNN/ORC	9/1-9/4	786 LV	47	49	Republicans +2
GWU/Battleground	8/28-9/1	1000 LV	45	43	Democrats +2
McClatchy/Marist	8/1-8/3	983 RV	49	41	Democrats +8
NBC News/Wall St. Jrnl	7/31-8/3	800 RV	47	43	Democrats +4
PPP (D)	7/29-7/30	1276 LV	47	44	Democrats +3
FOX News	6/26-6/28	1017 RV	46	41	Democrats +5

Figure 2 (continued).

minority in both the Senate (2012–2020) and House (2011–2018) in those elections and lost the White House in 2016. The tide against the Democrats only turned in the last few months of each election.

Why is that? This tide turned because of Weapon #1 the GOP used in this past decade to significantly damage Americans' ability to choose who governs them: unlimited dark money.

In most of these elections, the cumulative votes for Democrats exceeded those for the Republican candidates, but the Republicans still won a majority of seats.[9, 10, 11] So how is it that Republicans have won ten of the last twelve federal elections after Obama's tidal wave in 2008 despite not having a majority of voters supporting them? Let's follow the money.

The richest of the Republican donors were able to eliminate campaign contribution limits in 2010 so that they could literally now spend hundreds of millions—instead of a few thousand—in support of their political goals. By enabling that surprise attack of secret money in November 2010, Republicans won key districts that they otherwise would not have won.

Then Republicans targeted just enough legislative and congressional districts to flip key states from Democrat-controlled to Republican-controlled and gain veto-proof majorities in Republican states. Knowing that their victories would have been short-lived, Republicans continued to build their firewall against the popular will. Through an extraordinary campaign of gerrymandering and voter suppression in a handful of these states, they maintained control of Congress and various state legislatures even when Democrats received more votes.

In this chaos of an undemocratic Congress, Russia was able to step in to help throw the 2016 election to Trump. After Trump seized power, he blocked any repercussions for Russia's hack of our democracy. He then sought continued help from Putin, his oligarchs, and even the new Ukrainian president—for which Democrats finally impeached Trump.

But you know all this, right?

What you don't know is what happens next.

1. Will Trump be re-elected in November 2020?
2. Or will there be such a massive rejection of Trump and his allies in Congress that Democrats win the White House and the Senate?
3. Most importantly, if there is a massive rejection of the Trump party,

will the new Democratic trifecta in the White House, Senate, and House of Representatives focus on fixing our democracy, or will they simply chase the most popular issues of the moment according to their polling or corporate media?

The actual existential crisis facing our democracy is whether or not we will continue to have free and fair elections where the majority decides who governs them.

Unlike other seminal political books of the Trump era, my focus is on that third question. Because, even though this seems counterintuitive, the current crisis is not just about Trump. In fact, he is our best opportunity.

Notes

1.   Mark Murray. "Trump and His Family Could Save More than $1 Billion under House Tax Bill." NBC News, 16 Nov. 2017, www.nbcnews.com/politics/first-read/trump-his-family -could-save-more-1-billion-under-house-n821491.

2.   Ryan Grenoble, "Trump Takes Heat For Golfing During Pandemic, Blames Obama For Some Reason." HuffPost, 26 May 2020, www.huffpost.com/entry/trump-blames -golf-obama_n_5ecd77cac5b6658c20604c9e.

3.   Jeffrey M. Jones, "Democrats' 2008 Advantage in Party ID Largest Since '83." Gallup.com, Gallup, 8 June 2017, news.gallup.com/poll/113947/democrats-2008-advantage-party-largest.aspx.

4.   "Election Statistics, 1920 to Present." US House of Representatives: History, Art & Archives, history .house.gov/Institution/Election-Statistics/Election-Statistics/.

5.   Paul Singer, "Democrats Won Popular Vote in the Senate, Too," USA Today, 10 Nov. 2016, www.usatoday.com/story/news/politics/onpolitics/2016/11/10/democrats-won-popular -vote-senate-too/93598998/.

6.   Dylan Matthews, "The Senate's 46 Democrats Got 20 Million More Votes than Its 54 Republicans," Vox, 3 Jan 2015, www.vox.com/2015/1/3/7482635/senate-small-states.

7.   "What Billionaires Want: The Secret Influence of America's 100 Richest." The Guardian, Guardian News and Media, 31 Oct. 2018, www.theguardian.com/us-news/2018/oct/30 /billionaire-stealth-politics-america-100-richest-what-they-want.

8.   This phrase, used by Obama and MLK, originally came from the abolitionist Theodore Parker, a Unitarian minister.

9.   "Election Statistics," US House.

10.   Singer, "Democrats Won."

11.   Matthews, "The Senate's 46 Democrats."

CHAPTER 2

Understand That Elections ≠ Democracy

Corrupting an election to keep oneself in office is perhaps the most abusive and destructive violation of one's oath of office that I can imagine.

—Republican Senator Mitt Romney, voting to convict President Trump[1]

Let's not pretend that Democrats are the victims of Republicans here. In fact, this past decade has seen the perfect storm against our democracy. Republicans, fearing they will never govern again, have completely turned their back on democracy. Democrats, focused on chasing big dollar donors, have stopped doing the hard work of democracy: a mobilization of people who are loyal to democracy and who work to protect it from internal or external threats.

We are at this bizarre period in American history. Our democracy quite literally hangs in the balance in the next two to three years. Yet most Americans have no idea this is going on. The silence of our political leaders is either because they are causing it—in the case of the Republicans—or because they do not think that issue polls high enough—in the case of the Democrats.

It's an upside-down political world. Democrat leaders rush to the media to denounce the latest Trump tweet or insult. They don't even comment, however, when it is announced in January 2020 that individuals can now give almost $600,000 per year directly to Trump's campaign committees to support his 2020 re-election. This amount is up from just under $6,000 before the 2010 *Citizens United* case. When Republican election officials in Wisconsin began purging over 200,000 voters from their rolls in January 2020—a state Trump only won by 22,000 votes—not a single Democratic candidate for president highlighted it in the debates. No Democratic Party leader flew to Wisconsin to rally with voters over this Republican assault on democracy. There are dozens of these failures by Democrats each year.

As you can tell, I am an unhappy member of the Democratic Party. I can level almost as many criticisms against the Democrats as I can against the Republicans. After all, they both take massive amounts of money from the super-rich in our country. Our political parties are really just fundraising machines competing against each other. It's no surprise that both parties mostly focus on what the richest and most powerful care about: tax policy, trade policy, interest rates, and other monetary policies affecting the financial markets.

Oh, and don't forget wars. There is pretty much always bipartisan support for any war. We've been in Afghanistan since 2001 with no end in sight—like the bipartisan Vietnam War of the 1960s and 1970s. As in Vietnam, there is a muddled strategy and complete lack of transparency on the real costs and massive deaths and injuries of the people who live Afghanistan:

> The war has cost the US $1 trillion and led to the loss of 2,300 troops and 20,589 wounded in action.... 775,000 US troops have deployed to Afghanistan, many repeatedly.... Over 157,000 lives have been lost in Afghanistan as a consequence of the US invasion and of these, 149,898 are Afghans.... That number, though, does not include Afghans wounded, displaced and/or traumatized by the war.[2]

Which party do you think is against this madness? Who knows? Neither has done anything to stop it even though Bush, Obama, and Trump have all at one time or another have declared "mission accomplished" or the war over. Which party is in favor of creating what I would call a "democracy alliance" of nations who remain democratically governed? And then incentivizing other nations to move to democracy by giving members of the alliance special status in military, trade, and immigration agreements? It appears neither. Both parties are just as comfortable with alliances with authoritarian countries as they are with democratic ones as long as our corporate profiteers are making money, forced labor be damned![3]

Two Parts to the American Soul

No, don't worry, I am not about to say that Democrats and Republicans in 2020 are the same morally or that Obama or Trump are remotely equivalent. But to make this book as "fair and balanced" as Fox News, ahem, allow me to highlight the good in both parties for a moment.

Ideally each party represents different parts of the American soul. One part of our nation's soul has been the history of the individual's rise to greatness by relying on their own ideas, hard work, and determination. The other part of our nation's soul has been about taking care of each other and our neighbors and communities. Hero lieutenant colonel Alexander Vindman (retired) said it succinctly:

> Since the struggle for our nation's independence, America has been a union of purpose: a union born from the belief that although each individual is the pilot of their own destiny, when we come together, we change the world. We are stronger as a woven rope than as unbound threads.[4]

These two parts of the American soul have split into the two opposing political parties, with the Republicans (of yesteryear) championing the rights of the individual to be free of government restraint, and the Democrats (at their best) championing the caring community. It's like John Wayne versus Mister Rogers—there's benefit in having both sides strengthened and nurtured, and both make great TV.

In 2020, however, both parties believe that the other side is evil. Democrats (myself included) think Republicans have become selfish and mean and that they subscribe to a media bubble controlled by billionaires that mislead them into believing that Republicans—the party of the rich—are on the side of everyday Americans. Worse, they've allowed their party of the rich be taken over by a cult of an authoritarian leader. I may not accuse my Trump-loving parents of doing that on the daily, but you know I'm thinking it. Meanwhile, Republicans think Democrats are socialists who want to take all their stuff and give it away to those who have not earned anything, especially if those people are immigrants, Black, gay, or Muslim.

It almost seems radical to say that both sides of the American soul need to be represented and valued. Sometimes the government does trample on the rights of individuals and needs to be pushed back. Can a Democrat claim that's not true? And sometimes innocent people are denied fair opportunities and need to be helped. Do all Republicans think that is anti-American? Those seem to be principles that both sides should agree on. Don't worry. This is not an idealistic, utopian book. The rest of the book is so hard-hitting that I had to get an attorney to review the book to make sure I wouldn't get sued. But before we move on, let's give some thought to something we take for granted but really is revolutionary and responsible for everything good about our country: our democracy.

Our first problem is that we have been miseducated about what it means to be a citizen of a democracy. The elected officials in power—and the media apparatus that supports their power—need for us to believe that the peaceful transfer of power after an election signifies that we have a democracy. As such our role in a democracy is to simply exercise our "right" to periodically vote. But voting does *not* equal democracy. Just ask Russians who know they will have Putin as president until 2036 no matter the numerous elections that will take place between now and then.[5]

The mistake here is two-fold. First, the concept of a "right to vote" reverses the actual power dynamic that a real democracy would have. Politicians do not give us the right to vote. Voting is the exercise of our power. That power is inherent and foundational to democracy; it goes far beyond a mere right or privilege. We temporarily give our power to the officials we elect. They do not, however, have the right to restrict our power. The Republican Party currently believes the opposite is true. That the government magnanimously gives us the right to vote—a right they can take away based on their notions of who should exercise that right.

Second, exercising our power to vote is the end game, not the whole game. A more primary role citizens have in a democracy is limiting the power of those we elect so that they do not infringe on our ultimate power to decide who will be our elected stewards. This may mean we organize, we protest, or—in the case of the Civil War and World War II—we take up arms. At this present time, voting is simply not enough to protect our power. If we are to save American democracy, we must each take action.

The Three Fundamental Principles of American Democracy

Let's take a test. Do you agree with these three fundamental principles?

1. We love our country because it is a democracy.
2. We cherish the power for all citizens to vote in free and fair elections and have the majority vote decide who governs us.
3. It is better to lose an election and have the other party govern us than for our party to stay in power through cheating or destabilizing democracy.

There are many people—Republicans and Democrats—that might not agree with those three fundamentals of our country. Such people are not patriots; they are ideologues. They would be happiest in an autocratic country, either a right-wing authoritarian country or a left-wing socialist country that has no real elections. Of course, eventually these ideologies will succumb to the tendency of wealth and power to concentrate in the hands of those who govern (whether capitalist, socialist, or theocratic), and then they will realize the errors of their ways. Eventually things go bad in autocratic countries because they are so poorly governed. Those ideologues will find that there is no freedom to criticize their government, advocate for change, or protect themselves from the state. We need free and fair elections to protect those free speech rights. And when citizens exercise free speech rights, it helps governments course correct and improve.

This book was written for the people who agree with all three principles above. Because, fellow democracy-hugger, we are facing a crisis in our democracy; we've lost the rule of law that set the parameters for free and fair elections. Democrats are the permanent minority party regardless of being supported by more Americans than support Republicans. The only exception will be during the first two years of Democrats controlling the federal government after the Trump backlash election of 2020. That is, unless we revitalize democracy in 2021.

Democracy Is Unnatural

Governments...deriv[e] their just powers from the consent
of the governed.

−The Declaration of Independence

For the more than six thousand years of "civilization," almost all territories, city-states, nations, and empires were led by unelected individuals or families. And while democracy has been an idea for over 2,500 years, starting in Athens, Greece, very few governments have adopted it since then. After just minor experiments with limited forms of democracy for more than two thousand years, the most important moment for democracy came in the late eighteenth century. England, France, and Italy all began to experiment with letting some people vote. But it was the colonies on the east coast of America who were overthrowing the English empire that revived the idea of democracy as the philosophic underpinning of government. The founding of the United States began a momentous change to over six thousand years of uniformly repressive political governance.

In 6,000 years of civilization, people currently living under democratic governments are part of less than 1% of humanity privileged to live in a "majority-rules" democracy.[6] By decentralizing power to "we the people," our country has allowed individuals to achieve greatness. It is the sole reason that anyone proclaims we are the greatest nation on Earth. Of course, that's objectively not true at this point in our history by almost any measure.[7] Regardless, we owe all we are, all we have achieved, and all that we have to having, more or less, a functional democracy.

American democracy was limited for its first 140 years, extending to less than half the population of adult citizens. First it was white, male landowners representing only 6% of Americans who were allowed to vote. Then all white American males could vote in the mid-nineteenth century. Then in 1868, the vote was extended to Black American males.[8] Fifty years later, women were finally granted the vote—though not all women. In the south and in other areas, Black Americans continued to face discrimination and were again denied the vote. That was perhaps the main objective of Martin Luther King Jr.'s campaigns—to restore power to all Americans through removing obstacles that politicians had placed on voting. The civil rights movement won the last great victory for voting in 1965 when Congress passed the Voting Rights Act.

This is the real history of the United States. This is what matters. We have this tremendous and wondrous gift of being so fortunate to live in a democracy. Are we grateful for that gift? Humbled by it? Forget the dates and anniversaries of most events, forget the names of most of our presidents, don't even bother learning the capitals of the forty-nine states you don't live in. But don't you dare forget that "what makes us special" is that so many people have fought and struggled to extend democracy and the power to vote. It took mass movements and decades of struggles by women, Black Americans, and their allies, including a civil war, to expand democracy in the United States to more or less the current level.

Everything you have, you owe to these activists and movements.

Our largest wars have all been against governments that denied their own citizens voting rights and democracy: the old empires and kings of Europe in World War I; the dictators in Germany, Italy, and Japan in World War II; the Communist forces of Vietnam; and the Taliban theocracy of Afghanistan. This is what the American flag symbolizes: the fight for democracy against those who seek to limit or eliminate it. That's why we can simultaneously salute the flag to acknowledge the fight for democracy and then "take a knee" to protest the forces within our own country who refuse to respect the power and dignity of all Americans.

In fact, it has been America's written policy to promote democracy and justice throughout the globe. Or it used to be. Trump changed that as well. Trump removed the words "promoting justice and democracy" from the State Department mission statement in 2017. In response, Republican Elliott Abrams, deputy national security advisor for Global Democracy Strategy under George W. Bush, remarked, "We used to want a just and democratic world, and now apparently we don't."[9]

We're Never Really Taught What Democracy Means

In the larger march of humanity and 6,000 years of civilization, our political system is very special. But are we where we should be after 240 years as a country whose central organizing principle is democracy?

According to the most comprehensive comparative study on democracies worldwide, the United States is now considered a "flawed democracy," ranked only as the twenty-fifth most democratic in the world.[10] Indeed, the political system in the United States is misaligned with common-sense concepts of democracy.

- We have filibusters that require 60% of votes to pass almost any bill in the Senate.
- We give the 40 million voters of California the same number of senators as the half million voters of North Dakota.
- The Electoral College allows a minority of voters to pick our president.
- One billionaire can impact politics with his bank account as much as the combined contributions from millions of regular citizens.
- Russian dictator Vladimir Putin was able to involve himself in our politics, get caught, and suffer no consequences with very little effort aimed at preventing it again.
- The super-rich pay massive armies of lobbyists to promote their interests. This results in zero legislation being passed unless the economic and business elites support it.
- Almost all House members are being re-elected for life no matter what their records are as legislators.
- Leaders of the parties and committees in Congress are being promoted solely due to their ability to raise funds.

Yes, it's maddening and disheartening.

But despite this litany of easy-to-fix flaws in our democracy, we all still feel reassured by the fact that we live in a democracy and so we reassure ourselves that everything is going to be okay. For those of us who are passionate about democracy and reject would-be authoritarian leaders, however, it feels like we have not been winning many battles since the 1970s. This last decade has been particularly difficult.

We need to ask ourselves: Are the issues that we support so unpopular that Democrats who embrace them simply aren't electable? Or have certain people effectively conspired to dismantle the safeguards of our democratic system so that our country is now undemocratic?

Let's take a step back. It's not controversial to note that we have little education about democracy; it's just part of our assumed identity as a nation: we have always had democracy, we always will have it, and we are the best democracy around. That pretty much sums up everything our school system seems to think we need to know. It's this last concept that is perhaps our greatest weakness: a lack of humility. We simply assume our system is the best. As such, our representatives in government spend no time cultivating ideas or reforms that could improve or protect our democracy, our elections, or our system of governance. In fact, they barely register a complaint when our democracy is chipped away little by little.

Whose Responsibility Is It to Protect Democracy Anyway?

Representative, majority-rules democracy is built on two rules: first, the majority of citizens decide who will govern them; second, those citizens temporarily transfer their power to representatives through a free and fair election.

That's it.

Carefully looking at these two rules allows us to see the current crisis more clearly. Our system increasingly is allowing the party—or candidate—with a *minority* of support and votes to win. This is true at both the federal and state level, as we will explore in chapter 4. The second idea of democracy—citizens temporarily transferring power to representatives—shows us whose responsibility it is to rectify the violation of the first idea: the majority of citizens decide who will govern them. It is the responsibility of citizens to fix democracy; it is *not* the responsibility of our representatives to protect democracy.

We as citizens living under a democracy have chosen to temporarily give our power to our representatives. The representatives simply accept as much as we allow them to gain. Right now, we have allowed them to gain a whole bunch of power. In fact, we have let Republicans have so much power that they can stay in government even when they receive fewer votes due to gerrymandering; we have allowed them to restrict our power to vote through burdensome ID requirements, limiting voting to one work day, or massive purges of voters; and we have allowed the incumbents of both parties to have access to so much money that only 3% of them lost in the 2016 election.[11]

In other words, these representatives have taken for themselves all the power that we let them take. That's on us. The more power we let them take, the less likely our representatives will intervene to protect democracy. This is predictable human nature. If you are elected because an undemocratic provision of law facilitated your election, you will protect that undemocratic provision of law. That's true for all but the rarest of leaders.

For instance, if you were a Republican in a district where many Democratic voters were denied the power of voting would you be in support of restoring those rights? If a billionaire secretly funded an untrue and unfair but effective attack on your opponent, would you fight to stop that billionaire from spending unlimited amounts of money on your next election?

In other words, don't look to politicians to protect democracy. Not even Democrats. They will protect their power.

Democracy has to be protected by the people who lent their power to their representatives. That's the 99.99% of us who do not hold political office. It's our responsibility. We are responsible to limit the power our elected officials have. And we must do that collectively and strategically. In part 3, I provide the plan to restore democracy and outline the collective actions we must take to make that happen.

If the citizens who temporarily give up their power to their representatives do not keep control over those representatives, the citizens will permanently lose their power.

The moment we the people don't value democracy—or we take it for granted—we will stop protecting it. Then those in power will consolidate their power and concentrate it into the hands of the few. That could be an oligarchy, a theocracy, or a corporate autocracy; it could be a king or a dictator; it could be an authoritarian right-wing government or a communist left-wing government. International history, particularly that of the last 100 or more years, shows it really doesn't matter. Parties and movements of the people—right or left wing—will morph into an authoritarian government if the people don't protect their democracy.

Revolutions are co-opted, religious leaders are morally compromised, reform-minded army generals become despots, revolutionary leaders devolve into the dictator they overthrew. It's hard for democracy to take root in any country because it's not the responsibility of those in power to protect it. In fact, it's against their own self-interest.

Democracy is not the norm in human civilization; authoritarianism or autocracy is the norm. President Trump certainly understands this and powerfully speaks to people's innate comfort with strong men. Powerful people prefer to concentrate power in their own hands and not dilute their power with democratic institutions. Fearful people will accept that concentration if they think they are getting something from the bargain. This is where every authoritarian leader tricks their citizenry. They usually careen from one crisis to another, from one enemy to another, or from one threat to another, so that the people are too fearful to focus on how much it sucks to not live in a democracy.

Or sometimes, they will just pretend that their country is a democracy. Look at Russia, Iran, Venezuela, and Turkey. In those countries, the majority of their citizens vote, but no outside observer would say they are democracies.[12] They are electoral authoritarian regimes. They have exciting and highly contested elections, but the outcome is predetermined. Everyone, at least on the outside, knows which party will win in the end. The opposition party always comes up short. Sort of like what happened to Democrats in the 2010s.

Since 2010—with the exceptions of Obama's re-election in 2012 and the House in 2018—it's the Republicans who stay in power in the United States regardless of the popular will. Republicans have won ten of the last twelve elections to determine who governs the three branches of the federal government. This is despite receiving fewer votes in the majority of those elections, as explained in chapter 4. (See Figure 3.)

Simply put, we have to work and fight for democracy. It is the price we have to pay if we don't want a dictator to make all the decisions for our society. We had to literally fight for it in the 1770s. In the Civil War a century later, our nation was again confronted with who should be considered citizens and who should be left out of our democratic processes, and certainly the 1940s it was democratic societies (plus the U.S.S.R.) versus fascist societies.

Democratic Party Results

	House	Senate	White House
2010	LOST	LOST	
2012	LOST	LOST	WON
2104	LOST	LOST	
2016	LOST	LOST	LOST
2018	WON	LOST	

Figure 3. Source: CommonSenseDem.org.

This fight in 2020–2021 will not be a war—despite the sporadic violence of white nationalists, boogaloos, QAnon, and Christian Identity followers—but it will take more than a tweet or voting against Trump to protect democracy from the current threat. You simply don't get the benefits of democracy without taking responsibility to protect it. At least not anymore.

What Will America Look Like If Trends Continue?

Trump is not a rupture at all, but rather the culmination—the logical endpoint—of a great many dangerous stories our culture has been telling for a very long time. That greed is good. That the market rules. That money is what matters in life. That white men are better than the rest. That the natural world is there for us to pillage. That the vulnerable deserve their fate and the 1% deserve their golden towers. That anything public or commonly held is sinister and not worth protecting. That we are surrounded by danger and should only look after our own.

—Naomi Klein, author of *No Is Not Enough: Resisting Trump's Shock Politics*[13]

The whole point of democracy is for a population to stop policies that act against their interest. When those to whom we lend our power—elected politicians—must worry about our reaction to their policies, better policies are created.

When those elected politicians must answer to a small group of individuals or companies that help elect them, then democracy doesn't work that well. That's an apt description of the current crisis in American democracy. We get policies that no one—except the funders of elections—want, such as handing out $1.9 trillion in tax breaks to the richest individuals and corporations and cutting funding to health insurance.[14] According to a poll as reported in *USA Today*, a paltry 12% of Americans in 2017 supported the health care plan proposed by Senate Republicans as an alternative to Obamacare yet they kept pushing for it.[15]

When the popular will no longer decides elections, those in power can do whatever they want, no matter how unpopular it is. This is especially true when the media acts in the interests of their political parties (in the case of Fox News and Sinclair) or in the interests of their corporate ownership (in the case of ABC, CBS, NBC, etc.). But just because Republicans attack the media, Democrats should not mindlessly defend the media. Democrats need to tackle the problem with corporate-dominated media behemoths, and Republicans have certainly invited us to do so. To quote Elizabeth Warren, "I have a plan for that" in part 3.

Before we solve all these problems, we need to better grasp the stakes. What will happen in the next decade or two if the majority of Americans are unable to control who governs their states or the country? It's simple. Republicans will twist the rules of the political system even further against the Democrats. One-party rule will be the inescapable norm—another decade of McConnell in power with a GOP-controlled presidency, House, and Supreme Court beginning in 2022–2024. It's easy to imagine that our society will look a lot more like the religious vision of an older fundamentalist man (be they Christian, Muslim, Hindu, or Jew) than a vibrant, multicultural, liberal America.

As those in power lose support from an increasing number of Americans, our leaders will have to resort to greater demagoguery and authoritarianism. For hundreds of years, authoritarian rulers have had to contend with the fact that their policies favoring the elite who support them will eventually incite the masses against them. There's a playbook on how they deal with this: demagoguery, scapegoating, suppression, blaming immigrants, and criminalizing as many actions as possible. It leans on what I call diversionary propaganda, where followers are prepped to reject facts in order to remain loyal to their leaders by accepting their lies. George Orwell wrote about it extensively in the 1940s, having seen so many governments in his time do it.

There are dozens of governments worldwide following that playbook right now. You can see Fox News and Trump adapt this playbook for this current generation. If the playbook's central myth could be summarized in one sentence, it would be: All our problems would be solved if a strong leader would restore our country to our (alleged) former glory even if certain groups will be forced to pay a high cost.

So what happens when the economy goes bad? The public gets angry. So what do you do if you are in power and there's almost no way for you to be thrown out of power? You have to redirect the anger. You do that by starting wars, blaming immigrants, and letting some of your supporters blame Jews. You blame Democratic governors and mayors. You become more divisive, more fearmongering, more hateful.

It's obvious that the future of the Republican Party—after Donald Trump—is not former governor of South Carolina and UN Ambassador Nicki Haley or the re-emergence of former Speaker Paul Ryan of Wisconsin. It's the even more spiteful Donald Trump Jr. At the start of 2020, he was polling just behind sitting Vice President Mike Pence as the heir apparent to his daddy.[16] And that's before the Trump-re-election machine for 2020 has even begun promoting Donald the Junior. Junior's spite does not seem calculated. It comes from a true authoritarian, supremacist perspective. So we have that to look forward to.

Supporting Junior in 2024 will be the only game plan left for Trump-loving Republicans. Otherwise they would face a reckoning over how their economic policies impoverish the nation through the concentration of wealth into the hands of its very richest benefactors. Even during the pandemic, while Americans lost so much, the super-rich gained enormous sums of money due to policies put into place by Republicans.[17] But if they focus on killing democracy, they can avoid that reckoning. They will just need to escalate their authoritarian tactics.

The more that Republicans are able to maintain control over government despite the popular will, the less happy Americans are with our democracy. A 2019 study from the University of Cambridge's Centre for the Future of Democracy highlighted this sad fact. Using the largest international dataset on global attitudes to democracy ever made, they found that Americans' dissatisfaction with democracy has been on the rise this past decade:

> The US has seen a "dramatic and unexpected" decline in satisfaction. In 1995, more than three-quarters of US citizens were satisfied with American democracy. The deterioration is almost exclusively seen in the 2010 decade. Now, less than half of US citizens are content with their democracy.... Such levels of democratic dissatisfaction would not be unusual elsewhere. But for the United States it may mark an end of exceptionalism.[18, 19]

This is another special moment in American history.

> "The arc of the moral universe is long," [King said,] but "it bends toward justice," if there is a steadfast commitment to see the task through to completion.
>
> —Supreme Court justice Ruth Bader Ginsburg[20]

Our hopes, successes, dreams, voice, creativity, ability to rise up—those are all due to the democracy that others protected for us. Many of us were not alive for the five greatest battles our country has fought to extend rights and protect freedom:

- The Revolutionary War gave us the right to decide who governs us.
- The Civil War ended slavery and temporarily smashed white supremacy.
- The suffragette movement gave women the power of voting.
- The Second World War stopped the Nazis, who wanted to end everyone's power to vote.
- The civil rights battles secured the power of the vote for African Americans.

These fights were about ensuring that more and more people could exercise their power as citizens to vote and help determine the leaders of their country. Republicans want to take that power away from just enough people to remain the governing party. That is the key point to understand. The GOP is not seeking to end elections; rather, they simply seek to stay in power no matter what the full electorate would want. The West Coast and East Coast don't really experience this attack on democracy firsthand. Every swing state or purple state with Republicans in power, however, is a target for the dark money, gerrymandering, voter suppression, and diversionary propaganda.

It would be nice to believe that simply supporting Democrats would be enough to get us out of this mess.

It is not. Not at all.

Getting Democrats into power is an essential first step, but it actually does nothing to save democracy, nor our country. Even if the Republicans have a temporary setback in November 2020, Trump is much less of a problem than the structures Republicans have put in place to ensure they will always remain in power in DC. We are at the end of free and fair elections in the United States. We would have already lost our democracy if not for the grotesque presidency of Trump that created the blue waves of 2018 and 2020. Yes, our elections will stay competitive, but when all the votes are counted—of the citizens who are allowed to vote and whose votes are not thrown out—Republicans will generally prevail. It's a one-party country—unless we act immediately and strategically.

The Democratic Party pats itself on the back and says it puts the country over party. But really its governance priorities put country over democracy. By doing so, it has relegated itself to a servant of the rich and it just holds its breath, hoping that it can compete with Republicans in elections. That's why it has been unable to enact policy for over ten years—since November 2010, to be precise. That's a long time. Republicans have not passed much legislation either, but that's due to incompetence and greed. The Trump tax giveaway to billionaires is about the only thing they passed this decade. But that one tax bill was the principle goal of those who sought to end majority-rules democracy in the first place. This just happens to be the subject of our next chapter.

So why would anyone want to end majority-rules democracy? Let's follow the money.

Notes

1. "'The President Is Guilty': Romney Votes to Convict Trump – Video." *The Guardian*, 5 Feb. 2020, www.theguardian.com/global/video/2020/feb/05/the-president-is-guilty-romney-will-vote-to-convict-trump-video.

2. Sophia A McClennen, "The Real Outrage of the Afghanistan War Papers That No One Wants to Talk About." *Salon*, 13 Dec. 2019, www.salon.com/2019/12/14/the-bombshell-revelations-in-the-afghanistan-war-papers-no-one-wants-to-talk-about/.

3. Vicky Xiuzhong Xu et al., "Uyghurs for Sale: Re-education, Forced Labor, and Surveillance beyond Xinjiang," International Cyber Policy Center, February 2020.

4. Alexander S. Vindman, "Coming Forward Ended My Career. I Still Believe Doing What's Right Matters." The Washington Post, 1 Aug. 2020, www.washingtonpost.com/opinions/2020/08/01/alexander-vindman-retiring-oped/.

5. Patrick Reevell, "Here's What It Means if Putin Rules until 2036," ABC News, 5 Jul 2020, abcnews.go.com/International/means-russia-putin-rules-2036/story?id=71609840.

6. Technically, the United States qualified as a majority-rules country only from 1966 (the first election after the Voting Rights Act) until 2009 (the last election before Citizens United, extreme gerrymandering, and massive voter suppression), but it was a great forty-five-year run.

7. Annalisa Merelli, "The US Has a Lot of Money, but It Does Not Look like a Developed Country." *Quartz*, 21 Mar. 2017, qz.com/879092/the-us-doesnt-look-like-a-developed-country/.

8. Grace Panetta, "Today Is National Voter Registration Day. The Evolution of American Voting Rights in 242 Years Shows How Far We've Come - and How Far We Still Have to Go," *Business Insider*, 24 Sept. 2019, www.businessinsider.com/when-women-got-the-right-to-vote-american-voting-rights-timeline-2018-10#1776-and-before-only-men-who-owned-property-who-were-mainly-white-christian-and-over-21-had-the-right-to-vote-1.

9. Josh Rogin, "State Department: What's so Great about Democracy, Anyway?" *Miami Herald*, 2 Aug. 2017, www.miamiherald.com/opinion/op-ed/article165123342.html.

10. "The Economist Intelligence Unit." Democracy Index 2019, www.eiu.com/public/topical_report.aspx?campaignid=democracyindex2019.

11. John W. Schoen, "Incumbents in Congress Are Hard to Beat - and a Lot of It Has to Do with Money," CNBC, 26 Apr. 2018, www.cnbc.com/2018/04/26/here-is-why-incumbents-in-congress-are-hard-to-beat.html.

12. "Breaking Down Democracy." Freedom House, freedomhouse.org/report/special-report/2017/breaking-down-democracy.

13. Naomi Klein, "Daring to Dream in the Age of Trump." *The Nation*, 13 June 2017, www.thenation.com/article/archive/daring-to-dream-in-the-age-of-trump/.

14. Robert Frank, "Rich Could Get Nearly $2 Trillion Tax Cut under Trump's Tax Loophole." CNBC, 15 May 2017, www.cnbc.com/2017/05/15/rich-would-get-1-trillion-tax-cut-under-trumps-tax-loophole.html.

15. Susan Page and Emma Kinery, "Poll: Only 12% of Americans Support the Senate Health Care Plan," *USA Today*, 28 June 2017, www.usatoday.com/story/news/politics/2017/06/28/suffolk-poll-obamacare-trump-senate-health-care-plan/103249346/.

16. Martin Pengelly, "Donald Trump Jr and Ivanka Trump among Top Republican Picks for 2024." *The Guardian*, 4 Jan. 2020, www.theguardian.com/us-news/2020/jan/04/donald-trump-jr-ivanka-trump-2024-presidential-election-poll.

17. "Republicans Seek to Exploit COVID-19 Crisis to Cut Social Security Benefits," *Los Angeles Times*, 11 May 2020, www.latimes.com/business/story/2020-05-11/republicans-covid-social-security.

18. Eoin Higgins, "The End of American Exceptionalism? Study Indicates Failure of US Democracy Creating Wave of Self Doubt." *Common Dreams*, 29 Jan. 2020, www.commondreams.org/news/2020/01/29/end-american-exceptionalism-study-indicates-failure-us-democracy-creating-wave-self.

19.   Chris Riotta, "Millionaires Receive $1.7m in Coronavirus Relief as Most Taxpayers Get $1,200 Checks
      Thanks to Hidden Republican Loophole," *The Independent*, 15 Apr. 2020, www.independent.co.uk
      /news/world/americas/coronavirus-stimulus-checks-millionaires-wealthy-tax-break-loophole
      -a9466476.html.

20.   *Shelby County v. Eric H. Holder*, 570 U.S. 529, (2013) dissenting from the bench as quoted in Liptak,
      Adam. "Supreme Court Invalidates Key Part of Voting Rights Act," *New York Times*, 25 June 2013,
      www.nytimes.com/2013/06/26/us/supreme-court-ruling.html.

CHAPTER 3

Understand Why the GOP Has Almost Ended American Democracy

> The oldest and most important conflict in human societies is the battle over the concentration of wealth and power. The folks like us at the top have always told those at the bottom that our respective positions are righteous and good for all. Historically, we called that divine right. Today we have trickle-down economics.
>
> —Nick Hanauer, self-described zillionaire and entrepreneur[1]

The primary conflict in governments and nations is democracy versus the concentration of wealth and power. When protestors risked their lives in the Arab Spring or Tiananmen Square or on the streets of Hong Kong, they did it because they wanted democracy. They saw democracy as generating opportunities for all, not just for those who control the government. In nondemocratic countries, the autocrats who control everything are the people with wealth and power. The protestors against these regimes are seeking an end to domination by those with wealth or power.

Those who are opposed to democracy want to concentrate the wealth and power into their own hands. This is the real conflict in our society.

It's not socialism versus capitalism. Socialism concentrates wealth and power into the hands of the party leaders. Members of the Politburo in the Soviet Union and the Communist Party in China have been the richest and most powerful men in their societies. Capitalism, on the other hand, concentrates wealth and power into the hands of monopolies and the uberwealthy, a.k.a. those who own the capital.

The struggle is between those who seek to concentrate wealth and power versus those who want to democratize our society and create opportunities for everyone to live well and have autonomy over their lives.

Whether a country is capitalist or socialist, run by Wahabists from the Saudi royal family or the oligarchs of Putin's inner circle, only an ongoing commitment by a large group of people will allow democracy to exist, let alone flourish. It is as true today as it was when Julius Caesar and later Napoleon made themselves emperors and destroyed the experiment of democracy in Rome and France respectively. Likewise, it was true of the ancient Assyrian empires in the Middle East, the Incan empire of South America, the monarchy of Japan, or Haile Selassie of Ethiopia. Those in power do not willingly choose democracy; rather, it must be forced upon them.

The wealthiest and most powerful who run their societies generally see democracy as a threat to their interests. They fight it, they co-opt it, they undermine it, and they develop strategies to inoculate themselves against it.

This is what has been happening at an alarming rate in the United States since 2009. Other than fuzzy-thinking, idealistic feel-goodery, is there any reason to think that most of the rich and powerful wouldn't want to dismantle democracy in the United States if by dismantling it they could gain even more wealth and power?

This past decade has seen a concentration of wealth within our economy, accelerated by political policy. Here is what that trend will get us over the next two decades: as the middle class continues to shrink, we will see fewer home buyers and more renters, and the owners of housing inventory will be corporations, wealth funds, and real estate investment trusts (REITs) where the richest have invested their money and own a slice of thousands or even millions of homes.

That is certainly what happened in the 2010s, when 95% of the distressed mortgages from the 2008 housing crash were auctioned off to Wall Street investors. Over 200,000 single-family homes were purchased by these private equity funds. They rented them out so that the renters paid the mortgages. According to the *New York Times,* it's a "housing recovery without a homeowners' recovery."[2]

Most Americans will live paycheck to paycheck. Eventually it will drip down to individuals who don't own cars but instead use fleets centrally owned and provided on demand (another way to say rented) for a fee. Everything will be owned by a shrinking number of corporations and rented to us in order to grease the transfer of our earnings into their wealth funds.

Those at the top will send their kids to the best schools imaginable, have the finest health care—including gene therapies—to extend their lives, and live in pristine, safely policed communities. Their wealth will protect them against everything: climate change, war, poverty, failures of the health care system. Even pandemics. That's why fighting the GOP's 4 Weapons Against Democracy—or any of the previously mentioned problems—is not on the agenda of the most wealthy and powerful in our society.

We will continue to see independently owned stores die out in favor of chains, especially the 99-cent-type stores, paycheck loan sharks instead of banks, and more fast-food restaurants owned by a few corporations instead of mom-and-pop restaurants. There will be a homogenous, interconnected chain of stores that sell us cheap products and unhealthy food because we really can't afford anything else. We already see some of this when depressing strip malls seem to have the same five to seven stores in every retail zone. Or when entire minority communities are considered "food deserts" because grocery stores have been replaced by convenience stores selling more affordable but unhealthy food.

Sometimes it's hard to see this change in society. We adjust to the depressing milieu of cheap, corporate-owned storefronts. These in turn are spread out over the landscape with a precision dictated by an intersection of density maps and demographic profiles. Eventually every neighborhood will have the same sets of stores with their cash registers connected to a metaphorical funnel owned by a small number of corporate owners. We give over almost every penny; they control almost all the wealth. One doesn't need a Nobel in economics to grasp this.

Are the Super-Rich and Powerful Loyal to Democracy?

There is scarce a king in a hundred who would not, if he could, follow the example of Pharaoh, get first all the people's money, then all their lands and then make them and their children servants forever.

—Benjamin Franklin[3]

We would like to think every person in the United States is automatically loyal to democracy simply because we all pledged allegiance to the flag in grade school. But ask yourself: If the military committed a coup in the United States, is there a single board of directors of a major American company that would pledge resistance to this overthrowing of democracy? Would the billionaires of our country be more likely to take up arms against them or throw parties for those generals? Would K Street lobbyists resign en masse, or would they simply lobby the new power in the White House for their same super-rich clients? Would Fox News organize militias, or would it somehow justify the generals' coup and argue that they were actually preventing a coup by Hillary Clinton and Hunter Biden, son of the former vice president? Would Americans of all political stripes rebel, or would powerful interests flood social media with paid-for influencers and corrupted local officials who all work off the same lobbyist-created script justifying the coup?

The coup will not be televised.

We are unlikely to face that type of coup in the United States. Instead, we are experiencing a different coup—one where the rules of elections, the boundaries of district maps, and the funding of the campaigns are all changed so that the results almost always ensure one party wins while the other just barely loses.

The oil-magnate Koch brothers; the Amway-founding family of secretary of education Betsy DeVos; Fox News; and the Republican Party did not need to conspire with generals to end democracy in the United States. Instead, they simply amassed the 4 Weapons discussed in the next chapter. They created a media landscape where truth was obscured by the noise of diversionary propaganda. These elite then promoted a few American myths to their followers that sounded true but were really masks to cover up the assault on democracy. These American myths are powerful magnets for those who find themselves on the short end of the global economy. (See Figure 4.)

Autocrats in every country have their own myths that they promote. The myths are usually nationalistic with an infusion of religion and populated by alleged enemies (internal and external) who supposedly seek to keep that country down because they (inexplicably) hate the "fill-in-the-blank" (freedoms, history, values, culture, religion, whatever). It is a playbook that allows the rich and powerful of that country to maintain their wealth and power in partnership with global financial interests who are extracting wealth from those countries.

This used to be done with military invasions and the creations of colonies. Now it is done with strongmen in power in alliance with a global economic system whose goal is, you guessed it, to concentrate wealth and power into the hands of the few. This is the real globalism. The Occupy movement and Tea Party are both right to be alarmed by this aspect of globalism.

This global economic system was built to facilitate the rich not just getting richer but getting all the wealth in the world. Globalism is now so complex that we cannot even grasp the amount of wealth and power that international financiers wield. These international wealth funds are not passive investment instruments. They employ building after building of analysts, researchers, statisticians, accountants, copywriters, media trackers, pollsters, media experts, attorneys, and most importantly, political strategists and lobbyists. These apparatchiks are ready to create the myths in their respective countries to keep the masses from overthrowing their handpicked autocrat. Such professionalism of autocracy is why democracy is receding globally and autocrats are resurgent. Currently, only 45% of countries worldwide have a semblance of democracy.[4]

These international funds do not make democracy a priority. It doesn't matter if the funds are controlled by Saudi Arabia's royal family, the Chinese

Great American Myth	The Covered-Up Assault
The rich all earned their wealth.	Republicans cut the estate tax so the descendants of the super-rich maintain their position of power over the rest of us.
Tax breaks for the super-rich create jobs.	Republicans give tax breaks for the super-rich, concentrating wealth into the hands of the few while creating financial burdens for everyone else.
Immigrants come here to use our welfare system.	Republicans execute a divide-and-conquer strategy aimed to stoke hate against "the other" (like Reagan's "welfare queens") and scapegoat brown people for the problems created by Republican tax policies.
The United States has the finest health care system in the world, and if you work hard, you will be covered by it.	Our government takes our taxes to pay for its priorities, but refuses to support one of the highest priorities for every American: a health care system that would benefit us all.
Money in elections is free speech.	Republicans enable billionaires to massively outspend a regular citizen, literally a million-to-one, and control all politics.
Voting fraud is rampant, and so we need strict voter ID laws.	Republicans create as many obstacles for poor and minority voters as possible so that conservatives can disproportionately control elections.
The United States has the greatest democracy in the world.	The electoral college, two senators per state, and gerrymandering have so skewed elections that the majority is never in power.
Fox News is fair and balanced; corporate media protects the truth.	Both right-wing media and corporate-controlled media serve the interests and agenda of their owners first and foremost.
We all benefit when businesses in the stock market go up because so many of us own stocks.	The richest 10% of Americans own 84% of the stock,* and corporations often buy back their own stock when they get tax breaks. The ups and downs of the DOW is a game played only by the rich.
Democrats cater to people who want things for free.	Republicans cut the taxes for the super-rich, and then say we can't afford the social welfare net.

Figure 4. Source: CommonSenseDem.org.

* "The Richest 10% of Americans Now Own 84% of All Stocks." Money, money.com/stock-ownership-10-percent-richest/.

government, Russian mafia, or the Norwegian government pension fund. They all have the same interests: to attract more money to be sheltered from taxation. They then diminish regulations in the sectors that hold their investment to remove protections for people and the environment. Their armies of suits ensure the political environment is conducive to rigging the system in their favor. The great giant sucking sound of international commerce then slurps up everyone's money.

This is no Adam Smith, small-business capitalism at play. It is massively wealthy interests using their power to gain advantage over the rest of us. The invisible hand of the market has been slapped away by the professionals. Not even laws passed by democratically elected legislatures can withstand the rights of corporations to make money under our current Republican regime.

For example, one of the first decisions after Citizens United by the Republican-packed Supreme Court held that elected state legislatures could not prohibit pharmaceutical company marketers from buying confidential prescription data of doctors and patients. Their reasoning? Such laws violate the First Amendment rights of the corporations![5]

That is why corporate interests and their billionaire owners were so invested in removing campaign limits. With no limits, their ability to control the courts, government agencies, Congress, and the White House became near-complete.

Let's face it. Democracy is not necessary for the goals of rich and powerful monied interests. The government oversight that democracy creates is definitely unwelcome to them. Just ask any oil executive. In fact, democracy is against their interests. The more democratic the society is, the more likely the government will levy taxes or oversight against these giant money-hoarding and tax-evading instruments. Such fair taxation enables the democratic country to better provide more services to the other 99.99% of the population—you know, the majority.

It's not just wealth funds; sixty-nine of the world's largest one hundred economies are corporations.[6] Every one of these corporations has an incorporation charter that legally requires them to maximize profits for their shareholders and owners. When this is in direct conflict with regulations that will cost them profits, they are legally required to pursue those profits by any means necessary.

The Evolution of the Fight against Democracy

Congress should know how to levy taxes, and if it doesn't know how
to collect them, then a man is a fool to pay the taxes.

—J. P. Morgan[7]

So what does one do when profits are constrained by regulations meant
to protect the majority of the population? Hire lobbyists. Create astroturf
groups that pretend they are "concerned citizens." Fund think tanks to create policies that show more money should be left with rich people and that
"wasteful" social services should be cut for poor people. Unleash bots, trolls,
and extremist groups like when Betsy DeVos funded the Liberate! groups
protesting COVID-19 measures armed with assault weapons.[8] They will do
anything to gin up social and racial conflicts that serve as a smokescreen to
the policy changes that they truly care about. Lobby those in power—or just
bribe them—to promote policies that diminish regulations and taxation.
Without those regulations, the businesses reap the profits and society and
individuals must pay the costs.

Eventually these financial interests and corporations understand that
instead of lobbying against regulations one by one, it's simply easier to take
over a political party. Here in the United States, that is exactly what happened
with the GOP. But it doesn't make sense to stop with taking over one party.
The next logical step is to change the election system so that their party
maintains power. Once this is done, there are no more fights over regulations. The profits may continue unfettered by protections for the populace.
The funding of the redistricting project known as REDMAP (detailed in
the next chapter) is perhaps the clearest example of these steps taken here
in the United States. And yes, that was done in 2010 at the start of all this.

All this to say, you don't have to call yourself a socialist or follow anarcho-
syndicalist Noam Chomsky to be pissed off right now. You have permission
to be disgusted with our leaders. You can be appalled at the planned and
carefully shaped inequity of our economy. You can be disappointed that
democracy has been flung aside for the profits for the few.

If you think socialism is the alternative, however, just a quick reality
check. Socialism puts more power in the hands of the government. In

my five decades on Earth, our government has consisted of the following presidential administrations: Richard Nixon and the Vietnam War and Watergate; four years of a beautiful but ineffective Jimmy Carter and massive inflation; then eight years of Reagan and Iran-Contra; four years of "now he doesn't look so bad" George H. W. Bush; then eight years of Bill Clinton and the Monica Lewinsky scandal and speaker Newt Gingrich's Contract on America; then eight years of George W. Bush and his vice president Dick Cheney and a decade lost to wars and recession; finally we got Obama but with veto power held by speaker John Boehner, senate majority leader Mitch McConnell and chief justice John Roberts; and now we have Trump.

So at what point in the last fifty years would it have been better if those who actually have controlled the federal government were given *more* power? More democracy—not more government control or unfettered corporate power—is what we need.

The richest and most powerful in any country fear the populace that democracy empowers. If the populace acts in its own interests, then the promise of never-ending wealth and power to the few is jeopardized. The lobbyists, the armies of accountants, the tax evasion strategies, the cheating on the entrance exams to elite universities for their kids, the inherited vacation homes in the Hamptons, and the simple buying of politicians and elections are all somewhat blunted. Democracy is the only thing that can reverse the concentration of wealth and power.

What You've Been Waiting For: An Essay on Taxes!

I don't pay taxes, because I'm smart.

—Donald Trump[9]

Most of you by now are surely hoping that I get into tax law and policy in this book. Because the only thing better than paying taxes is reading about taxes. But seriously, taxes are the *central* battle in our political system, so it's pretty important you see some numbers. I promise to make it interesting, even Stephen King like.

In the golden ages of the American economy—the 1950s—the overall tax rate for the richest 400 households was 70–91%.[10] Now, it's just under 23%. Amazingly, this 23% is currently the lowest tax rate of any group in America. Meaning: the other 99%-plus of us all pay a higher percentage of our income in our taxes than do the richest Americans.

How is this possible?

Income is taxed differently based on its source. The most penalized income is that which is earned through a salary, which is how the vast majority of us gain money. The least penalized income is that which is earned passively through one's investments and wealth. Better still is wealth that is sheltered from taxes by loopholes not relevant to most people.

When democracy is weakened, as has happened here in the United States, the concentration of wealth accelerates. Policies are passed to promote this by, for instance, lowering the tax rates on investment and wealth or abolishing the inheritance tax. Instead of the middle-class society we once had, we now have these almost unbelievable inequities:

- The top 0.1% of the population in the United States is worth on average $73 million. They own 22% of the nation's wealth. The bottom 90% percent owns 22% of the nation's wealth. So the top 0.1% and the bottom 90% of US households own the same share of the nation's wealth.[11]
- The Walton family, which owns Walmart, has the same amount of wealth as the bottom 42% of Americans combined. That's 138 million people.[12] In fact, the 400 richest people in the nation—just .00025% of the population—own more than the 150 million adults in the bottom 60%.[13]

Worldwide we see this phenomenon:

- The richest 1% in the world now own half the world's total household wealth. The poorest half of adults—3.9 billion—controls less than 1% of the world's wealth.[14]
- There are now, in 2020, over 2,800 billionaires.

But it's not just individuals who are vacuuming up the money. We no longer have small businesses. Or at least, we only have half as many as we used to before Reagan deregulated the economy. (See Figure 5.)

SHARE OF COMPANIES LESS THAN A YEAR OLD

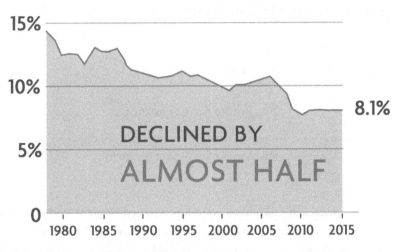

Figure 5. Source: Buchanan, Leigh. "American Entrepreneurship Is Actually Vanishing. Here's Why." *Inc.com*, Inc. com, 1 Apr. 2015, www.inc.com/magazine/201505/leigh-buchanan/the-vanishing-startups-in-decline.html.

The Prince and Princess Economy

We don't pay taxes. Only the little people pay taxes.

—Leona Hemsley, billionaire and frenemy of Donald Trump[15]

The enormity of those statistics is difficult to grasp. The wealth of the richest people on the planet is obscured from us because of the enormity of the gap between their wealth and that of a typical human. The super-rich are not just richer than us, they are living a fantasy life as princes and princesses while the rest of us have to work harder every year just to stay afloat. It's the creation of a "prince and princess economy," where the gap is as stark now as it was five hundred years ago in feudal Europe.

Democracy was supposed to end this corrupted system that promoted the concentration of wealth and power into the hands of the few. Indeed, the Founding Fathers created a democracy for this very purpose. But now the capture of our American democracy in the twenty-first century is so complete that we have royalty and serfs again in all but name. Are we all so jaded that individuals toiling in the fields for less than the minimum wage and living twenty to a room seems okay? Or people having to take part-time work as taxi drivers using their own cars now seems normal? Renting out a room in our home to a stranger—yes, please!

Pearl Harbor for the Rich and Powerful

Only morons pay the estate tax.

—Gary Cohn, Trump's National Economic Council director and former president of Goldman Sachs[16]

Election Night 2008. Political watchers grasped that the demographic changes were finally accruing to the Democrats' benefit. The trend was set to continue for the next few decades. Obama had put together the coalition that Republicans most feared—one that would grow more powerful simply as older white people died and the diversity of American youth aged into voters. Republicans looked to be the minority party for decades.

The country's richest power brokers who fund Mitch McConnell and the Republican Party woke the next day and angrily sent their servants to the other wing of their estates so that they could strategize. (Okay, I'm just imaging the servants were sent away.) They saw that this Obama coalition would slow down their noble quest to have all the money for themselves. A government led by Obama, Pelosi, and then–senate majority leader Harry Reid seemed poised to be responsive to the demands of the American public.

Indeed, in his first year of power, Obama reinstated the inheritance tax, which applied a 35% tax rate to estates worth over $5 million for individuals. This was done through special surcharges included in the Affordable Care Act.[17] That is the primary reason why Republicans kept trying to repeal Obamacare—it was the tax on the super-rich that paid for health care for 20 million Americans[18] that they were really trying to repeal. In addition, congressional Democrats were pushing hard to repeal tax breaks that President Bush had given to the richest 2% of American families.

These might seem like just another set of numbers and statistics, but to the richest and most powerful, this aimed at the heart of what they spent their lives doing: hoarding immense wealth—often inherited—at the expense of almost all else in their lives. It must have seemed so unfair to them; I can't imagine. As a *Guardian* report revealed, "Most of the wealthiest US billionaires...are extremely conservative on economic issues. Obsessed with cutting taxes, especially estate taxes—which apply only to the wealthiest Americans. Opposed to government regulation of the environment or big banks. Unenthusiastic about government programs to help with jobs, incomes, healthcare, or retirement pensions."[19]

Before we move on, we need to understand the libertarian argument for lowering taxes on the super-rich: they've earned what they accumulated, so leave them the hell alone. The logical extension of that argument is that the rich should pay no taxes. On the other hand, there's a social equality argument that says if you have a lot, you should be contributing so that those who have less can be part of our beneficial society. The logical end to that argument is basically something akin to communism. Which is better?

That's the wrong question. The real questions are what are our country's priorities? How much will it cost to achieve those priorities? And who should pay which amount? That is what should drive tax policy. In digging our way out of the Depression, Franklin Roosevelt redirected our national budget to pay for our collective priorities and lift everyone up. After he left, in the 1950s under Republican President Dwight Eisenhower, the top marginal tax rate was even increased to 91%. It's currently 37%, although if any rich person were actually paying that, they'd probably sue their accountant. The percentages dropped from 91 to 37 because the super-rich have changed the priorities of Congress. If you share their priorities, then your side is winning. For those who root for the rich even though such fans pay higher rates in taxes than do the rich, well, there's a sucker born every minute apparently.

The Democrats underestimated the danger of making the super-rich their enemy. It only took a few families at the very top to exact their revenge. This was thanks to the Republican Supreme Court's *Citizen United* decision.

To say these issues—Democratic majorities, worsening demographic trends for the Republican Party, tax increases on the wealthy—were a wake-up call for the brains and money behind the GOP is a gross understatement. This felt like the apocalypse had arrived. The four horsemen were ready to bring death, famine, and war to man, and worse, taxes to the super-rich.

Republicans understood their proportion of support in the electorate would decrease further.

What do you do if you and your billionaire friends realize that the Democrats, the party of wealth redistribution and targeted taxes, might become the semipermanent government? You use your money to change the playing field. In America that means undermining democracy. Instead of coming up with better policies to attract more voters, Republicans found a way to govern with the support of a shrinking percent of voters. Billionaires literally pay protection money to the Republican Party now to stop our political and tax system from being fixed.

Most people, including most elected Democrats, still haven't grasped how effective the Republicans' changes were. Because of this, Democratic strategies since 2010 to win elections and govern again have been destined to fail.

There is almost nothing that Republican leaders fear more than Democrats—and other American citizens—waking up to what Republicans have done to American democracy in the 2010s. The next chapter will give you a full understanding of exactly what has happened and how the Republicans managed to stay in power despite minority support. That understanding—and your subsequent reaction—is the only power that can strip them of their minority rule. The 2010s will always be a lost decade, but if it helps us revitalize American democracy, it may be worth the price.

Manipulating the Whites

The super-rich are not paying people to vote. How is it that Republicans are still managing to get a sufficient number of voters to the polls? There are not enough millionaires to elect Republicans. But there are *almost* enough white men and their wives.

We know the motivation for the super-rich: to concentrate wealth and power into their own hands so they can live like modern-day princes and princesses. But why are so many white Americans joining in with those rich people?

In some ways there's a great dividing line in life. This is true in every country, culture, and philosophy. There is a really simple question that will help you know which side of the line you fall: Is every human life on Earth as sacred as yours? If you believe that to be true, it will follow naturally that you believe in democracy and multiculturalism. You are empathetic and want to take care of people or have them cared for, at least. You probably root for the underdog and want everybody to get a fair shake and have an abundance of opportunities. I definitely prefer to be surrounded by people like this, so let's hang out after all this is done.

The other type of person believes their life is more sacred than that of the poor kid born in the slums of Mumbai, the shanty towns outside of Johannesburg, the favelas of Rio de Janeiro, or the hills of Appalachia. If you believe your life is somehow more important than their lives, then you would naturally find yourself superior to them and others. These inferior people certainly shouldn't have an equal voice in deciding how your tax dollars are spent or who controls your government. The culture and habits and language of these others would appear to you as inferior.

Under this worldview, democracy is a system to subvert in order to keep your group in power. But when your group can no longer obtain majority support, then you need to make changes. Chapter 4 discusses the changes that Republicans began making in 2010 to stay in power.

How do the Republican elite keep whites in solidarity with their cause? The primary techniques are ramping up fear and tamping down empathy. It's not loving thy neighbor as oneself. It's fearing thy neighbor and buying a gun to protect yourself from people who are different. Their motto seems to be that we shouldn't embrace the reality of our country's multicultural-ism, nor is it kosher to add to the fabric of American society. Instead, they define "real Americans" in a narrow manner to exclude as many people as possible. They then believe themselves to be superior. White, Christian heterosexuals with conservative values and a love of guns and country (but no understanding of democracy) are the only ones courted for the GOP's small tent.

Republicans in Congress currently serve one ultimate purpose: to help the richest people accumulate more wealth. The strategic coalition the rich pulled together in the 1980s focused on welcome into their forces Evangelical Christians. The most politicized of these Christians try to create a world where men dominate women and where white Christians are the chosen people who follow a European-looking Jesus, not the Palestinian Jew of the New Testament. Most of the Republican financial elite have different priorities but certainly don't question the privileges that flow their way from this nineteenth-century worldview.

The Republican elite uses constant propaganda from Fox News, the Limbaugh radio network, Sinclair Broadcasting, Breitbart, pre-woke Drudge, et cetera, to invoke fear in their chosen people. Fear they are being replaced. Fear that they are under threat (somehow) from racial diversity. Fear that immigrants are ripping apart the American way of life. Fear of crime from Black Americans. Fear that secular America—or Muslims or Jews—will oppress Christians. Fear that Democrats want to take their money and give it to their alleged coalition of lazy welfare queens. Fear that Democrats are using this "hoax" of a pandemic to cripple the economy without legitimate public health concerns. And don't forget fear of gay people, feminists, and college-educated intellectuals; they are all divergent in this Fox News worldview. The idea is that none of these groups are real Americans, and so their votes are illegitimate and should be dealt with instead of protected.

This value system provides cover for the Republican Party to do whatever it takes to keep the "libs" and the un-American Americans out of power. The *New York Times* perhaps explains this most succinctly: "A party built on demonizing and attacking marginalized people is a party that will have to disenfranchise those same people if it is to survive."[20]

As angry white people decrease as a percentage of the US population, it becomes almost impossible for Republicans to win a majority of votes in a national, democratic election. In fact, they have only done so at the presidential level once since 1990: Bush's victory in 2004. Despite this, they've occupied the White House for almost half the years since 1990.

Who needs democracy when you can stay in power despite receiving fewer votes?

Get on the Gravy Train

I think not having the estate tax recognizes the people that are
investing—as opposed to those that are just spending every darn
penny they have, whether it's on booze or women or movies.

—Republican senator Chuck Grassley of Iowa[21]

In a comprehensive study of three decades of congressional legislation, Cambridge researchers found that policies supported by economic elites or the business lobby became law two-thirds of the time. But policy changes favored by a majority of all citizens passed less than one-third of the time. Even when laws supported by the majority of citizens passed, these laws were also supported by the super-rich or business elites almost 100% of the time.[22] That means *only* laws supported by economic and business elites ever pass. Yes, there is a reason the super-rich and corporations invest in congressional campaigns. It enables them to benefit at the expense of the majority of Americans. It's more "investment portfolio" than democracy.

The 600-plus billionaires in the United States understand that changes in governmental policy enable them to accumulate unimaginable wealth. It's not as if a billionaire is a thousand times smarter or harder working than a millionaire. Just like a millionaire is not a thousand times smarter or harder working than your average American with no money in the bank. The argument can be made that these billionaires are visionaries and they deserve their billions. Because of their genius, productivity, and perhaps luck, they have earned every penny. Of course, this is one of the Great American Myths.

Many of these billionaires have never worked a day in their life; six of the ten wealthiest Americans inherited their wealth. As wealthy seniors die, an estimated $30 trillion will go to their children over the next three decades.[23] Republicans will allow all of this to go untaxed. Such policy has helped the richest 1% to control more wealth than the bottom 90% of Americans. It will get worse as these intergenerational, untaxed fortunes are passed along.

Putting such economic power into the hands of a relatively small number of people who have never worked or built companies from scratch will continue to transform our economy. Taxes will have to be higher on wages

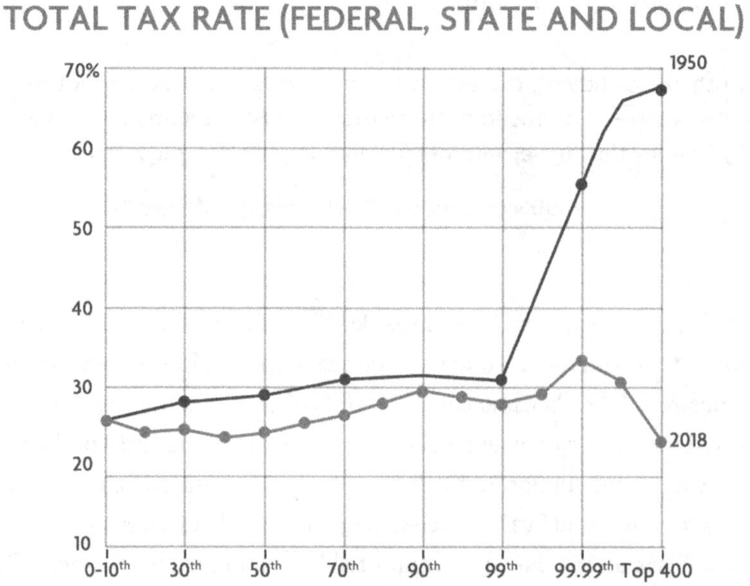

TOTAL TAX RATE (FEDERAL, STATE AND LOCAL)

New York Times columnist David Leonhardt's graph showing how in 2018, for the first time in U.S. history, the 400 richest Americans paid less in taxes than any other income group.

Figure 6. Credit: Leonhardt, David. "The Rich Really Do Pay Lower Taxes Than You." *The New York Times*, The New York Times, 6 Oct. 2019, www.nytimes.com/interactive/2019/10/06/opinion/income-tax-rate-wealthy.html?action=click&module=Opinion&pgtype=Homepage.

while government investments and earned benefits will decrease as fewer taxes are paid by the super-rich. It's a never-ending, self-perpetuating aristocracy no different than the Russian oligarchy. Democracy has no value in that system. (See Figure 6.)

Not surprisingly, the wealthier you are, the healthier you can be and the longer you can live. Currently, the richest 20% of Americans live ten to fifteen years longer than the poorest 20% of Americans who are mostly minorities.[24] Remarkably, we just accept this early death rate for minorities, pretending that political decisions bear no responsibility for it. Likewise, no one will have a problem as that gap dramatically increases in the next twenty to fifty years. Most of the gains we have from curing diseases as well as better nutrition, technology, and understanding of the body and human health, all incur for the richest Americans and trickle ever so slightly to the middle class (what's left of it).

These inequities are compounded by structural racism and lack of access to health care for all. The poor basically die sooner from the psychosocial, environmental, physical, and material stressors of being poor (called "weathering" by Dr. Arline T. Geronimus).[25] The grossly disproportionate impact of COVID-19 on minorities is just the latest example of this. The rich are therefore able to accumulate more money because they live and are productive for longer. This financial advantage becomes even more exacerbated due to the virtual elimination of inheritance taxes.

When anyone earns their first million or two, they invariably do so through hard work, sometimes through talent or genius as well. Kudos to them. May we all reach that tax bracket, because that is when the real wealth starts coming in. There is now in place a well-established intersecting network of policies designed by lobbyists, accountants, and attorneys that helps the "modest wealth" of a few million dollars accelerate more quickly than the *very* modest wealth of people earning salaries for their work. Once you have wealth, you can now earn more money through passive investments that are taxed less than the salary of the working class. Finally, you begin to benefit from tax-free shelters available to the wealthy.[26] Our tax system takes a higher percentage out of a $40,000-a-year paycheck than a $40,000-per-week dividend.[27] Not surprisingly, this system was created by politicians who have to rely on millionaires and billionaires to get them elected.

This reverse–Robin Hood tax world is also true for corporations. As explained earlier, many of the largest corporations in America pay almost no taxes. Meanwhile mom-and-pop businesses struggle under the weight of local, state, and federal fees, levies, costs, and taxation. I speak from experience. There were so many government costs and fees for my little business of well under one hundred employees that I wanted to vote Republican for the first time in my life—but then I remembered that I wasn't a Fortune 500 company, so the tax loopholes didn't help me. Just kidding. Lincoln was probably the last Republican for whom I would have voted.

Elected representatives cater to the rich and ignore the plight of the poor—whether it's lead in the drinking water of Flint, Michigan, school shootings, or opioid addiction. Luckily for these elected officials, the poor struggle just to get through the day and end up voting less. Meanwhile, those who want low taxes on capital income or easy regulations on polluting industries or the banks they own are strategically engaged in the political process with money and lobbying.

Under President Trump's 2017 tax breaks, the effective tax rate of the richest is now lower than the effective tax rate of the poorest in our country.

He lowered the taxes for how the richest families, including his own, increase their wealth: stocks and inheritance. Based on his tax returns from 2005—the most recent ones so far discovered—Trump's tax bill will be cut by $1.1 billion overall.[28] With the repeal of the estate tax set to take place in 2023, Trump's heirs will save $600 million. In fact, the heirs of the fifteen wealthiest Trump administration officials will save $1.7 billion.[29] Trump grabbed the issue of "draining the swamp" when in fact he is the swamp monster![30]

It gets better. The Trump administration and the then-Republican-controlled Congress passed a $300 billion repeal of estate taxes. Only one out of five hundred families—as in the richest .2% of Americans—were eligible to benefit from this repeal. At the same time, the Republicans were promoting their health care plan that would remove 24 million people from Obamacare for a $300 billion savings.[31] Can anyone say with a straight face that the rich don't get richer because of government policy?

The better economic strategy is to give tax breaks to the poor. If one cuts the working class's taxes and lets them keep an extra $10,000 per year, that money will immediately be reinvested into the economy. That means more money goes into businesses, which means businesses can create more jobs. Cut a billionaire's taxes by $50 million, and there will be zero increases in the economy. It's not as if that person were waiting to buy another car until they had a tax cut. This is the exact opposite economic theory from the Republican's trickle-down policies. But as Nobel prize winner in economics Paul Krugman said, "There isn't anybody doing serious work supporting GOP tax ideas because the evidence is overwhelmingly against those ideas."[32]

Some may want to say I'm talkin' class warfare here. I'll let Berkshire Hathaway CEO Warren Buffet respond: "There's class warfare, all right, but it's my class, the rich class, that's making war, and we're winning."[33]

Corporations who can now spend unlimited money in politics also benefited "bigly" under Trump's tax changes:

> The Institute on Taxation and Economic Policy found that 91 of the 379 companies analyzed took advantage of loopholes to effectively not pay federal income taxes in 2018 despite making a combined profit of $101 billion. That list of companies includes prominent corporate giants such as Amazon, Halliburton, Chevron, Starbucks, and Delta Air Lines…. Another 56 companies paid effective tax rates

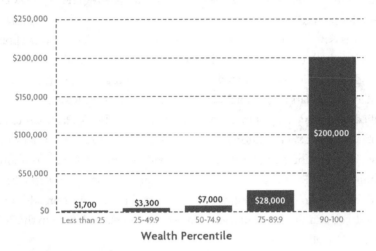

VALUE OF STOCK HOLDINGS BY NET WORTH

Median value among households in each wealth bracket that own stocks

Figure 7. Source: Kiersz, Andy. "Alexandria Ocasio-Cortez Said Cheering for Soaring Stock Prices While Wages Stay Low Is 'Inequality in a Nutshell.' We Made 6 Charts to Show Why She's Right." *Business Insider*, Business Insider, 15 Jan. 2020, www.businessinsider.com/alexandria-ocasio-cortez-tweet-stock-market-and -average-americans-2020-1#however-most-americans-dont-directly-own-any-stocks-at-all-2.

between 0 percent and 5 percent on their 2018 income. Their average effective tax rate was 2.2 percent. Thanks to the Republican tax law, which Trump signed in 2017, Bank of America, J.P. Morgan Chase, Wells Fargo, Amazon, and Verizon raked in a combined $16 billion in tax breaks in 2018.[34]

No taxes on $101 billion in profits. Did you have the same experience paying your taxes this year? No? Well, perhaps we all get rich when those companies do well because we own stock? Unfortunately, this is just another Great American Myth. The bottom 90% of people in America on average own less than $10,000 of stocks. Stocks are owned, not surprisingly, by the rich. (See Figure 7.)

Meanwhile, the Republican tax plan creates another *trillion* dollars of debt. And we all know how Republicans tackle debt: by claiming that Social Security; Medicare and Medicaid; nutrition assistance for women, infants, and children; grants for teachers; affordable housing; or scientific research are all bankrupting America and need to be cut: "You also have to bring spending under control.... The driver of our debt is the structure of Social Security and Medicare for future beneficiaries." — Republican senator Marco Rubio of Florida speaking just after passing the 2018 tax cuts for billionaires.[35]

This is not a book on tax policy. It is, however, a book on how tax policy puts hundreds of millions of dollars into the hands of a small group of elite, mostly Republican campaign donors. Those donors then put hundreds of millions of dollars into Republican election efforts. It's the Republican's well-lubed circle-jerk. As just one example, Sheldon Adelson's Las Vegas casino businesses got $700 million in tax breaks due to the 2017 Republican tax law. He then donated $113 million (and perhaps more to the dark-money nonprofits) to Republicans for the 2018 midterm.[36] Guess what Republicans did for Adelson's family? Eliminated the estate tax to save him additional hundreds of millions for his heirs. Guess what Adelson will do in the 2020 election? Well, you get it.

Eventually we will live in a world where just a small group of families own so much wealth that they dominate all politics, media, and entertainment. It will be their world; we'll just rent space in it.

Republican elites are not looking to put an old-school tyrant dictator into power. They won't call for an end to regular elections. No need to suppress the opposition, although fake investigations, like those into Benghazi and the Hunter Biden probe, are a great way of cutting your opponents down. Instead, the elite simply want to convince the populace—through diversionary propaganda and conservative media networks—that the country's Republican leadership is doing a great job. With enough propaganda, an effective autocrat can convince the population that up is down. The goal of modern autocrats and their backers is to have enough citizens who don't think they live in a dictatorship. But first you have to take away democracy. So what are the weapons you would use to do that besides diversionary propaganda? I am so glad you asked!

We're finally at the 4 Weapons Against Democracy that Republican elites and elected officials used during the 2010s. Hold onto your hat, because it is a wild ride.

Notes

1. Nick Hanauer et al, "The Pitchforks Are Coming...For Us Plutocrats." Politico, www.politico.com/magazine/story/2014/06/the-pitchforks-are-coming-for-us-plutocrats-108014.

2. Francesca Mari, "A $60 Billion Housing Grab by Wall Street," *New York Times*, 4 Mar. 2020, www.nytimes.com/2020/03/04/magazine/wall-street-landlords.html.

3. "American Author, Printer, Political Theorist, Politician, Postmaster, Scientist, Inventor, Civic Activist, Statesman, Diplomat, Founding Father, and a Therapist." Wikiquote, Wikimedia Foundation, Inc., 31 July 2020, en.wikiquote.org/wiki/Benjamin_Franklin#:~:text=There is scarce a king,(June 2, 1787).

4. "Populists and Autocrats: The Dual Threat to Global Democracy." *Freedom House*, freedomhouse.org/report/freedom-world/2017/populists-and-autocrats-dual-threat-global-democracy.

5. *Sorrell v. IMS Health Inc.*, 564 US 552 - 2011.

6. Global Justice Now, 11 Mar. 2019, www.globaljustice.org.uk/news/2018/oct/17/69-richest-100-entities-planet-are-corporations-not-governments-figures-show.

7. Peter Rush, "Class Tax and Then the Mass Tax." *New York Times*, 15 Apr. 1981, www.nytimes.com/1981/04/15/opinion/class-tax-and-then-the-mass-tax.html.

8. Adam Gabbatt, "Thousands of Americans Backed by Rightwing Donors Gear up for Protests." *The Guardian*, 18 Apr. 2020, www.theguardian.com/us-news/2020/apr/18/coronavirus-americans-protest-stay-at-home

9. Daniella Diaz, "Trump: 'I'm Smart' for Not Paying Taxes," CNN, 27 Sept. 2016, www.cnn.com/2016/09/26/politics/donald-trump-federal-income-taxes-smart-debate/index.html.

10. Mary Papenfuss, "400 Richest Americans Own More Than 150 Million Of The Nation's Poorest: Study," HuffPost, 11 Feb. 2019, https://www.huffpost.com/entry/400-richest-own-more-than-150-million-poorest_n_5c60f627e4b0eec79b250c34.

11. National Bureau of Economic Research.

12. Bernie Sanders et al., "Bernie Sanders, in Madison, Claims Top 0.1% of Americans Have Almost as Much Wealth as Bottom 90%." *Politifact*, www.politifact.com/factchecks/2015/jul/29/bernie-s/bernie-sanders-madison-claims-top-01-americans-hav/.

13. Papenfuss, "400 Richest Americans," HuffPost.

14. Global Wealth Report.

15. "Top 10 Tax Dodgers." Time, 15 Apr. 2009, content.time.com/time/specials/packages/article/0,28804,1891335_1891333_1891317,00.html.

16. The Editorial Board, "'Only Morons Pay the Estate Tax,'" *New York Times*, 21 Nov. 2017, www.nytimes.com/2017/11/20/opinion/estate-tax-trump-republicans.html.

17. Floyd Norris, "Merely Rich and Superrich: The Tax Gap Is Narrowing," *New York Times*, 18 Apr. 2014, www.nytimes.com/2014/04/18/business/merely-rich-and-superrich-the-tax-gap-is-narrowing.html?_r=0.

18. "Chart Book: Accomplishments of Affordable Care Act," Center on Budget and Policy Priorities, 21 Mar. 2019, www.cbpp.org/research/health/chart-book-accomplishments-of-affordable-care-act#:~:text=Thanks to the Affordable Care,people have gained health coverage.

19. Benjamin I Page, Jason Seawright, and Matthew J. Lacombe, "What Billionaires Want: The Secret Influence of America's 100 Richest," *The Guardian*, 31 Oct 2018, https://www.theguardian.com/us-news/2018/oct/30/billionaire-stealth-politics-america-100-richest-what-they-want.

20. Noah Berlatsky, "The Trump Effect: New Study Connects White American Intolerance and Support for Authoritarianism," NBC News, 21 Aug. 2019, www.nbcnews.com/think/opinion/trump-effect-new-study-connects-white-american-intolerance-support-authoritarianism-ncna877886.

21. Brent D. Griffiths and Brian Faler, "Grassley Derides Those Who Spend All Their Money 'on Booze or Women or Movies,'" Politico, 4 Dec. 2017, www.politico.com/story/2017/12/03/grassley-tax-booze-women-movies-277764.

22.   M. Gilens, and B. Page, "Testing Theories of American Politics: Elites, Interest Groups, and Average Citizens," *Perspectives on Politics, 12*(3), 564-581, 2014. doi:10.1017/S1537592714001595.

23.   Robert Reich, "Only Morons Don't Make the Wealthy Pay Taxes," *Baltimore Sun*, 30 May 2020, www .baltimoresun.com/opinion/op-ed/bs-ed-op-0920-reich-20170919-story.html.

24.   Raj Chetty, "The Association Between Income and Life Expectancy in the United States, 2001-2014," PhD1 *JAMA*, 2016; 315(16):1750-1766. doi:10.1001/jama.2016.4226.

25.   Arline T. Geronimus et al, "Do US Black Women Experience Stress-Related Accelerated Biological Aging?: A Novel Theory and First Population-Based Test of Black-White Differences in Telomere Length." *Human Nature*, U.S. National Library of Medicine, 10 Mar. 2010, www.ncbi.nlm.nih.gov /pmc/articles.

26.   Jesse Drucker and Eric Lipton. "How a Trump Tax Break to Help Poor Communities Became a Windfall for the Rich," *The New York Times*, 31 Aug. 2019, www.nytimes.com/2019/08/31/business /tax-opportunity-zones.html.

27.   "Taxes on Ordinary and Qualified Dividends." How Much Is Taxed on Dividend Income and How to Report It? Ordinary Dividends, Qualified Dividends, www.efile.com/ordinary-qualified-dividends -tax-rates-stock-income/. "IRS, Federal Income Tax Brackets by Tax Year." 2019, 2020 Income Back Taxes Income Tax Rates and Brackets, www.efile.com/irs-income-tax-rates-and-brackets/.

28.   Jesse Drucker, and Nadja Popovich, "Trump Could Save More Than $1 Billion Under His New Tax Plan," *New York Times*, 28 Sept. 2017, www.nytimes.com/interactive/2017/09/28/us/politics /trump-tax-benefit.html.

29.   Michael Tanglis, "Trump's Tax Cut Is a Big Payday for His Family: Heirs Stand to Save $600 Million." *Salon*, 4 Nov. 2017, www.salon.com/2017/11/04/trumps-tax-cut-is-a-big-payday-for-his-family -heirs-stand-to-save-600-million /.

30.   Get your T-shirt here: https://www.amazon.com/IMPEACH-Trump-Drain-Impeach-Monster/dp /B07B3VXZ1T

31.   Tanglis, "Trump's Tax Cut," *Salon*.

32.   Paul Krugman, "The Economics of Soaking the Rich," *New York Times*, 5 Jan. 2019, www.nytimes.com /2019/01/05/opinion/alexandria-ocasio-cortez-tax-policy-dance.html.

33.   Ben Walsh, "16 Insights on Politics And Taxes From Warren Buffett," *Business Insider*, 13 Jan. 2012, www .businessinsider.com/warren-buffetts-best-quotes-on-politics-and-taxes-2012-1#class-warfare-12.

34.   "Corporate Tax Avoidance in the First Year of the Trump Tax Law." *ITEP*, itep.org/corporate -tax-avoidance-in-the-first-year-of-the-trump-tax-law/.

35.   Nicole Goodkind, "Republicans Will Cut Social Security and Medicare after Tax Plan Passes, Says Marco Rubio," *Newsweek*, 1 Dec 2017, https://www.newsweek.com/tax-plan-social -security-medicare-welfare-republicans-rubio-729133

36.   Robert Reich, "Why We Must Get Big Money Out of Politics," *Robert Reich*, 5 Jan. 2019, robertreich.org /post/181719843490.

PART 2

Your Warning: Democracy Won't End with Tanks Rolling Down DC Streets*

*This may be too optimistic

The death of democracy is now typically administered in a thousand cuts. In one country after another, elected leaders have gradually attacked the deep tissues of democracy—the independence of the courts, the business community, the media, civil society, universities and sensitive state institutions like the civil service, the intelligence agencies and the police.

—Larry Diamond, eminent democracy scholar[1]

1. "The Threat." Protect Democracy, protectdemocracy.org/the-threat/.

CHAPTER 4

Understand the GOP's Four Weapons Used to Almost End American Democracy

I don't want everybody to vote.... Our leverage, quite candidly, goes
up as the voting populace goes down.

—Paul Weyrich, cofounder of the conservative Heritage
Foundation and, with Jerry Falwell, of the Moral Majority[1]

Starting in 2010, the GOP built a firewall against the popular vote by
wielding 4 Weapons Against Democracy: unlimited dark money,
extreme gerrymandering, voter suppression, and diversionary
propaganda.

In quick succession after the 2008 election, the following eight events
took place:

1. Betsy DeVos—Trump's reviled Secretary of Education—and the Koch
    brothers funded a group called Citizens United to initiate lawsuits
    aimed at overthrowing the limits on campaign spending by billionaires
    and corporations.
2. In early 2010, the five Republican-appointed members of the Supreme
    Court outvoted the four Democratic-appointed members and approved
    unlimited—and untraceable—money in elections in *Citizens United v.
    FEC*. It allowed this spending to begin immediately, before Congress
    or the Federal Election Committee could require any transparency for
    those expenditures.
3. Democrats were winning at the polls in the 2010 congressional elec-
    tions as late as five months before the election. In the final few months
    of the 2010 election, and after the *Citizens United decision*, the billion-
    aire funders of the GOP sent a tsunami of money against Democrats.

This shocked the campaigns of both sides. In some traditional Democratic areas, the Democrats were suddenly outspent 20-1. Not only did the GOP pick up 63 House seats and 6 Senate seats, but—more importantly—they flipped 30 state legislatures to Republican control.[2] Flipping these states is what enabled them to enact their second and third weapons, as explained below.

4.   The 2010 election was the first election to be bought by Republicans post–*Citizens United*. The buying of the election was not an indiscriminate free-for-all. In fact, most seats were not targeted at all. For the vast majority of Americans, nothing changed. The Republican State Leadership Committee targeted key seats in a plan called REDMAP. By flooding those elections with money from billionaires and corporations after the *Citizens United* decision, they successfully targeted fewer than 200 of the 5,000 legislative seats up for election that year. Those seats gave them majorities in previously blue states (Wisconsin, Pennsylvania, Michigan, etc.).[3]

5.   After the election, the dominant media spin was that the GOP gains were in reaction to an unpopular Obamacare. This is appallingly incorrect. Just a few months before the election—immediately after the passage of Obamacare—the public favored its passage 49–40%, according to Gallup.[4] Not a single part of Obamacare was implemented in the short time between the passage of it and the 2010 election. And the new federal health care program certainly would have had no negative impact on state legislatures in Wisconsin and Michigan and other blue states that favored Obamacare. The 2010 Republic-dominated election was a direct result of the avalanche of money fueled by the *Citizens United* case.

6.   The REDMAP program—and its obscene funding from the Koch brothers, Walmart, the US Chamber of Commerce, and so on—gave the GOP legislative majorities that implemented two additional weapons: extreme gerrymandering and voter suppression. Republicans also used diversionary propaganda to flood the media with controversies, misinformation, and conspiracies to keep attention away from their attacks on democracy.

7.   The unlimited dark money and voter suppression in key states such as Wisconsin, Michigan, Florida, North Carolina, and Pennsylvania, to name just a few, then led to the rise of Trump.

8. Trump then encouraged Russian interference in the election. Russian President Vladimir Putin famously obliged.

Understanding the Republicans' 4 Weapons is crucial to understanding why the Democrats will completely lose all power on November 8, 2022. Understanding these 4 Weapons will also be the precursor to the actions outlined in part 3 needed to fix our democracy before it is too late.

Weapon #1: Dark Money Turning Elections into Auctions

The 2010 decade was by far the most expensive in the history of US elections. Independent groups spent billions to influence crucial races, supplanting political parties and morphing into extensions of candidate campaigns. Wealthy donors flexed their expanded political power by injecting unprecedented sums into elections. And transparency eroded as dark-money groups, keeping their sources of funding secret, emerged as political powerhouses.[5]

With the Supreme Court's 5–4 ruling in *Citizens United* in early 2010, individuals and corporations were allowed to spend unlimited amounts of money on politics for the first time. They can do so through something called "super PACs." There are also nonprofit groups called "501(c)(4) groups" that can accept unlimited contributions from individuals, corporations, and unions to spend on political activities such as TV commercials or Facebook ads.

Imagine if the Supreme Court took David's sling away and gave it to Goliath. Now you understand Citizens United.

How did America's wealthiest respond to *Citizen United's* "freedom of speech for billionaires?" Well, in the 2010 midterm, there was a 400% increase in expenditures from super PACs compared to the previous midterm election.[6] In the 2016 presidential campaign, fewer than 400 families accounted for almost half the money raised.[7]

The average top-end contribution by individuals to PACs went from $5,000 in 2008 to over $1 million in 2010.

In the 2012 election cycle, 97% of the contributions to the super PACs would have been illegal prior to *Citizens United*.[8] The massively wealthy began to apply as much political muscle with their fortunes as they wanted. It really is chump change to them. At long last, billionaires could get their way in American politics! According to the Republican-appointed Supreme Court majority's logic, our elections were neither fair or free previously because billionaires and corporations could not spend as much money as they wanted. So in that view, our democracy was only "actualized" in mid-2010 once we stopped the shackling of wealth in politics. Thank you, Chief Justice John Roberts, for making America so great in the 2010 decade.

Ironically, Roberts has given us the path to real democracy. In 2021, we can fix this avalanche of dark money and rein in lobbyists while we are at it, no constitutional amendment necessary. More on that in part 3.

But why do we call it "dark money"? The money given to the nonprofit 501(c)(4)s does not have to be reported. An investigation by the *New York Times* uncovered hidden contributions of over $1 million from American Electric Power, Aetna, Prudential Financial, Dow Chemical, Merck, Chevron, and MetLife to Republican 501(c)(4) groups.[9]

Well, it can't be that dark if the *New York Times* found it, right? Wrong. It actually took journalists seven years of investigation and lawsuits to piece together who was behind the $20 million or more spent against Democrats and Obama from 2010 to 2012 from just one nonprofit group, Americans for Job Security. Spoiler alert, it was a bunch of billionaires: securities dealer Charles Schwab, founders of clothing retailer the Gap, the DeVos family, real estate magnate Steve Wynn, and the Bass Pro Shop guy, to name just a few.[10]

How great that these billionaires can donate unlimited money to pursue their special interests in tax breaks for the rich and be hidden from any accountability. Please feel free to return your Baby Gap clothes now—or at least make masks out of them to protect us from Trump's COVID-19 bungling.

Another fun example of election auctioning was in Alabama in 2010. Democrats had controlled both houses in the state legislature for over 130 years straight. Sure, many of those Democrats had been white supremacists, but not so much in the past thirty years. Democrats held a 60–43 majority in Alabama's House of Representatives and a 20–15 majority in the state senate until 2010. The head of the Republican Party—Mike Hubbard, who later would be jailed for illegal political activities—figured out how to launder money from a local Native American casino controlled by the Poarch Band of Creek Indians. In Alabama, money from gambling is toxic due to conservative Christian principles. So under the lawless *Citizens United* scheme, Hubbard funneled over $1 million of campaign contributions to the Republican State Leadership Committee (RSLC)—the same people who ran REDMAP. The RSLC then donated almost the exact same amount to the Republican candidates in Alabama, effectively laundering the money.

This laundered money was such a huge sum for the normally low-spend state elections that the Republicans overturned the historic Democratic majorities. Incredibly, the Republicans in Alabama were able to achieve two-thirds majorities in both houses of their state legislature in just one election cycle.[11]

Because of the dark-money mechanism, no one in Alabama was aware of this scheme until it came out years later.[12] And that's not why Hubbard was convicted, either—this money laundering scheme is now legal in the United States, thanks to the Supreme Court. Let freedom ring!

What did the Alabama Republicans then do with this money-bought majority? This is detailed in the second and third weapons below—extreme gerrymandering and voter suppression.

If this wave of money just gave Republicans a majority in Alabama, then I'd probably not have written this book. So let's look at the rest of the 2010 midterms—the first election after *Citizens United*—since it is not well understood. First, conservative super PACs were poised to strike as soon as the Supreme Court took the sheath off their sword. They quickly spent almost $90 million in the months after *Citizens United*, compared to less than $10 million for liberal super PACs. The liberals were completely in the dark about the new reality and were outspent 11–1 with this new weapon during this campaign cycle.[13] But in the areas the Republicans were targeting through REDMAP, the numbers were often 20–1.

This was a perfectly executed sneak attack on free and fair elections that succeeded more wildly than any of the Republican strategists had dared dream. Try to imagine the impact at the local or state level. One side—led by the outside groups supporting Republicans—suddenly have twenty times the staffers, twenty times the TV commercials, twenty times the mailers of the Democrats. And none of it was being reported. That's enough to turn a 55% Democratic district to a 51% Republican vote. Targeted Democratic legislators all over the country were facing a barrage of attacks from unknown sources aimed at soiling and degrading their reputations. The effort was successful and led to a massive swing of legislatures from blue to red, including Congress: the GOP picked up sixty-three House seats and six Senate seats and flipped a remarkable twenty state legislative houses.

All through the 2010 elections and continuing throughout most of the decade, the Republican-affiliated 501(c)(4)s and super PACs have massively outspent Democrats. In the 2016 election, for instance, the Koch brothers' network alone spent close to $900 million on the Republican cause in Congress.[14] Give the devils their due: they refused to support Trump. The Democrats' biggest network—unions—spent just over $100 million combined.[15] That included the money on behalf of Hillary Clinton's presidential campaign. In the 2014 election, the incumbent Democratic senator from North Carolina, Kay Hagan, was defeated by more than $28 million of dark money spent against her. The Democrats could only muster $2.3 million of dark money to support her.[16] She lost by only 45,000 votes, approximately 1.5%.

Money in politics is the great black hole of democracy—every elected body gets sucked into its spiral of destruction; no issue can escape its gravitational pull. This is just wrong. And grotesque. We still have elections, but do they strike you as free and fair? (See Figure 8.)

Can Democracy Survive Big-Money Elections?

We are mostly blind to the impact of the grotesque amount of money in campaigns. First, it doesn't happen in the safe seats—which are a majority of seats, especially on the coasts. But if you live in a swing district, you see some of the money in extra commercials on TV. This is not, however, the extent of how or where the money is spent. So much of the money is spent on behind the scene efforts for expenses like pollsters, buying information on voters, paying for staff, and countless campaign infrastructure expenses.

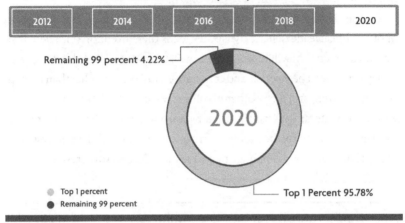

SUPER PAC DONORS
(2012 - 2020)

The percentage of money going to super PACs from the top 1 percent of super PAC donors has increased in every full cycle since 2012.

2012	2014	2016	2018	2020

Remaining 99 percent 4.22%

2020

○ Top 1 percent
● Remaining 99 percent

Top 1 Percent 95.78%

Figure 8. With permission from Center for Responsive Politics https://www.opensecrets.org/

Imagine two cars racing in NASCAR. One has a seasoned, professional pit crew. The other has a bunch of volunteers from the local high school using their dads' wrenches. One has a professional videographer crew; the other is trying to figure out how to record video on their Android phone. That's what those political races felt like.

Republicans have continued to use this dark-money advantage to prop up the otherwise uninspiring Republican congressional candidates in the 2012, 2014, and 2016 elections. Polling in the months before the 2010, 2012, 2014, and 2016 elections showed the Democrats winning, as the charts show in figure 2. But the GOP's 4 Weapons—particularly the money advantage—rendered polling irrelevant. The money hydrant flowed hardest in the last month of the election.

This money also helped Republicans retain control of the Senate starting in 2014. It helped them limit their losses in the House in what should have been an even greater tsunami in 2018. But big money can't always buy an individual election. Some billionaires lose when they run—ask Michael Bloomberg. California won't elect a Republican senator no matter how much money is poured into that race. But in the aggregate, money does buy governing majorities where they are within reach. We should not feel reassured that democracy might survive an avalanche of money in a few individual races. We need to get angry that our elected leaders—Democrats as much as Republicans—allow the system to continue when there is such an easy solution as explained in part 3.

Even aside from elections, no one can say that money doesn't set the agenda for our political leaders. It sets what they focus their attention on. There is almost no difference in willingness between Democrats and Republicans to take money from the richest people and corporations in America (other than perhaps Sanders, Warren, and a few other notables). Most of these big donors have a reason to donate, and it's usually not for good government. Yet Democrats did not even attempt to fix the problems in our campaigns and election system in 2009–2010 when they held huge majorities and Obama was president.

While Democrats are our only hope right now, the fight in 2021 will be against any Democrats who care more about their cushy jobs than they do the fate of democracy.

Weapon #2: Extreme Gerrymandering

> The practices challenged in these cases imperil our system of government. Part of the Court's role in that system is to defend its foundations. None is more important than free and fair elections. By substantially diluting the votes of citizens favoring their rivals, the politicians of one party succeeded in entrenching themselves in office. They had beat democracy.
>
> —Supreme Court Justice Elena Kagan's dissent in the *Ruch v. Common Cause* decision that allowed Republican states to use extreme gerrymandering

Gerrymandering is the political process by which the boundaries of political seats are drawn to benefit the party in charge of drawing the maps. Generally, seats need to be drawn with proportionate numbers of individuals in them. Other than that, there are very few rules that have survived the Republican Supreme Court's rulings. Thanks to gerrymandering, Republicans were able to slow Obama's ability to appoint federal judges, and then they packed the courts with Trump appointees. These Republican-appointed judges have now concluded that gerrymandering aimed at stopping Democrats from being elected is no longer unconstitutional. Go figure.

Let's take a step back though. Who draws these boundaries? Remarkably, it's the politicians themselves. It would be as bad as if they could set their own tax rate—oh, wait, they can do that too.

In America, elected representatives choose their voters, not the other way around.

In a few states, like California, the voters have taken this self-serving, ass-preserving power away from the politicians. But in most states, the politicians continue to have such power. So then why is this such a powerful GOP weapon?

It goes back to the 2010 election. Remember the one where Republicans swamped Democrats, outspending them 20–1 in many key seats due to the new *Citizens United* free-for-all campaign financing scheme? That election was key because it determined who would draw the congressional and legislative maps for the entire next decade—the decade we've just slogged through. The Republicans flipped so many states in that election from blue to red—and captured supermajorities in many states—that Republicans were able to draw the maps without having to compromise with Democrats. Because the states draw the maps both for themselves and for congressional seats, it was a twofer. And because these maps last ten years, it screwed up the entire 2010 decade for majority-rules democracy.

Political consultant Karl Rove, the Einstein of disenfranchisement, figured out that the Republicans only had to flip 107 state seats in sixteen states to gain an inordinate amount of legislative majorities or even supermajorities. Republicans could then redraw the district lines for 190 congressional seats![17] That's not just math, that's calculus, baby.

There are almost 7,400 state seats in the entire country, but it only took flipping about 1% of them to ruin Obama's presidency. Spending obscene amounts of money on 1% of state legislative seats gave Republicans control of Congress and almost two-thirds of the states despite ever-shrinking support.

So the money that poured into GOP groups after the *Citizens United* decision focused on those 107 key state legislative seats plus a few dozen others for insurance. That's how Weapon #1 (unlimited dark money) created Weapon #2 (extreme gerrymandering).

The redrawing of district maps after the 2010 election was so powerful because the Republican mapmakers were able to use advanced mapping technology. This technology did not exist in previous decades. For the first time, they could draw maps and exclude certain houses on the same block based on a full profile of the people in those houses. As the man who has tried so hard to educate Democrats on gerrymandering, senior advisor of FairVote David Daley, pointed out:

> Gerrymandering from 1790 through 2000 is really just...politicians working from memory about which neighborhoods are friendly, and they've got magic markers and giant pieces of parchment paper. In 2010, gerrymandering moved into its steroids era. It is highly sophisticated computer software.... Magazine subscriptions, information that can be gleaned off of social media, the kinds of things we leave about ourselves as we travel around the Internet that marketers and political firms and mapmakers can buy up for pennies on the dollar.[18]

Partisan mapmaking in 2010 became the most important factor in determining which party won which seat. It also made it nearly impossible for Democrats to regain control. In many states it simply doesn't matter now if a majority of the state votes for Democrats, Republicans will still win more seats and govern. Republicans have found a way to twist democracy to keep themselves in power despite having less support from voters.

Right now in America, Republican mapmakers have more power to determine which party controls the majority of states than do voters.

Wait until the 2021 redistricting when Republicans can use machine learning, AI, and neural networks when creating their maps. It will be Democrats versus robots. My money is on the robots.

To illustrate how this works, imagine a state with ten political seats and 1,000,000 voters, 600,000 of whom are Democrats and 400,000 who are Republicans. Democrats should have six representatives and the Republicans should have four, you say? Ha! You will never make it as a Republican legislator. When a Republican official sees that split, they think Republicans should control seven—not four—of those ten seats. They hire the Republican mapmakers who travel all over the country, kind of like Lewis and Clark, but with a laptop instead of a canoe. They then draw the maps so that seven of the seats have 55,000 Republicans to 45,000 Democrats. So they win those seven seats. The other three seats end up having 95,000 Democrats and just 5,000 Republicans. The Republicans gain a 7–3 advantage even though they only have 40% support, compared to the Democrats' 60% support.

I know what you are thinking. Can we go back to talking about tax policy please?

Or maybe you are thinking my example above is too extreme. No way could that be real. I take that as a personal challenge.

Let's start at the federal level. Remember that 2012 election? Obama cruised to an easy victory over Romney. But the Democrats got killed in the House of Representatives 234–201. The news media talked about how the American public wanted a check on Obama by giving control of the House to Republicans. But did Democrats really lose the House? Actually, the Democratic House candidates got 1.4 million more votes than Republican candidates; yet the Republicans still won 54% of the House seats. That was due solely to the gerrymandering of 2011. Republicans are now guaranteed at least a seventeen-seat majority in the House of Representatives when the vote is evenly split.[19]

That meant that instead of Obama passing policy after we elected him president again, all we got were government shutdowns, votes to repeal Obamacare, and investigations into Benghazi and Hillary's "missing" 33,000 emails. Republicans shrug and say, "Elections matter." Of course, they mean *we will make sure voting doesn't matter.*

Onward to the states! Wisconsin, Pennsylvania, Michigan, North Carolina, Virginia, Ohio, and Texas, oh my. I won't have to cherry-pick from elections in the 2010s because they all had upside-down results. Nor am I gonna give you all the stats on all the elections. This isn't inside baseball. But here's a little taste of what Republicans managed to pull off in each of those states.

Wisconsin

In 2012, Democrats won 53% of the votes statewide, but the Republicans won over 60% of the seats. That's the power of gerrymandering to destroy democracy. This is the same election where Obama won the majority of votes in Wisconsin. In 2016 Republicans received just over 50% of the vote statewide—a majority due to the power of voter suppression and dark money—but won almost two-thirds of the seats.

In 2018, Democrats swept every single statewide office, including governor. Democrat Tammy Baldwin won re-election to the US Senate by eleven percentage points. Democratic assembly candidates captured 200,000 more votes statewide than Republicans. Despite Democrats winning 53% of the votes, Republicans won a 63–36 majority in the state assembly. Republicans won 64% of the seats, even though they won 47% of the vote. The Democrats' vote share of 53% only gained them 36% of the seats. Democrats need to beat Republicans by over ten points statewide to win just 50% of the seats in the assembly.

Pennsylvania

In 2012, Democrats won 51% of the statewide vote for Congress. Yet Republicans won thirteen of the eighteen seats because of the maps that they had drawn the year before. C'mon, those are some genius mapmakers. You have to acknowledge that they really perfected making voting irrelevant to the outcome. Mission accomplished. Similar results happened for the rest of the decade.

Michigan

In the 2016 election, Republicans won 50% of the vote for the House but garnered nine of the fourteen seats (64%). Democrats won the majority of the votes for the state house, but Republicans won 57% of the seats. Similar results occurred during the entire 2010 decade.

North Carolina

In the 2016 US House races in North Carolina, Democrats won 47% of votes but only three out of thirteen seats. I told you my hypothetical above was not an exaggeration! In the 2018 midterms, the GOP picked up nine of thirteen US House seats with only 50% of the statewide vote. In their state legislature, the Democratic candidates for the North Carolina house and senate won a solid majority of the statewide vote, but Republicans won 54% of the state house seats and 58% of the state senate seats. Remarkably, pundits keep repeating that North Carolina is now a Republican state. #lamestreammedia

Virginia

The great 2017 Democratic victory in Virginia is a great case analysis. It was described as a blue wave, and pundits marveled that the Democrats won 49% of the seats in the Virginia House of Delegates. Celebrate good times! But this is just another case of Democrats being willfully blind (see chapter 5). In the delegate race, 55% of Virginians voted for Democrats, yet Republicans still managed to maintain control of their state house despite losing by 10%. In other words, Democrats need about 58% of the vote to win 50% plus one of the seats.

Not a single Democratic Party official or journalist that I could find mentioned this in any of the coverage after that election. No one. I can't even add a footnote because I am the one who had to add the voter count on all one hundred of those election results. Help me out here, Democrats! This is the stuff that we should be obsessing over, not Drumpf's latest tweet. Too few Democratic leaders have woken up to the impact of these GOP Weapons Against Democracy. Instead they actually celebrate staying in the minority even when they win a majority of votes. I, on the other hand, get angry about it and write a book. Not sure which is the better coping mechanism.

Ohio

In 2012, Republicans received 52% of the vote but 75% of the congressional house seats (12 of 16). Two years later, Democrats won 48% of the vote and thus should have won eight of the sixteen seats. No. Due to the brutal gerrymandering during the 2011 mapmaking, they won only 25% of the state's house seats—four of the sixteen. It's startling. C'mon LeBron, stop dribbling and speak up.[20]

Texas

In 2018, Democrats won 47% of congressional votes in Texas, but barely won a third of the seats, winning only thirteen seats to the Republicans' twenty-three seats. A great example within Texas is Travis County. Ultraliberal Austin is in Travis. The county voted for Clinton over Trump by nearly thirty-nine points (66 to 27 percent). That county has six congressional seats. All the Democrats (representing almost two-thirds of the voters) have been packed into one seat. The Republicans won the other five seats. They do things big in Texas. As Republican Texas governor Greg Abbott candidly explained: "Our redistricting decisions were designed to increase the Republican Party's electoral prospects at the expense of the Democrats."[21] You're darn tootin'.

Missouri

In Missouri in 2019, 63% of voters supported an initiative to have the maps drawn by a nonpartisan committee. The Republican legislature gutted the reform in 2020 to steal back the mapmaking for the GOP. They are also test-running an idea to only count people eighteen years old and above when drawing maps. This gives people in cities and minorities—who have more kids per capita—less representation and makes states much redder.

Overall, in the seventeen states where Republicans controlled gerrymandering, Republicans won 53% of the congressional vote yet came away with a remarkable 72% of the congressional seats. This represented 40% of the entire US Congress.[22] This is the primary reason Republicans have maintained control of Congress through most of the 2010 decade. Voilà!

After the 2018 House election, Democrats celebrated as though they had won everything, yet almost sixty million Americans continued to live under minority rule in their state legislatures.[23] So in those states—all Republican-led—the party with fewer votes in the 2018 election controls a majority of seats in the legislatures as of early 2020.

Due solely to gerrymandering, Republicans start each election cycle with approximately more seventeen seats in the US House of Representatives than they should have relative to their share of the popular vote. It takes approximately a 55% vote for the Democrats to win a bare majority of the seats. In other words, it takes a *landslide* for Democrats to achieve a majority. Trump delivered a landslide for Democrats in 2018. What happens when he is no longer embarrassing himself in the White House? How would Democrats continue to count on landslides?

As a good-hearted and trusting American, your first instinct is "Let's sue the bastards! That can't possibly be legal." Well, four Supreme Court justices agreed with you in the 2018 *Gill v. Whitford* case from Wisconsin. Unfortunately, the five Republican-appointed Supreme Court justices thought the examples above were perfect. The Supreme Court held that partisan gerrymandering that allows the minority party to keep control of the government is constitutional. Had it gone the other way, it would have immediately swung the majority of American states back to majority Democrat legislatures and created an even larger majority in Congress for Democrats. But these five Republican justices didn't get appointed to the Supreme Court by Trump and George W. Bush to allow such results. As one court noted: "The Court finds that in many election environments, it is the carefully crafted maps, and not the will of the voters, that dictate the election outcomes in a significant number of legislative districts and, ultimately, the majority control of the [government]."[24, 25]

This is not democracy. It is a rigged political system that uses elections to hide the fact that we have become a one-party nation. When Republicans can control states, the Congress and the presidency—without having a majority of voters support them—it is an end to American democracy. Plain and simple. Democracy in America is ending. Say it our loud until you hear it. Now say it again, but this time say it to your Democratic Party senators and candidates until *they* grasp it. Don't be too surprised if they aren't too receptive; remember, they won their respective seats with these rules. But don't fret. The second half of this book solves all the problems from the first half of the book.

Before we get to the plan, however, there are two other weapons we need to understand beyond the unlimited dark money and extreme gerrymandering. These additional weapons help act as an additional firewall for Republicans to stay in power despite being so damn unpopular.

Weapon #3: Voter Suppression

> Voter ID, which is gonna allow Governor Romney to win the state
> of Pennsylvania, done.
>
> —Pennsylvania Republican house leader Mike Turzai[26]

Once the GOP began capturing states (thirty-three by 2017) with their dark money and gerrymandered districts, they went from having half as many states as Democrats had in 2010 to controlling four times as many just six years later. With control over these states, they began implementing Weapon #3: voter suppression. Voter suppression is almost as powerful as the unlimited dark money or extreme gerrymandering. It gives Republicans an undemocratic artificial boost that may lower Democratic voter turnout by more than 5% in many key districts.[27]

Using diversionary propaganda, Republicans constantly talk about voter fraud and Democrats stealing elections even though it is Republicans attacking free and fair elections. It's as if we've all been dropped into the world of *The Matrix* suddenly. Or, if you prefer books over movies, perhaps *Animal Farm*.

For those of us in blue states or cities, it is impossible to gauge the effectiveness of the Republican campaign to rob the power of certain US citizens to vote. It's unimaginable. Even the dark money and gerrymandering could be excused as dirty politics. Denying people the vote, however, seems like treason. It strikes at the very heart of what it means to be American in this democracy: one person, one vote.

Before Obama's election in 2008, there were no strict voter ID laws in the United States, nor were there any states cutting back on early voting. These restrictions on voting started after the 2008 election, which saw record numbers of young voters and record participation by people of color. All of these voting restriction laws have been passed in states controlled by the Republican Party. In 2011–2012, nineteen states—all Republican (have I mentioned that?)—made it harder to vote by passing very similar laws regarding:

- photo ID laws and documentary proof of citizenship requirements;
- voter purges and restraints on voter registration;

- cuts to early voting and restrictions on the casting and counting of absentee and provisional ballots; and
- highly targeted polling place closures.

These laws disproportionately impact young people, people of color, and poor people—a.k.a. the Obama coalition.

How much of an impact?

For years, white voters and Republicans disproportionately used early voting. But in 2008, due to the Obama campaign's emphasis on early voting, that changed significantly. That year, more than 50% of African Americans voted early in Florida, and more than 70% of African Americans voted early in North Carolina. College students also voted early. Obama won North Carolina by only 15,000 votes in 2008. When Republicans captured the government in North Carolina after the *Citizens United* decision, they passed HB 589. This bill eliminated early voting and same-day registration, even though almost a million North Carolinian voters would vote during that week of early voting. It also stopped seventeen-year-olds from filling out voter registration forms in order to be automatically registered upon reaching eighteen. Those kids are seventeen years and nine months too old for Republicans to care about them.

Almost all of the states controlled by Republicans adopted these tactics for similar reasons. As Doug Preisse, Republican chair of Ohio's second-largest county, argued for ending the state's early voting: "I guess I really actually feel we shouldn't contort the voting process to accommodate the urban—read African American—voter-turnout machine."[28] [The "read African American" clarification is his.]

The Republicans also set up onerous ID requirements even though more than 200,000 registered voters in North Carolina didn't have driver's licenses. They prohibited college students from using college IDs, even state-issued ones. It is estimated that 25% of Black Americans nationally lack a government-issued photo ID, compared to just 8% of whites.[29] These are numbers that can tip presidential elections and majorities in state government. A North Carolina Republican official, Don Yelton, admitted that these North Carolina's voting restrictions are "going to kick Democrats in the butt."[30]

That's what restrictive voter ID laws are intended to do, obviously.

Twenty-first-century voter disenfranchisement looks different from the first century of vote suppressions between 1865 and 1965. In that first hundred years, mostly Southern Democrats sought to take away the vote from Black Americans because of white supremacy. Now it is Republicans who are taking the vote away from as many people as possible, regardless of the color of their skin. The focus is on disenfranchising the members of the Obama coalition—many, of course, who are African American. But the Republicans will also dutifully suppress the vote of youth, Native Americans, and any other member of the Obama coalition. They are equal opportunity vote suppressors.

Of course, we've fought wars or supported coups to stop people from voting when they vote for someone we don't like. Think Iran in 1953, Guatemala in 1954, Chile in 1973, Nicaragua in 1985, Haiti in 2004, and Honduras 2009, to name just a few. Perhaps it is not surprising then that Republicans do this in the United States. Putin is definitely smirking over Republicans using American empire tactics against American citizens.

So what are the tactics Republicans have used to suppress votes in the 2010 decade? There are four.

Vote-Denying Tactic #1: Purging Voter Rolls

> This [voter purge] will lead to people distrusting election administration in Wisconsin. If people feel like a system is rigged, it has a pretty profound impact on whether or not they feel it's even worthwhile to participate in an election.
>
> —Neil Albrecht, Milwaukee Election Commission[31]

Voter suppression since 2010 has been done with software programs instead of white hoods. Republicans developed the Interstate Voter Registration Crosscheck Program, commonly called Crosscheck. It allows Republican secretaries of state to purge hundreds of thousands of voters from voting rolls. Crosscheck was started by the then-chair of the Kansas Republican Party Kris Kobach. Thirty other Republican-controlled states enrolled in this Kansas state program, making it a national program despite not being passed by Congress. Kind of like that group of Democratic states who entered into a multistate compact to buy life-saving materials to fight COVID-19. Like that, except opposite.

Crosscheck searches for people who registered twice using only voters' first and last names and date of birth. It generates thousands of false matches. In a 2016 paper, researchers at Stanford University and the University of Pennsylvania found that for every voter registered twice and removed, two hundred legitimate voters may be stopped from voting.[32] Even when a person is registered twice, however, it doesn't mean they vote twice! Duh.

A fun—as in knife-to-the-eyeball fun—exchange occurred in a court case where the ACLU was trying to block a massive voter purge in Kansas. Kris Kobach's "expert" witness, Jesse Richman, testified that he flagged "foreign-sounding" names as examples of illegal voters. The ACLU attorney asked, "What about a name like 'Carlos Murguia'?" "Yes," Richman replied. The ACLU attorney then informed him that Carlos Murguia is a federal district judge (or was at the time).[33] You can't make this stuff up, folks.

As a legacy from slavery when enslaved people were given the last names of the white supremacists who enslaved them, Black Americans are much more likely to share the same name than white Americans. Republicans have lost their moral compass. Only they would find a way to extend that shameful Southern heritage in order to hurt descendants of those enslaved.

Twelve million voters were purged nationally between 2006 and 2008 ostensibly because they died, moved, et cetera. This was a normal purge, useful for a base count. Republican states have now led so many purges since then that 16 million voters were purged from the rolls between 2014 and 2016,[34] and between 2016 and 2018, 17 million voters were purged.[35] That's an extra 9 million voters in just four years than would have been predicted using the 2006–2008 numbers. Nine million voters are enough to swing a whole host of elections. It can even get Donald J. Trump elected and re-elected. This is especially true considering the disproportionate number of purged voters among African Americans rolls, Latino communities, students, and poor people.

Let's get back to Kobach. As any of the listeners to my podcast *Your Daily Trump* can attest, I was pretty obsessed with Kobach, a 2020 contender for the Republican nomination for Senate in Kansas. I considered him to be the worst American politician alive. I know, that seems harsh considering the accomplishments of Trump, Hannity, or Presidential Medal of Freedom whiner Rush Limbaugh. But you can't choose all of them.

Kobach is best known for lying about millions of "illegals" voting. When President Trump claimed that he won the popular vote if you were to subtract all of the illegal immigrants that voted for Hillary Clinton, he was citing Kris Kobach's numbers. Kris Kobach used an invalid interpretation of the Cooperative Congressional Election Study (CCES) to come to this unsupported conclusion. That was a study commissioned by the new Republican Congress that was attempting to prove illegal immigrants were commonly voting in elections. The three political scientists who coordinated the original CCES study, however, concluded, "The best estimate of the percentage of noncitizens who vote is zero."[36] But facts do not stop Trump or Kobach from repeating the false claim.

In Georgia, Republican Governor Brian Kemp—who stole the election from Stacey Abrams in 2018—disqualified almost 600,000 voters that had not voted in the previous three years before his election, 800,000 in the years before that. He converted the power of voting into a "use-it-or-lose-it" right. The equivalent would be if you don't shoot a gun every three years, the government takes away your guns.[37] Something makes me think that would not go over well. As the remarkable Abrams noted after the election:

> My opponent was a cartoon villain who stole the voices of Georgians when he purged 1.4 million voters and oversaw the shutdown of 214 precincts that left 50,000 to 60,000 people without the ability to vote, when Georgia had the longest lines in the nation and the highest rejection rates of absentee ballots and provisional ballots.[38]

In Wisconsin, a conservative law group appealed to a Republican-appointed judge to purge over 200,000 voters from the voting roll in 2019. Nine of the ten areas with the highest concentration of voters slated to be purged voted for Clinton.[39] The judge agreed and threw 234,000 voters off state rolls.[40] Trump won Wisconsin by just 23,000 votes. The three Democratic members of the Wisconsin election board refused the judge's order and were held in contempt and personally fined for not moving the voter purge forward quickly enough.

The battle is real. There are heroes and victims. As Alan King, Democrat appointed to Trump's Voter Fraud Committee in 2017, stated: "The less affluent in our society are more prone to move.... But that does not mean that officials in government should 'game the system' to deprive the less affluent from voting, simply because they may have moved from one election to another only to be stricken from the active voter list."[41]

In 2016, Arkansas purged thousands of voters for so-called felony convictions, even though some of the voters had never been convicted of a felony at all. Voters typically learn they've been purged when they show up at the polls on Election Day. It's usually too late for them to do anything about it.

Vote-Denying Tactic #2: Restrictive Voter ID Laws

> I was in the closed Senate Republican Caucus when the final round of multiple Voter ID bills were being discussed. A handful of the GOP senators were giddy about the ramifications and literally singled out the prospects of suppressing minority and college voters.... Elected officials planning and happy to help deny a fellow American's constitutional right to vote in order to increase their own chances to hang onto power.
>
> —Republican Todd Allbaugh, a staff aide to a Republican state legislator, who quit his job in 2015 after that meeting[42]

Republicans also intensified other voter suppression laws, such as restrictive ID laws. They openly admit these laws make it more difficult for Democrats to vote. Republican-led states are making it impossible to vote with Native American IDs or college IDs—even if it is a state college—but allow gun permits to suffice as IDs in places like Texas. Basically, just look at the Obama coalition, and Republicans will target that demographic.

Can this tactic alone change election outcomes and who controls the federal government or state legislatures? *Yes.*

Before Obama was elected, no state required photo ID to vote; now ten states, all Republican, have strict requirements. Twenty-three other states now have some version of restrictive voter identification laws.[43] The gap between white voters and minority voters significantly increases with these ID laws. (See Figure 9.)

The Government Accountability Office estimated that restrictive voter ID laws reduce total voter turnout by 2.5%.[44] But it's not as if this

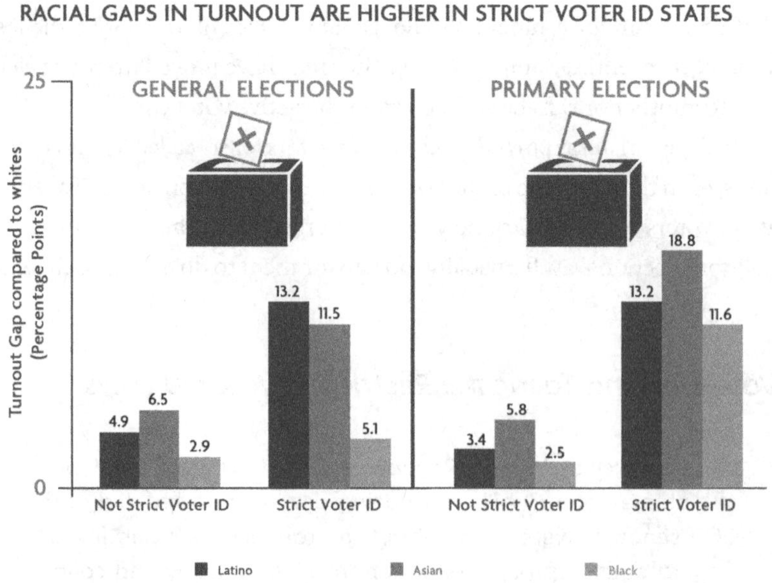

RACIAL GAPS IN TURNOUT ARE HIGHER IN STRICT VOTER ID STATES

Figure 9. Source: Zoltan L. Hajnal, Nazita Lajevardi. "Analysis | Do Voter Identification Laws Suppress Minority Voting? Yes. We Did the Research." *The Washington Post*, WP Company, 18 Apr. 2019, www.washingtonpost.com/news/monkey-cage/wp/2017/02/15/do-voter-identification -laws-suppress-minority-voting-yes-we-did-the-research/.

amount could ever make a difference in an election or even the chase for the presidency, right? (Spoiler alert: Trump won Wisconsin, Michigan, and Pennsylvania, all states with strict voter ID laws, by an average of less than 1%.) More than 21 million US citizens do not have government-issued photo identification.[45] Obviously they don't deserve to vote, damn commies.

In Wisconsin, after the Republicans passed their strict voter ID laws, a federal court found that more than 300,000 registered voters—disproportionately Democrat and African American—lacked the required ID for voting in that state. The restrictive voter ID law worked exactly as the Republicans intended: 41,000 fewer voters voted in 2016 than in 2012, just in the Democratic stronghold of Milwaukee.[46] Trump only "won" Wisconsin by 21,000 votes. Ironically the only person ever convicted under the strict voting laws in Wisconsin was a registered Republican who voted for Republican governor Scott Walker multiple times.[47]

Black Americans, students, young adults, elderly residents, and low-income voters are the ones most likely not to have the required citizenship documents. By the time many of these voters learn of the ID requirements—at the polls—it is too late to obtain them in time to vote. If they live in an area in which Republicans have closed voting locations, then they often would not have enough time to even return home and wait in line again if they did have the IDs at home. It's a perfect system. As a *Washington Post* study showed:

> By instituting strict voter ID laws, states can alter the electorate and shift outcomes toward those on the right. Where these laws are enacted, the influence of Democrats and liberals wanes and the power of Republicans grows.[48]

In North Dakota, Republicans were able to defeat incumbent Senator Heidi Heitkamp after creating restrictive voter ID laws. Thousands of Native Americans—who were strong supporters of Democrat Heitkamp—were prevented from voting because they could not show their current residential address. Native Americans who live on reservations mostly do not have street names and instead use PO boxes. So no vote, regardless of whether your family has been here for 30,000 years.[49] Part 3 of this book has a plan to not only fix voter suppression but also to restore some power to the more than five million Native Americans in the United States.

Prior to the 2018 election, Republicans held the trifecta in New Hampshire. They tried to block residents with out-of-state driver's licenses from voting in New Hampshire elections. This was targeted at college students, 60% of whom come from outside of New Hampshire.[50]

Kansas was the first state—starting in 2013—to require proof of citizenship to register to vote. Kris Kobach was the secretary of state. Don't get me started! This rule has blocked one in seven Kansans from registering to vote, with nearly half of them being under the age of thirty. Birth certificates and passports are not things most Americans carry around with them. Not everyone brings these documents down to the long wait at the DMV where they theoretically could register to vote. And if you go to the farmers market, apparently you must remember to bring your birth certificate as well as your reusable tote bag in case a League of Women Voters volunteer is there helping people register to vote.

There are entire books written about how and why Democrats have lost the Midwestern states. None of them that I've read mentioned voter suppression. Go figure.

In late April 2020, during the COVID-19 pandemic, Republicans in Kentucky overrode the Democratic governor's veto of a hastily passed voter ID law. Republicans were for the first time requiring that voters bring a narrow list of IDs to vote in the election in November 2020. That election will have both Mitch McConnell and Trump on the ballot. The Republicans did this after *all* of the DMVs and county clerk offices in the state—which are where you would get the ID—were closed because of COVID-19. The Republican secretary of state said they were doing this to "make it easier to vote."[51] Obviously he said that to give people like me a stroke. Of course, the need for this regulation was only seen after a Democratic governor was voted into office in November 2019.

Vote-Denying Tactic #3: Making Voting and Registering to Vote Difficult

> We want to do everything we can to help our side. Sometimes we think that's voter ID, sometimes we think that's longer lines—whatever it may be.
>
> —Scott Tranter, Republican political consultant[52]

Another weapon to deny the vote is by simply making it more inconvenient to vote. Since 2010, Republican states have begun restricting early voting, same-day registration, and—even worse—closing polling places in Democratic areas while expanding them in Republican districts. These cuts create four- or five-hour long voting lines in these Democratic Party strongholds.

It's fair to say that Democrat Stacey Abrams, an African American woman, lost her race for governor in Georgia in 2018 due to voter suppression. This suppression was spearheaded by her opponent—the man who remained in charge of overseeing his own election, Republican then-secretary of state and now the Great Usurper Governor, Brian Kemp. Leading up to his 2018 election against Abrams, Kemp's office refused to approve 53,000 voter registration forms—80% of which were from voters of color[53]—because of the law he helped pass, called the "exact match" law. This allowed him to reject names with nonidentical hyphens, middle initials, or accent marks. These US citizens were not allowed to vote on Election Day. Kemp also purged 1.4 million voters between the 2012 and 2016 elections. He then kept on purging, and a remarkable 70% of the Georgia voters purged in 2018 were African American.[54]

Only in America. Well, probably in apartheid South Africa as well, back in the day.

Some states just make it difficult to vote by closing polling places. Not just a few polling places—hundreds. Mostly in Black and Latino communities.

Texas, Arizona, Louisiana, North Carolina, Mississippi, and Alabama, to name just a few, all have a disgraceful history of discriminating against minority voters. They had been subject to US Civil Rights Commission oversight for decades. In 2013 the Supreme Court, led by its Republican-appointed justices, removed all such oversight from all states when it threw out some of the most important parts of the Voting Rights Act in the *Shelby County v. Holder* case. Those states celebrated by closing polling places in minority areas.[55] Of course that's how they responded. They were ruled by Republicans in the 2010s, and that's what Republicans now do.

Hervis Rogers is the "last man standing" voter in Texas—at least he was on Election Day March 2020. Rogers waited seven hours in line to vote after massive polling closures in his mostly Black American area.[56] In fact, the fifty Texas counties that gained the most Black and Latino residents from 2012 to 2018 eliminated 542 polling sites after the *Shelby* decision, while the fifty counties that gained the fewest Black and Latino residents during that time eliminated only thirty-four sites.[57]

But that might not be enough to keep Texas red. So on April 14, 2020, in the midst of the COVID-19 pandemic, Republican Texas attorney general Ken Paxton declared that fear of contracting COVID-19 is not a valid excuse for applying for an absentee ballot. He warned that anyone telling voters to apply on that basis could face "criminal sanctions" under state law prohibiting election fraud and the encouragement of "false information" on ballot applications.[58] To give me a break from writing this book, I engaged in some Twitter civil disobedience:

CommonSenseDemocracy · 4/15/20

hey #texas - if u fear COVID-19 & assume @GregAbbott_TX prioritizes politics above ur health, get your absentee ballot. now. BTW @KenPaxtonTX @TXAG go ahead and arrest me, you are corrupt/incompetent and I don't mind the legal battle. v.gd/ O7hk4F vote @JoeBiden

Texas AG threatens to criminally sanction any group that tells voters...
rawstory.com

Clearly the Republicans want me to finish this book because they didn't arrest me.

By midsummer 2020, Trump's re-election campaign had allocated $20 million in legal fees trying to prevent widespread use of absentee ballots filing more than a dozen lawsuits thus far.[59]

Texas and other red states have closed 16% of their polling locations in counties under the federal civil rights supervision once the Supreme Court's *Shelby* decision allowed racial discrimination again. Every one of these polling closures was done under Republican legislatures and Republican governors.

It is worth taking a moment to see that even in states that are considered red states, Republicans are so concerned about losing their power that they must rely on voter suppression. Imagine what the United States would look like if everybody got to vote. Georgia State speaker of the house David Ralston, a Republican, did imagine that in April 2020 in responding to the proposal to let all voters in Georgia vote by mail due to COVID-19:

> So, here, you know, the process keeps going up and up and up and so a multitude of reasons why vote by mail in my view is not acceptable," Ralston incoherently rambled, before adding, "the president said it best, this will be extremely devastating to Republicans and conservatives in Georgia.[60]

Sounds peachy to me.

You've been with me through philosophical treatises on taxes and explorations of the algorithms of gerrymandering. But I'm not going to subject you to a lengthy essay on poll closures. Maybe J. J. Abrams can do a movie on poll closures now that he's done directing *Star Wars* movies. But bear with me for just two more examples, pretty please.

Hard to imagine now, but Obama won Indiana in 2008. Republicans continued, however, to control the legislature. Fun fact: from 2008 to 2016—Pence was governor there until 2016—the GOP expanded early voting stations in Republican-dominated Hamilton County and decreased them from three to one in the state's biggest Democratic county, Marion, which has a large African American population. GOP stronghold Hamilton saw a 63% increase in early voting after expansion of voting stations there while Marion saw a 26% decrease.[61]

We end with a COVID-19 era example: Wisconsin, of course. Weeks before the April 7, 2020, election, the Democratic Party went to court to try to delay the election because we were in the midst of the COVID-19 outbreak, and everyone in the country was sheltering in place. The Democratic governor tried to delay the election but was opposed by the Republican-controlled state legislature. Eventually, the US Supreme Court sided with the Republican legislature. The court even went further and rolled back the vote-by-mail program that the Democratic governor had created. The Supreme Court thus prevented people from voting by absentee ballot and instead forced them to vote in person at the polls, at the exact same time that the government was telling them to stay at home or risk a life-threatening illness.

Thousands of people who had asked for absentee ballots in the weeks prior to the election never received them because the agencies that were to send them out had been shut down. The United States Supreme Court couldn't give a whit about this. In a moment of typical Republican hypocrisy, the Supreme Court took their vote to disenfranchise voters remotely because they were fearful of contracting COVID-19.

Why was this done? There was an important race on the ballot involving the Wisconsin Supreme Court, and a small turnout favored the conservative incumbent. Most polling locations were closed—175 out of the normal 180 in Milwaukee alone were closed—and those that were open had much fewer workers.[62]

Thanks to anger at the Republican shenanigans in the election, however, the progressive Democratic candidate beat the incumbent Republican Supreme Court member. Nothing like being pissed off to turn out voters! If only Democrats had understood this since 2010. It's hard to fight everything Republicans do, but as Marc Elias, the premier election rights litigator, wrote on Twitter in 2020: "There are paralyzingly long lines in TX, CA, and elsewhere. If Democrats and progressives don't prioritize solving this between now and November, we will lose. The GOP knows this, which is why they are closing polls and funding litigation to purge voters and block voting access." Florida State Republican Party chairman Jim Greer agrees: "The Republican Party, the strategists, the consultants, they firmly believe that early voting is bad for Republican Party candidates.... We've got to cut down on early voting because early voting is not good for us."[63]

Vote-Denying Tactic #4: Denying the Vote to Citizens with Felonies

Another denial of the vote is seen in Republicans reviving the old felon-disenfranchisement laws passed in most Southern states soon after the emancipation of those enslaved by Southern Christians. Almost 6 million voters with past felonies—and in some states, misdemeanors—are not allowed to vote in the United States.

How big are these numbers? Across the country, one in thirteen Black Americans cannot vote. In the following states it's nearly one in four[64]:

- Florida (21 percent)
- Kentucky (26 percent)
- Tennessee (21 percent)
- Virginia (22 percent)

Black Codes like these date back to angry slave owners who lost the Civil War and wanted to keep African Americans in chains and prevent them from voting. What is a felony? After the Civil War, a Black man convicted of looking at a white woman would receive a felony and lose his vote—for life. Now, stealing a cell phone or anything over $400 is a felony in most states. The second possession of a marijuana cigarette—or first if your baggie of pot is big enough—is a felony. DUIs, violations of curfew, loitering laws, public drunkenness, and disorderly conduct can all be felonies and can strip you of your power of voting depending on the circumstances. It doesn't really matter if you're guilty or not. Imagine being charged with felony assault and then being offered a plea for creating a public disturbance with no time in jail. Of course you accept that. But the upshot is that you lose your power of voting.

In states like Florida, Iowa, and Kentucky, 20–25% of Black men permanently, for life, cannot vote.[65] Due to racial bias in both the criminal justice system and state legislatures, felony disenfranchisement laws disproportionately affect Black Americans. This is especially true considering that Black Americans face harsher sentences than whites for the same offenses. These laws are in the same states that blocked Black Americans' power of voting for the hundred years after the Civil War by enforcing poll taxes, literacy tests, and other barriers that were nearly impossible to meet. I'm not saying they are the Confederate States of MAGA, but I'm not disagreeing with you if that's what you call them. Actually, that name does seem fitting in the summer of 2020.

Remember the Afghanistan and Iraq wars that we started after Saudi Arabian men attacked the Twin Towers? And the Great Recession of 2007–2009 under George W. Bush? Bush won the presidency in 2000 based on his 537-vote victory in Florida. Florida is one of the states that has always disenfranchised ex-felons—or at least they have since slaves were freed and allowed to vote. Florida passed laws aimed at those same Black voters. Right before the infamous Gore versus Bush election, the Republican secretary of state purged over 10,000 voters, mostly African Americans, "mistakenly" claiming they were felons. Oopsies. The US Civil Rights Commission found that approximately 4,752 Black Gore voters—almost nine times Bush's margin of victory—could have been prevented from voting.[66]

The fight over the power of voting for US citizens with a felony continues in Florida; more than 10% of the adult population in Florida is permanently barred from voting. In 2018, voters approved an initiative 64–36% to stop denying the power of voting to US citizens with a felony.[67] Republicans in the legislature immediately changed the law so that these citizens would still be ineligible to vote unless they paid all fees, fines, and restitution costs from their conviction. The problem is that not only can these ex-felons not afford to pay these fines and costs, the state has no records of the amounts or who has paid and who has not.[68] So these 1.5 million citizens in Florida are still without the power of voting, despite the ballot initiative. The Republican Supreme Court then sided with Florida Republicans, and those ex-felons won't get to vote against Trump regardless of what Florida voters had decided.

To sum up, Republicans are okay with voting, but if you live in a Democratic area, be prepared to pay for identification cards that you otherwise would never need, travel far from your home to find a voter location that is open for limited hours on one workday where the lines may be extremely long and that will have few poll workers—and none of those know how to troubleshoot antiquated, hacker-friendly machines—while you are being challenged by armed Republican observers dressed like cops who claim you don't have a right to vote there. Be sure to bring your kids to show them how American democracy works.

Weapon #4: Diversionary Propaganda

The Republicans' three weapons above could not have flown under the radar for ten years if not for their fourth weapon: diversionary propaganda used to cover up the Republicans' destruction of our democracy. Weapon #4 does not require a suppression of the truth by legal means (though the Department of Justice has begun to arrest those who seek to publish un- flattering books about Trump like Michael Cohen).[69] Rather, the strategy is to overwhelm the public discourse with scandals, lies, misinformation, and distractions.

Throughout this book I criticize Democrats for constantly taking the bait—Trump tweets something mean, Democrats clamor to get in front of the cameras to denounce his ridiculousness. While Democrats and the media are distracted, Republicans make some other move against democracy or give some other corporate tax giveaway to supporters. While numerous books have been written about the problematic Fox News—Al Franken's *Lies and the Lying Liars Who Tell Them* (2003) being the most appropri- ately named among them—the effort is no longer restricted to Fox News opinionators.

Republicans and the right-wing media sphere use a whole host of tactics to hide Republican attacks on democracy. I'm not going to harp on the right- wing propaganda of Fox News and other billionaire-owned outlets. There are enough books on those ministers of disinformation already. Instead, I want to connect three otherwise disparate diversionary tactics that are effectively making it difficult to sound the alarm on Republican attacks on democracy: preemptively branding Democrats as threats to our democracy; weaponizing trolls and bots to "flood the zone with shit";[70] and covering up Putin's election interference to ensure its continuation.

Diversionary Tactic #1: While Destabilizing Democracy, Fox News and the GOP Elite Brand Democrats as the Real Threats to Democracy

Branding. Gotta hand it to Republicans. Starting with Ronald Reagan, Republicans have spun a myth that their team represents the real Americans: the patriotic, red-white-and-blue crew. USA! USA! USA! I guess the American public forgot about Watergate pretty quickly. I have a lovely history of just how obscene Republicans have been for the past forty years in appendix 10 if you want some more red meat.

Republicans brand, they don't follow polls.

Remember the Republicans campaigning on Obamacare's alleged death panels and Hillary's missing emails in the first half of the 2010 decade? Do you think Republicans polled on these issues and found that Americans were deeply concerned about them? Hardly. No one knew of either of these false fabrications until the Republicans focused on them. Republicans control the agenda by bringing focus to an issue. Republicans are also smart enough to bring focus to the various misdeeds they are currently engaged in. But they pre-emptively blame the Democrats for those same misdeeds.

Republicans, and Trump in particular, understand that if they accuse the other side of that of which they themselves are guilty, it will muddy the issue. They prime their supporters to focus on the sin but not to understand that the Republicans are in fact the sinners. And Democrats are frustratingly still unable to effectively counterattack. Look at how Democrats' refusal to go after Republican corruption allowed Trump to grab the issue of "draining the swamp" in DC. The swamp is made of corporate lobbyists giving campaign money to congressmen in exchange for bills designed to help those companies at the expense of the American public. The swamp also refers to enriching oneself by using one's position of power. Trump's "drain the swamp" campaign promise allowed him to dominate that issue, despite being the swampiest administration in the history of the country.

The Republicans' effectiveness in blaming Democrats for "the swamp" and similar branding—no matter how absurd—impacts voters. Since 1964, *CBS News* has annually polled voters on this question: "Is the government run by a few big interests looking out for themselves or for the benefit of all the people?"

- In 1964, 30% said our government was run by a few big interests.
- By 2018, 92% said it was run by a few big interests.[71]

Thanks to the effectiveness of Republican branding, more Republicans than Democrats believe the government is now run by and for a few big interests.[72] That's how poorly Democrats have blown the whistle at Republican corruption.

Another current example of the effectiveness of Republican branding is that nearly half of Americans believe voter fraud is widespread.[73] It doesn't exist—at all—according to numerous government investigations.[74] But Republicans are masters at manufacturing a problem, then coming up with the so called solutions. So Republicans and later Trump have been hammering on it for the entire 2010 decade. They spread this false message to justify their voter ID laws and voter purges that disenfranchise millions of voters. They do this to make it harder for people to vote during a pandemic, when polling locations are very limited. Polling did not determine their message and their need to divert attention from their misdeeds. Rather, their goal of voter suppression determined their message. That then drove the public's sentiment. It also kept Democrats basically silent on the issue of voter suppression relative to its importance.

Republicans' unbelievable focus on these issues planted "scandals" deeply into the minds of voters. Republicans know how to penetrate voters' consciousness through focus, repetition, and simple explanations. They repeat their issues over and over until a very large group of the American populace believes them.

After the 2016 election, these same problems plagued the Democrats again. Democrats in Congress were afraid of talking about Putin's work with Trump's campaign. There was so much hand-wringing among Democratic Party leaders that they were "overplaying the Russia story."[75] They feared that it was interfering with their poll-tested messaging about health care. They chose to bury this story by leaving it to Robert Mueller to conduct his investigation in secret. Democratic leaders refused to even consider a more public investigation through an impeachment process until a whistleblower reported Trump's extortion of the Ukrainian president.

Because Democrats have not prepared the American public regarding how much Republicans are willing to destroy democracy, Democrats self-censor. Republicans then get to brand Democrats as the ones attacking democracy.

Trump's first term is the price we have paid for Democrats' failure to focus sufficiently on the corruption of our democracy. If Democrats don't do a better job of sounding the alarm on Republicans' continued corruption and attacks on democracy, the price we may pay will be a second Trump term and/or a Republican takeover of Congress in 2022.

Republicans then escalate their branding to turn Democrats into the Evil Empire.

Look at any of your Republican friends' Facebook feeds, and you will see how they treat Democrats as if we were somehow traitors, the enemy, less American. At Trump rallies, there are signs that say, "I'd rather be Russian than a Democrat."

Republicans have branded Democrats as the enemy of the United States for forty years. Lee Atwater. Roger Ailes. Karl Rove. Grover Norquist. Newt Gingrich. Rush Limbaugh. Glenn Beck. Bill O'Reilly. Sean Hannity. Roger Stone. The Koch brothers. The Mercers. Sinclair Broadcasting. Laura Ingraham. Steve Bannon. Q. And now Trump and Trump Jr. Every one of these people has made a career at branding Democrats as traitors, American-haters, socialists, communists, degenerates, weak.

> Joe Biden and the Radical Left want to Abolish Police, Abolish ICE, Abolish Bail, Abolish Suburbs, Abolish the 2nd Amendment — and Abolish the American Way of Life. No one will be SAFE in Joe Biden's America!
>
> —Trump tweet from July 15, 2020[76]

> "Democrats want to → Deface, → Destroy, and → Dismantle our country."
>
> —Kevin McCarthy, Republican house leader, tweet from July 17, 2020[77]

> The leaders of today's Democratic Party...despise this country. They have said so. They continue to. That is shocking but it is also disqualifying. We cannot let them run this nation because they hate it. Imagine what they would do to it.
>
> —Fox News's most popular host Tucker Carlson and 2024 presidential contender on July 7, 2020[78]

Many Evangelical Christians even consider Democrats to be possessed by Satan or demons.[79] But they've always thought that about non-Southerners. The religious right comes straight from the Confederacy's delusion that it was a Christian nation. When one side has not gotten over their defeat in the Civil War and thinks the other side is associated with "rulers of the darkness," democracy is not all that important to them anymore. Preventing citizens from voting who might be fooled by the devil becomes the moral thing to do.[80]

Indeed, Republicans are more motivated by stopping Democrats than they are in supporting their own party's candidates.[81] They have been taught to fear and loathe Democrats. At least asking for Tofurky is no longer the main source of conflict at the family dinner table during Thanksgiving.

Republican demonization of Democrats and journalists is necessary in order to delegitimatize the media and its reporting.

> The Democrats don't matter. The real opposition is the media. And the way to deal with them is to flood the zone with shit.
>
> —Steve Bannon, Trump's 2016 campaign manager, on the campaign's strategy for 2020[82]

Republicans can get away with anything when their followers have been trained to not believe any of it. The shocking wrongs of the Trump administration—keeping immigrant children in cages, deploying para-militaries against our own citizens, enabling Russian election interference, Trump's sexual assault of almost two dozen women—are then cast aside as #fakenews. As my dear great-uncle-in-law Ray wrote to my wife in Facebook: "When are you going to stop the hate of the president and listen to Fox News to find out what's really going on. I don't care how much you hate Donald Trump, if you vote Democrat on November 3, you are voting to transform your country into a communist state. You had better think long and hard before you do. There will be no turning back!" Hard for any real news and facts to penetrate that fog of lies and diversionary propaganda.

Republicans have already begun branding their hoped-for coup in November 2020.

Starting in May 2020, Trump began attacking the legitimacy of voting at home, a.k.a. absentee voting. Unless Biden wins by a landslide, that's step one of a slow-motion coup. Even though over 25 million Americans voted using absentee ballots in 2018—including Trump himself—and five states, including Republican Utah, exclusively use absentee voting, his attacks continued. On July 21, 2020, he again laid the groundwork for his planned coup, tweeting: "Mail-In Voting, unless changed by the courts, will lead to the most CORRUPT ELECTION in our Nation's History! #RIGGEDELECTION." Meanwhile, Fox News reports that Trump is skeptical of election results because Democrats have a "history of cheating."[83]

If Trump loses the vote in November 2020 (which he will), he's hoping that the election will be close enough that by flipping Wisconsin, Michigan, North Carolina, and Pennsylvania from Biden to him would be enough for a second term. If on Election Night he's winning in those states because absentee votes have not yet been counted, he will declare victory. Just like he did on November 12, 2018, in the 2018 Senate race in Florida when he tweeted: "The Florida Election should be called in favor of Rick Scott and Ron DeSantis in that large numbers of new ballots showed up out of nowhere, and many ballots are missing or forged. An honest vote count is no longer possible—ballots massively infected. Must go with Election Night!" That's step two. It takes a few days—or even weeks—for absentee ballots to be counted, especially if there is a greater number than normal due to COVID-19.

The Republican legislatures will then immediately declare they will send Republican electors' votes to the Electoral College in those states in which Trump declares victory. That's step three. Remember, these are the same state legislatures that took away the powers of the new Democratic governors. A few days later, the overly cautious Democratic governors will finally call the election for Biden after all the votes are counted. Trump claims fraud from the absentee voters. McConnell states the Senate will not accept the electors from the Democrats. That's step four.

Trump blows his dog whistle again, and the heavily armed militias respond. That's step five. In April 2020 he tweeted, "Liberate!" and the armed militias showed up in those states ready to fight COVID-19 precautions aimed at saving lives; that was a practice run. Maybe some good-hearted citizens counterprotest, and Trump's militia assaults or kills one or two of these "terrorist antifas." Maybe some government buildings where ballots are held are burned down. That's step six. Arson has always been a favorite tool of those seeking to oppress their fellow Americans. Think KKK burning Black churches. Or the arson against the Democratic Party headquarters in Arizona as recently as July 2020.[84] Trump declares an emergency or even martial law and mobilizes his paramilitary forces, like he did in DC in June 2020 to suppress peaceful protestors and continued to do in Portland throughout July 2020. That's step seven.

Do the Democratic Party leaders or Biden talk about Trump and Republicans in a way that has prepared the country for this possible coup? Not yet, at least. However, this is so easy to see four months before it happens. If history is any teacher, the Democrats will respond to Trump's coup not by talking about Republican corruption and attacks on democracy but by simply saying, "Let's let the courts decide this." As if this version of the Supreme Court won't do exactly what the 2000 version did—make the Republican loser the president. Let's hope I'm wrong about all of this—especially the outcome.

What I'm not wrong about, though, is that Republicans are using branding to lay the groundwork needed to declare themselves the winners of the 2020 election and to delegitimize another Democratic president.

Diversionary Tactic #2: Republicans Weaponize Trolls and Bots to Flood the Zone with Shit

Online discourse is horrendous...

Every political writer and elected official—or at least the liberal or left-wing ones—knows how quickly anything they post, or that is posted about them, will be met with ugly and abusive troll commentary. Many nonpoliticians who just want to express an opinion know this as well. If you don't know it, here's a fun test: post a very liberal comment on your local newspaper's site about an issue. Warning: the comments this will generate will sicken you. Now imagine this impact magnified by thousands of vulgar attacks daily. This creates a self-censorship to avoid anonymous trolls. That's an attack on democracy. Without debate, flow of ideas and an airing of facts, democracy is diminished. As David Frum said in the *Atlantic*, "Americans remain as free to speak their minds as ever—provided they can stomach seeing their timelines fill up with obscene abuse and angry threats from the pro-Trump troll armies that police Facebook and Twitter. Rather than deal with digital thugs, young people increasingly drift to less political media like Snapchat and Instagram."[85] We live in an America where free speech is increasingly punished. Usually the punishment is doled out by anonymous posters, many of whom are bots. Some are Russian and some come from various MAGA groups. There's a growing coordination among these efforts.

As political as I have always been, I was very careful for most of my ten years leading a high-profile immigration law firm to keep my online mouth shut. I was afraid that if I bashed Republicans too much, my law firm would get a whole bunch of negative reviews from anonymous people or bots in retaliation. Who needs government censorship when such abuse causes self-censorship?

Once I learned that Russia was behind much of this online doxing—and assuming they would not bother to research my business interests—I took a chance and began cross-posting my podcast called *Your Daily Trump* onto Facebook. The good news is my business was never attacked. The bad news is that I would regularly get vile and abusive messages in the comments section within minutes of me posting the podcast. I had to report dozens of inappropriate comments to Facebook each time I reposted my podcast.

It was gross and frustrating. It also made it impossible to have real conversations about political issues. So much of the Internet is permeated with abusive and threatening language, full of disinformation, lies, and attacks. It has made a mockery of the concept of the great American public square. This is all part of a larger disinformation campaign waged by Russian bots and Trump's version of the Committee to Re-Elect the President (CREEP).

...And that's the point

No debate means no change of hearts and minds, just vitriol and ever-increasing doses of anger. Republicans benefit when our nation is divided, radicalized, and full of hate before, during, and after elections. Trolls and bots help amplify messages of hate. Whether it's the "Mexican rapists" that Trump focused on in his 2016 campaign, or the caravans of Central Americans from the 2018 campaign, or now the supposed American youth terrorists from the Black Lives Matter protests that he is so focused on in 2020. He sets the target on the backs of his enemy, and the trolls and bots work overtime to amplify that message of hatred.

And it's going to get worse. According to Harvard cybersecurity expert Bruce Schneier, "AI-driven personas will be able to write personalized letters to newspapers and elected officials, submit individual comments to public rule-making processes, and intelligently debate political issues on social media."[86] If we do not get a handle on this *now*, we will be drowned out in every debate and in every forum on the Internet, not by fellow citizens but by programmed attack bots. Who knew that when the Terminator came for us, it would be with diversionary propaganda meant to obscure the truth?

Steve Bannon, Trump's onetime campaign strategist, first used the phrase "flood the zone with shit" to describe Republican efforts to drown out the media's coverage of Republican campaigns and actions.[87] I use the term "diversionary propaganda," but once again, the Republican comes up with the better branding. The idea is to have so much controversy and mis-information that the unpopular policies of Republicans to suppress votes is hidden. Instead, there is more cultural and racial conflict to distract. There is no better tool than the trolls and bots for spreading the flood of shit all over the Internet and even into mainstream media.

These bots have been infecting social media discourse for years. About 20% of all tweets about the 2016 presidential election were written by bots.[88] Bots have been weaponized by Russian and certain corporate and political forces to spread propaganda in fifty countries as of 2019.[89] Even during the COVID-19 pandemic bot networks were responsible for five million views of misinformation on COVID-19 in a ten day period.[90]

The Republicans benefit from the anonymity of the web. Journalists, professors, elected officials, and anyone who expresses ideas or beliefs counter to Trump are targeted. And these targets never learn the real iden-tity of their attackers and know its futile to respond.

The GOP's last chance to stay in power is a breakdown of democracy.
The pattern for disinformation by trolls is already well established but ever evolving. Some fake news outlet created by Russians or the Trump campaign spouts disinformation. This gets spread by adoring fans of the president or by artificial intelligence and bots, and then it's amplified through some paid media buys. Eventually it becomes widespread enough that it's covered in the right-wing echo chamber that treats the original fake news as real.

If critiqued, there is an avalanche of comments abusing the person who critiques it. This further amplifies the spread of disinformation with the claim that the critique is #fakenews. Not exactly how the founders intended the First Amendment to play out!

Bots and trolls obscure what is actually by attacking the messengers. The Republicans need these distractions and heat because they have run out of ideas and policies. Worse, they are now against many of the issues they had previously embraced for years. Remember when Republicans from Reagan to Romney thought Russia was a threat, deficits were bad for the economy, and free trade was good? Those have been Republican positions for decades, until they were not. What do Republicans stand for now? Fear of Democrats is pretty much the only campaign issue for Trump. If you can't defend—or articulate—your positions, then bots and trolls can provide the diversionary propaganda to focus attention elsewhere. Controversies, personal attacks, conspiracies, and misinformation are all the tools of this online diversionary propaganda.

The Russian military handbook on information war teaches Russian operatives to create web or Facebook pages that reach people "organically."[91] Looking at just 6 of the 470 publicly known Russia-linked political Facebook pages, researchers found that their posts had been shared 340 million times.[92] Obviously their Republican Party allies have taken note of this strategy. But Putin's leadership of the modern-day Republican Party goes much further than attacking the truth.

Diversionary Tactic #3: Republicans Cover Up Putin's Interference to Ensure Its Continuation

> Democrats face a national security problem without parallel in the annals of American democracy. The president of the United States, Donald Trump, has made clear not only that he will remain passive in the face of foreign interference in the 2020 US election—a threat his current and former directors of national intelligence have called the most serious facing the country—but also that he will actually solicit such interference if it serves his interests.
>
> —Thomas Wright, Brookings Institution[93]

The Republicans' diversionary propaganda has perhaps been most shockingly effective in allowing Russia to interfere in America's 2016 presidential election without any repercussions. Russian President Vladimir Putin's goal in interfering with American elections is obvious: make democracy seem like an unattractive option for Russia or to the populace of Russia's client states (formerly called Soviet Republics). Putin is creating an axis of evil—or more precisely, an axis of autocracies—with Russia at the center. These will be countries led by the rich and elite, a.k.a. oligarchs, with no democratic guardrails limiting their rapacious appetites. Trump's fantasy of being a strong man makes America Russia's primary target for recruitment. Can anyone seriously doubt that Trump would prefer an authoritarian America more than a democratic one?

In addition to these political endeavors, there's a special personal relationship between Trump and Putin—probably money laundering.[94] As the former leader of the KGB and current richest man in the world,[95] Putin operates on a zero-sum philosophy. Russia can only win if the United States loses. Trump gives those victories to Putin because he has no interest in the geo-political positions of nations. He is much more focused on his domestic fortune, in both meanings of the word.

Putin's interest is to continually undermine America's "moral superiority" and attack our democracy. Trump's rationale is to win at all costs—including but not limited to treason, bribery, and other high crimes. They are in many ways a perfect match.

Russia's interference in the 2016 election was an unexpectedly powerful weapon for Republicans in taking the presidency away from the Democrats. Putin provided just enough support to change the outcome of the 2016 election in favor of Trump. To understand how he did this, we have to go back to 2015. That's when Russian intelligence services hackers illegally gained access to the Democratic Party computer networks. They not only obtained emails but had access to the most important election strategy documents the Democrats possessed. That same summer, the FBI opened an investigation of contacts between Russian officials and Trump associates. Meanwhile, Putin directed the Russian Internet Research Agency to amplify messaging aimed at turning the American electorate against each other. They used fake online personas, a.k.a. trolls, and helped organize and pay for rallies and protests, both right wing and extreme left wing.

Then, on July 22, 2016—the day after Trump was caught on tape admitting to routinely groping women—nearly 20,000 emails that had been stolen from the Democratic National Committee by the Russian Intelligence Service were posted online by WikiLeaks. These were obtained through Russian intelligence agents. The media, however, kept reporting the non-profit WikiLeaks connection, not the Russian source. Obviously, the timing of the release by Russia was intended to blunt the effect of America learning that Trump was a sexual predator. This is a great example of diversionary propaganda. Russia succeeded in moving the media coverage away from Trump's admission of sexual assaults and onto the petty squabbles in the Democrats' emails.

Starting in August 2016, Trump began to claim that the election would be rigged against him. Sound familiar? This clearly was a tactic to make it more difficult for Obama and Clinton to act on the Russian interference just like it's now a tactic to pave the way for his hoped-for coup in 2020. This was classic diversionary propaganda. Any public actions on the part of Democrats would be evidence of Trump's theory of "deep state" political interference into his inevitable victory.

In the summer of 2016, Obama ordered the Homeland Security secretary to help secure US voting systems against Russian hackers. Multiple Republican state officials rejected the plan to safeguard our election apparatus, calling it a federal takeover. The Democrats backed down. The resistance to safeguarding the patchwork of voting mechanisms was led by Georgia's Republican then-secretary of state Brian Kemp, and later by Senate majority leader Mitch McConnell.

In both July and October 2016, Trump publicly asked Russia to steal more emails from Hillary Clinton and the Democrats. Days before the election—on October 28, 2016—FBI Director James Comey announced an additional investigation into Clinton's emails. What prompted the investigation were emails that Russian intelligence had falsified. The fake emails purported to show attorney general Loretta Lynch promising to kill any investigation of Hillary. Comey knew they were fake but feared they would be leaked and believed.[96] That shows the effectiveness of Republican's diversionary propaganda. Within a week of Comey's announcement, Hillary Clinton's lead shrank from 5.9% to 2.9%.

The most comprehensive academic study of the election concluded that Russia delivered the election to Trump. They did this by carefully synching their campaign to Clinton's campaign targets.[97] Russia spread false information about Clinton to keep her voters home—especially African American voters. Having stolen Democratic Party emails, Russia possessed the Democratic voter targeting, polling, and strategy for the campaign. They also targeted the group of anti-Trump independent voters. The Russian goal was to persuade these voters to vote for third-party candidates. Clinton lost Pennsylvania, Michigan, and Wisconsin by a combined total of 80,000 votes. Remarkably, 660,000 voters voted for third-party candidates in those three states. If only 12% of those third-party voters targeted by Russian were persuaded by Russian propaganda not to vote for Clinton, that would have delivered the presidency to Trump. It was that easy.

Putin has continued his offensive to date. America's National Intelligence Services expects Russia to be even more aggressive in 2020.[98] Putin now knows there are zero repercussions for Russia as long as they ensure a Trump election—or a Republican Senate. In fact, Republicans in the Senate removed the requirement that presidential campaigns report offers of assistance from foreign governments in June 2020.[99] Trump has continued to solicit Russian assistance, even after his impeachment in 2019. In December 2019 Trump's treasury, run by sycophant Steven Mnuchin, suddenly overruled Congress and lifted sanctions against Russian oligarch Oleg Deripaska.[100] These sanctions were put on Deripaska at the end of Obama's administration due to the national intelligence community's assessment that Deripaska funded Russia's interference in the 2016 election on orders from Putin. Gotta protect your own.

You see, there are no consequences when the bad you do is on behalf of the winner. That's a corollary to the well-known phrase "history is written by the victors."

The GOP's Future Weapon #5, Currently Delayed by Trump

Ironically, Trump saved us from the fifth and most powerful weapon that the Republicans were going to use to forever change our country. The wheels were set in motion for our country's first constitutional convention since the original one in the eighteenth century.

Say what now?

Yes, the Koch brothers were using the 4 Weapons Against Democracy to take over enough states that they could call a constitutional convention. That was their goal the entire time. The Koch network wanted to literally rewrite our United States Constitution, this time with them cast in the role of our Founding Fathers.

As detailed in the *Washington Post* and the *Hill* in September 2017, the Koch brothers funded training for Republican state legislators to call for a constitutional convention.[101, 102] Republican representatives from seventeen states showed up to the Koch brothers' one-week training in Arizona. No Democrats were invited. Republicans almost controlled enough states to call for this constitutional convention. They were one state short of the required thirty-four. Then Trump won the election and made the Republican brand toxic. Instead of gaining that final state they needed in 2018, Republicans lost a few states. The Koch brothers' constitutional convention was put on hold at least until their network could capture more states in 2022. That is, assuming Trump is not weighing down the Republicans anymore.

The rules of a constitutional convention are such that a majority of the attending delegates can change the US Constitution with simple majority vote. Of course, the majority of the delegates would have been Republican. They could have written into and rewritten anything in the Constitution.

What would they want to rewrite, you ask? A lot of it would have focused on keeping taxes low for the rich, no doubt. You can imagine how they would have inserted as many cultural and social restrictions, and voter suppression measures, as Jerry Falwell Jr. and Sean Hannity could dream up.

Republicans continue to plan for this constitutional convention. Former Oklahoma senator Tom Coburn was spearheading the group "Convention of States," one of three major Republican groups supporting a constitutional convention, until his death in March 2020. Speaking in 2018 at the American Legislative Exchange Council (ALEC)—a powerful right wing organization that creates "model" conservative laws for states to copy and pass—Coburn stated, "I think we're three or four years away [from holding a constitutional convention]."[103]

His analysis of the timing is exactly the same as mine. In 2022—after Trump is no longer on the ballot—the Republicans will likely recapture all the states they lost in 2018 as well as the House and Senate. Then we all get to watch the constitutional convention unfold before our disbelieving eyes. And there's nothing a president Biden would be able to do about it. That is, unless the Democrats enact the necessary reforms to American democracy found in part 3 of this book.

But why haven't the Democrats just come up with a plan and fought back against the 4 Weapons? There are a couple of things about Democrats that I am afraid I have to now share with you.

Notes

1. Carol Anderson et al., "GOP Takes Advantage of Coronavirus for Voter Suppression." *Time*, 8 Apr. 2020, time.com/5817380/voter-suppression-coronavirus/.

2. "State Legislative Elections Results, 2010," Ballotpedia, ballotpedia.org/State_legislative _elections_results_2010

3. Daley, David. "The Decade Republicans Hijacked Our Democracy, via the Gerrymander." *Salon*, Salon.com, 31 Dec. 2019, www.salon.com/2019/12/30/the-decade-republicans -hijacked-our-democracy-via-gerrymandering/.

4. Lydia Saad, "By Slim Margin, Americans Support Healthcare Bill's Passage." Gallup, 16 May 2019, news.gallup.com/poll/126929/slim-margin-americans-support-healthcare-bill-passage.aspx.

5. "More Money, Less Transparency: A Decade under Citizens United," OpenSecrets, www.opensecrets.org /news/reports/a-decade-under-citizens-united.

6. "Money in Politics 101: What You Need to Know About Campaign Finance After Citizens United," Brennan Center for Justice, www.brennancenter.org/our-work/research-reports/money -politics-101-what-you-need-know-about-campaign-finance-after.

7. Nicholas Confessore, Sarah Cohen, and Karen Yourish, "Small Pool of Rich Donors Dominates Election Giving," *New York Times*, 1 Aug 2015, https://www.nytimes.com/2015/08/02/us/small-pool -of-rich-donors-dominates-election-giving.html

8. "Money in Politics 101: What You Need to Know About Campaign Finance After Citizens United." *Brennan Center for Justice*, www.brennancenter.org/our-work/research-reports/money -politics-101-what-you-need-know-about-campaign-finance-after.

9. Mike McIntire & Nicholas Confessore, "Tax-Exempt Groups Shield Political Gifts of Businesses," *New York Times*, July 7, 2012, at A1.

10. Michela Tindera, "At Least 20 Billionaires Behind 'Dark Money' Group That Opposed Obama," *Forbes*, 27 Oct. 2019, www.forbes.com/sites/michelatindera/2019/10/26/at-least -20-billionaires-behind-dark-money-group-that-opposed-obama/#2b0c9a856c6.

11. David Daley, "How a Dark-Money Scam Created Alabama's Hard-Right Legislature - and the Abortion Ban." *Salon*, 2 June 2019, www.salon.com/2019/06/02/how-a-dark-money-scam-created -alabamas-hard-right-legislature-and-the-abortion-ban/.

12. David Daley, "How a Dark-Money Scam Created Alabama's Hard-Right Legislature - and the Abortion Ban." *Salon*, 3 June 2019, www.salon.com/2019/06/02/how-a-dark-money-scam-created -alabamas-hard-right-legislature-and-the-abortion-ban/.

13. "2010 Outside Spending, by Group." *OpenSecrets.org*, "2010 Outside Spending, by Group." *OpenSecrets.org*, www.opensecrets.org/outsidespending/summ.php?cycle=2010&chrt=V&disp=O&type= &.https: //www.issueone.org/wp-content/uploads/2019/01/Post-CU-Dark-Money-Mini-Report.pdf

14.   Bill Hewitt, "David Koch, Billionaire Industrialist Who Influenced Conservative Politics, Dies at 79," *Washington Post*, 23 Aug. 2019, www.washingtonpost.com/local/obituaries/david-koch-billionaire-industrialist-who-influenced-conservative-politics-dies-at-79/2019/08/23/91c29a20-a264-11e8-83d2-70203b8d7b44_story.html.

15.   Ryan Cooper, "How the Democratic Party Can Become a Labor Party Again," *The Week*, 22 Nov. 2016, theweek.com/articles/661874/how-democratic-party-become-labor-party-again.

16.   Editorial Board, "Dark Money Helped Win the Senate," *New York Times*, 8 Nov 2014, https://www--.nytimes.com/2014/11/09/opinion/sunday/dark-money-helped-win-the-senate.html.

17.   David Daley, "Democrats Just Blew It in Wisconsin: Elections Likely to Stay Rigged in Favor of GOP." *Salon*, 28 Apr. 2019, www.salon.com/2019/04/28/democrats-just-blew-it-in-wisconsin-elections-likely-to-stay-rigged-in-favor-of-gop/.

18.   Miles Parks, "Expert Warns Of 'Real Festival of Partisan Gerrymandering' In 2021," NPR, 19 Apr. 2020, www.npr.org/2020/04/19/836260800/expert-warns-of-real-festival-of-partisan-gerrymandering-in-2021?ft=nprml&f=1032.

19.   Michael Li, "Extreme Maps." Brennan Center for Justice, 9 May 2017, www.brennancenter.org/our-work/research-reports/extreme-maps.

20.   Emily Sullivan, "Laura Ingraham Told LeBron James to Shut Up and Dribble; He Went to the Hoop," NPR, 19 Feb 2018, https://www.nytimes.com/2015/08/02/us/small-pool-of-rich-donors-dominates-election-giving.html

21.   Ian Millhiser, "Texas Brags To Court That It Drew District Lines To 'Increase The Republican Party's Electoral Prospects'." ThinkProgress, 14 Aug. 2013, archive.thinkprogress.org/texas-brags-to-court-that-it-drew-district-lines-to-increase-the-republican-partys-electoral-bdda4aff58bf/.

22.   Sundeep Iyer, Keesha Gaskins, *Redistricting and Congressional Control: A First Look*, Brennan Center for Justice, 2012 http://www.brennancenter.org/sites/default/files/legacy/publications/Redistricting_Congressional_Control.pdf

23.   Arnold Schwarzenegger, David Daley, "Too Many Voters Live under Minority Rule. Here's Why," *The Washington Post*, 9 Sept. 2019, www.washingtonpost.com/outlook/2019/09/09/schwarzenegger-too-many-voters-live-under-minority-rule-heres-why/.

24.   Wake County Superior Court in a 2018 North Carolina gerrymandering case, *Common Cause v. Lewis*, 18 CVS, 014001 in Savannah Behrmann.

25.   "'Extreme Partisan Gerrymandering': North Carolina Judges Rule Legislative Maps Violate State Constitution," *USA Today*, 4 Sept. 2019, www.usatoday.com/story/news/politics/2019/09/03/north-carolina-judges-toss-maps-partisan-gerrymandering/2204294001/.

26.   Kelly Cernetich, "Turzai: Voter ID Law Means Romney Can Win PA," *PoliticsPA*, 25 June 2012, www.politicspa.com/turzai-voter-id-law-means-romney-can-win-pa/37153/.

27.   Alex Tausanovitch, "Voter-Determined Districts," Center for American Progress, 9 May 2019, www.americanprogress.org/issues/democracy/reports/2019/05/09/468916/voter-determined-districts/.

28.   "Race, Party and Early Voting in Ohio," *Washington Monthly*, 20 Aug. 2012, washingtonmonthly.com/2012/08/20/race-party-and-early-voting-in-ohio/.

29.   "African American Early Voting Is Way down in North Carolina. Why Is That?" www.insight-us.org/blog/african-american-early-voting-is-way-down-in-north-carolina-why-is-that/.

30.   Maya Rhodan, "Republican Activist Resigns After Racially-Charged 'Daily Show' Comments," *Time*, 25 Oct. 2013, nation.time.com/2013/10/25/republican-activist-resigns-after-racially-charged-daily-show-comments/.

31.   Ari Berman, "GOP Voter Purges in Wisconsin and Georgia Could Tip the 2020 Election," *Mother Jones*, 17 Dec. 2019, www.motherjones.com/politics/2019/12/gop-led-voter-purges-in-wisconsin-and-georgia-could-tip-2020-elections/.

32. Christopher Ingraham, "Analysis: This Anti-Voter-Fraud Program Gets It Wrong over 99 Percent of the Time. The GOP Wants to Take It Nationwide," *Washington Post*, 20 July 2017, www.washingtonpost.com /news/wonk/wp/2017/07/20/this-anti-voter-fraud-program-gets-it-wrong-over-99-of-the-time -the-gop-wants-to-take-it-nationwide/.

33. Bryan Lowry, "His Own Witness Doesn't Back Kobach Claims That Illegal Votes Cost Trump Popular Vote," *Kansas City Star*, 13 Mar 2018, https://www.kansascity.com/news/politics-government/article 204976839.html

34. Kevin Morris, Myrna Perez, "Purges: A Growing Threat to the Right to Vote," Brennan Center for Justice, 20 July 2018, www.brennancenter.org/our-work/research-reports/purges-growing-threat-right-vote.

35. "Voter Purge Rates Remain High, Analysis Finds," Brennan Center for Justice, 8 May 2020, www .brennancenter.org/our-work/analysis-opinion/voter-purge-rates-remain-high-analysis-finds.

36. Ari Berman, "The Man Behind Trump's Voter-Fraud Obsession," *New York Times*, 3 Jun 2017, https: //www.nytimes.com/2017/06/13/magazine/the-man-behind-trumps-voter-fraud-obsession.html.

37. Sarah K. Burris, "Georgia Purges 591K Voters - Simply Because They Didn't Vote in the Last 3 Years," *Raw Story*, 2 Aug. 2017, www.rawstory.com/2017/08/georgia-purges-591k-voters -simply-because-they-didnt-vote-in-the-last-3-years/.

38. Kevin Powell, "Stacey Abrams Has Ascended to Political Prominence. How Has She Harnessed so Much Power in so Little Time?" *Washington Post*, 14 May 2020, www.washingtonpost.com /magazine/2020/05/14/stacey-abrams-political-power/?arc404=true.

39. Berman, Ari. "GOP Voter Purges in Wisconsin and Georgia Could Tip the 2020 Election." *Mother Jones*, 17 Dec. 2019, www.motherjones.com/politics/2019/12/gop-led-voter-purges -in-wisconsin-and-georgia-could-tip-2020-elections/.

40. Terry H. Schwadron, "How Republicans Have a Coordinated Attack to Assure an Electoral Victory in 2020." *Raw Story*, 31 Dec. 2019, www.rawstory.com/2019/12/how -republicans-have-a-coordinated-attack-to-assure-an-electoral-victory-in-2020/.

41. Judge Alan King, *Presidential Election Integrity Commission, Statement of Issues/ Recommendations*, 6 Sept. 2017, https://www.whitehouse.gov/sites/whitehouse.gov/files/docs/pacei-submission-alan -king_statement-issues-recommendations.pdf

42. Michael Wines, "Some Republicans Acknowledge Leveraging Voter ID Laws for Political Gain," *New York Times*, 16 Sept. 2016, www.nytimes.com/2016/09/17/us/some-republicans-acknowledge-leveraging -voter-id-laws-for-political-gain.html.

43. Zoltan L. Hajnal, Nazita Lajevardi. "Do Voter Identification Laws Suppress Minority Voting? Yes. We Did the Research," *Washington Post*, WP Company, 15 Feb. 2017, www.washingtonpost.com/news/monkey-cage /wp/2017/02/15/do-voter-identification-laws-suppress-minority-voting-yes-we-did-the-research/.

44. "Elections: Issues Related to State Voter Identification Laws," US Government Accountability Office, 27 Feb. 2015, https://www.gao.gov/products/GAO-14-634.

45. "Oppose Voter ID Legislation - Fact Sheet." *American Civil Liberties Union*, www.aclu.org/other /oppose-voter-id-legislation-fact-sheet.

46. Ari Berman, "A New Study Shows Just How Many Americans Were Blocked from Voting in Wisconsin Last Year." *Mother Jones*, 26 Sept. 2017, www.motherjones.com/politics/2017/09/a-new-study-shows -just-how-many-americans-were-blocked-from-voting-in-wisconsin-last-year/.

47. Stephanie Condon, "Scott Walker Supporter Claims Amnesia in Voter Fraud Case," CBS News, 26 June 2014, www.cbsnews.com/news/scott-walker-supporter-claims-amnesia-in-voter-fraud-case/.

48. Zoltan L. Hajnal, Nazita Lajevardi. "Analysis | Do Voter Identification Laws Suppress Minority Voting? Yes. We Did the Research." *The Washington Post*, WP Company, 15 Feb. 2017, www.washingtonpost.com/news/monkey-cage/wp/2017/02/15/do-voter-identification -laws-suppress-minority-voting-yes-we-did-the-research/.

49. Robert Lee Hotz, "Mexican Cave Find Hints That People Lived in North America 30,000 Years Ago," *Wall Street Journal*, 22 July 2020, www.wsj.com/articles/mexican-cave-find -hints-that-people-lived-in-north-america-30-000-years-ago-11595430002.

50. "ACLU News & Commentary," American Civil Liberties Union, 3 Feb. 2020, www.aclu.org/news civil-liberties/block-the-vote-voter-suppression-in-2020/.

51. Sam Levine, "Kentucky Republicans Quietly Tighten Voter Restrictions as US Focuses on Covid-19." *The Guardian*, 20 Mar. 2020, www.theguardian.com/us-news/2020/mar/20/kentucky-voter-restrictions -photo-id-republicans?CMP=Share_iOSApp_Other .

52. Maryalice Aymong, "See It: GOP Consultant Says Voter ID, Long Lines Help 'Our Side,'" MSNBC, 22 Aug. 2013, www.msnbc.com/hardball/see-it-gop-consultant-says-voter-id-long-li.

53. Ari Berman, "Republican Voter Suppression Efforts Are Targeting Minorities, Journalist Says," interview by Teri Gross, *Fresh Air*, NPR, 23 Oct 2018, https://www.npr.org/2018/10/23/659784277 /republican-voter-suppression-efforts-are-targeting-minorities-journalist-says.

54. P. R. Lockhart, "Georgia Put 53,000 Voter Registrations on Hold, Fueling New Charges of Voter Suppression." Vox, 12 Oct. 2018, www.vox.com/policy-and-politics/2018/10/11/17964104/georgia -voter-registration-suppression-purges-stacey-abrams-brian-kemp.

55. The Leadership Conference Education Fund, "The Great Poll Closure," Nov. 2016, http://civilrightsdocs .info/pdf/reports/2016/poll-closure-report-web.pdf

56. Ja'han Jones, "Texas Officials Want To Suppress Democratic Voters. Super Tuesday Shows It's Working," HuffPost, 6 Mar. 2020, www.huffpost.com/entry/texas-super-tuesday-rigged-election_n _5e601c1dc5b644545ea4c2cc .

57. Richard Salame, "Texas Closes Hundreds of Polling Sites, Making It Harder for Minorities to Vote," *The Guardian*, 2 Mar. 2020, www.theguardian.com/us-news/2020/mar/02/texas-polling -sites-closures-voting.

58. Letter from Attorney General of Texas Ken Paxton to Chairwoman Stephanie Klick, 14 April, 2020, https://www.texasattorneygeneral.gov/sites/default/files/images/admin /2020/Press/4.14.20%20Letter%20to%20Rep.%20Klick.pdf?utm_content=&utm _medium=email&utm_name=&utm_source=govdelivery&utm_term=

59. Elise Viebeck and Robert Costa, "Trump's Assault on Election Integrity Forces Question: What Would Happen If He Refused to Accept a Loss?" *The Washington Post*, 22 July 2020, www.washingtonpost .com/politics/trumps-assault-on-election-integrity-forces-question-what-would-happen-if-he -refused-to-accept-a-loss/2020/07/22/d2477150-caae-11ea-b0e3-d55bda07d66a_story.html.

60. Aris Folley, "Georgia's GOP House Speaker Says Vote-by-Mail System Would Be 'Devastating to Republicans,'" The Hill, 2 Apr. 2020, https://thehill.com/homenews/state-watch/490879 -georgias-gop-house-speaker-says-vote-by-mail-system-would-be-devastating.

61. Fatima Hussein, "Republicans Limiting Early Voting in Marion County, Letting It Bloom in Suburbs," *Indianapolis Star*, 10 Aug. 2017, www.indystar.com/story/news/2017/08/10/silencing -vote-data-shows-unequal-barrier-indiana-polls/435450001/.

62. Dan McCready, "Take It From Me, Voter Fraud Is Part of the G.O.P. Playbook," *New York Times*, 24 Apr. 2020, www.nytimes.com/2020/04/24/opinion/voter-fraud-republicans.html.

63. Dara Kam, "Former Florida GOP Leaders Say Voter Suppression Was Reason They Pushed New Election Law," Palm Beach Post, 27 Nov. 2012, www.palmbeachpost.com/article/20121125/NEWS /812021098.

64. The Sentencing Project: Research and Advocacy for Reform, "6 Million Los Voters: State-Level Estimates of Felony Disenfranchisement, 2016," https://www.sentencingproject.org/wp-content /uploads/2016/10/6-Million-Lost-Voters.pdf.

65. "Voter Restoration." American Civil Liberties Union, www.aclu.org/issues/voting-rights/voter-restoration.

66. "This Election Is Being Rigged - But Not By Democrats." BillMoyers.com, 18 Oct. 2016, billmoyers. com/story/election-rigged-not-democrats/.

67.   Tim Mak, "Over 1 Million Florida Felons Win Right To Vote With Amendment 4," NPR, 7 Nov. 2018, www.npr
      .org/2018/11/07/665031366/over-a-million-florida-ex-felons-win-right-to-vote-with-amendment-4.

68.   Daniel Rivero, "Voting Rights For Hundreds Of Thousands Of Felons At Stake In Florida
      Trial," NPR, 27 Apr. 2020, www.npr.org/2020/04/27/844297011/voting-rights-for-hundreds
      -of-thousands-of-felons-at-stake-in-florida-trial.

69.   Benjamin Weiser and Alan Feuer, "Judge Orders Cohen Released, Citing 'Retaliation' Over Tell-All
      Book," New York Times, 23 July 2020, www.nytimes.com/2020/07/23/nyregion/michael-cohen-trump
      -book.html.

70.   Michael Lewis, "Has Anyone Seen the President?" Bloomberg, 9 Feb. 2018, www.bloomberg.com
      /opinion/articles/2018-02-09/has-anyone-seen-the-president.

71.   Ken Forsberg, "Eye-Catching Poll Results Show New High in Voter Distrust of Government," Fix
      Democracy First, 6 Dec. 2016, www.issueone.org/poll-shows-new-high-in-government-distrust/.

72.   "General Opinions about the Federal Government." Pew Research Center - U.S. Politics & Policy, 30 May 2020,
      www.pewresearch.org/politics/2015/11/23/2-general-opinions-about-the-federal-government/.

73.   Emily Guskin and Scott Clement. "Poll: Nearly Half of Americans Say Voter Fraud Occurs
      Often," Washington Post, 15 Sept. 2016, www.washingtonpost.com/news/the-fix/wp/2016/09/15
      /poll-nearly-half-of-americans-say-voter-fraud-occurs-often/.

74.   Christopher Ingraham, "7 Papers, 4 Government Inquiries, 2 News Investigations and 1 Court Ruling
      Proving Voter Fraud Is Mostly a Myth," Washington Post, 9 July 2014, www.washingtonpost.com
      /news/wonk/wp/2014/07/09/7-papers-4-government-inquiries-2-news-investigations-and-1-court-
      ruling-proving-voter-fraud-is-mostly-a-myth/?arc404=true.

75.   See, e.g., Sean Sullivan, David Weigel. "Democratic Leaders Face Pressure to Counter Trump's
      Attacks on Mueller's Russia Investigation," Washington Post, 23 May 2018, www.washingtonpost
      .com/politics/democratic-leaders-face-pressure-to-counter-trumps-attacks-on-muellers-russia
      -investigation/2018/05/23/b9f61414-5ea2-11e8-a4a4-c070ef53f315_story.html.

76.   Donald J. Trump, Twitter, 15 July 2020, twitter.com/realdonaldtrump/status/1283429106768662528.

77.   Kevin McCarthy, Twitter, 17 July 2020, twitter.com/gopleader/status/1284108549673582593?lang=en.

78.   David Bauder, "Fox's Carlson Criticized for Saying Democrats Hate America," Associated Press, 7
      July 2020, https://apnews.com/76e2893f2397eb61f9bbe61c4941c729

79.   Chauncey DeVega, "Trump and the Christians: Evangelical Historian John Fea on Decoding the Great
      Paradox," Salon, 9 Mar. 2020, www.salon.com/2020/02/19/trump-and-the-christians-evangelical
      -historian-john-fea-on-decoding-the-great-paradox/ .

80.   Heather Digby Parton, "Bill Barr, Warrior for Theocracy: Why Didn't We Know This until Now?"
      Salon, 5 Jan. 2020, www.salon.com/2020/01/03/bill-barr-warrior-for-theocracy-why-didnt
      -we-know-this-until-now/.

81.   Matthew Sheffield, "Poll: Republicans Voters More Motivated to Beat Democrats than Back Their
      Candidate," The Hill, 1 July 2019, https://thehill.com/hilltv/what-americas-thinking/450884-poll
      -republicans-like-their-partys-candidates-less-than .

82.   David Remnick and Adrian Chen. "Trump vs. the Times: Inside an Off-the-Record Meeting,"
      The New Yorker, 30 July 2018, www.newyorker.com/news/news-desk/trump-vs-the-times
      -inside-an-off-the-record-meeting.

83.   Brooke Singman, "Trump Claims Mail-in Voting Will Lead to 'Most Corrupt Election' in
      US History," Fox News, 21 July 2020, www.foxnews.com/politics/trump-mail-in-voting
      -will-lead-to-most-corrupt-election-in-us-history.

84.   Lee Moran, "Arizona Democratic Party HQ 'Completely Destroyed' In Arson Attack," HuffPost,
      25 July 2020, www.huffpost.com/entry/arizona-democratic-hq-arson-attack-phoenix
      _n_5f1be9b3c5b6128e68263d0c.

85.   David Frum, "How to Build an Autocracy," The Atlantic, 2 June 2020, www.theatlantic.com/magazine
      /archive/2017/03/how-to-build-an-autocracy/513872/.

86.   Bruce Schneier, "Bots Are Destroying Political Discourse As We Know It," *The Atlantic*, 7 Jan. 2020, www
      .theatlantic.com/technology/archive/2020/01/future-politics-bots-drowning-out-humans/604489/.

87.   Michael Lewis, "Has Anyone Seen the President?" Bloomberg, 9 Feb. 2018, www.bloomberg.com
      /opinion/articles/2018-02-09/has-anyone-seen-the-president.

88.   Alessandro Bessi, Emilio Ferrara, "View of Social Bots Distort the 2016 U.S. Presidential Election
      Online Discussion," First Monday, firstmonday.org/article/view/7090/56

89.   Samantha Bradshaw, "The Global Disinformation Order: 2019 Global Inventory of Organised Social
      Media Manipulation," Computational Propaganda Research Project, 2019, https://comprop.oii.ox.ac.uk
      /wp-content/uploads/sites/93/2019/09/CyberTroop-Report19.pdf.

90.   Taylor, Josh. "COVID-19 Misinformation: pro-Trump and QAnon Twitter bots found to be
      worst culprits," The Guardian, 31 May 2020, https://www.theguardian.com/media/2020/jun/01/
      covid-19-misinformation-pro-trump-and-qanon-twitter-bots-found-to-be-worst-culprits

91.   Peter Pomerantsev, "Inside the Kremlin's Hall of Mirrors," *The Guardian*, 9 Apr. 2015, www.theguardian
      .com/news/2015/apr/09/kremlin-hall-of-mirrors-military-information-psychology.

92.   Craig Timberg, "Russian Propaganda May Have Been Shared Hundreds of Millions of Times, New Research
      Says," *Washington Post*, 5 Oct. 2017, www.washingtonpost.com/news/the-switch/wp/2017/10/05
      /russian-propaganda-may-have-been-shared-hundreds-of-millions-of-times-new-research-says/.

93.   Thomas Wright, "Democrats Must Act Now to Deter Foreign Interference in the 2020
      Election," Brookings, 4 Oct. 2019, www.brookings.edu/blog/order-from-chaos/2019/10/04
      /democrats-must-act-now-to-deter-foreign-interference-in-the-2020-election/.

94.   Nick Givas, "Trump Is 'Owned by Putin' and Has Been 'Laundering Money' for Russians,
      Claims MSNBC's Donny Deutsch," Fox News, 24 Oct. 2019, www.foxnews.com/media/donald
      -trump-russian-asset-msnbc.

95.   Sam Dangremond, "How Much Is Vladimir Putin Actually Worth?" *Town & Country*, 16 Jul 2018, https:
      //www.townandcountrymag.com/society/money-and-power/a14480615/vladimir-putin-net-worth/.

96.   Jane Mayer and Evan Osnos. "How Russia Helped Swing the Election for Trump," *The New Yorker*,
      www.newyorker.com/magazine/2018/10/01/how-russia-helped-to-swing-the-election-for-trump.

97.   Kathleen Hall Jamieson, *Cyberwar: How Russian Hackers and Trolls Helped Elect a President What We
      Don't, Can't, and Do Know,* Oxford Univ. Press, 2020.

98.   Martin Matishak, "Intelligence Heads Warn of More Aggressive Election Meddling in 2020,"
      Politico, 29 Jan 2019, https://www.politico.com/story/2019/01/29/dan-coats-2020-election
      -foreign-interference-1126077.

99.   Jeremy Herb, "Senate Strips Provision from Intelligence Bill Requiring Campaigns to Report Foreign
      Election Help," CNN, 30 June 2020, https://www.cnn.com/2020/06/30/politics/senate-removes-ban
      -foreign-election-help/index.html.

100. "U.S. Treasury to Lift Sanctions on Companies Linked to Russian Oligarch Oleg Deripaska,"
      The Daily Beast, 19 Dec. 2018, www.thedailybeast.com/us-treasury-to-lift-sanctions
      -on-companies-linked-to-russian-oligarch-oleg-deripaska.

101. Niv Elis, "GOP State Lawmakers Meet to Plan Possible Constitutional Convention," *The
      Hill*, 18 Sep 2017, https://thehill.com/homenews/state-watch/351204-gop-state-lawmakers
      -meet-to-plan-possible-constitutional-convention.

102. "We're Surprisingly Close to Our First Constitutional Convention since 1787. Bad Idea." *The Washington
      Post*, 6 Apr. 2017, www.washingtonpost.com/opinions/were-surprisingly-close-to-a-new-constitutional
      -convention-bad-idea/2017/04/06/f6d5b76a-197d-11e7-855e-4824bbb5d748_story.html.

103. Jamiles Lartey, "Conservatives Call for Constitutional Intervention Last Seen 230
      Years Ago," *The Guardian*, 11 Aug. 2018, www.theguardian.com/us-news/2018/aug/11
      /conservatives-call-for-constitutional-convention-alec.

CHAPTER 5

Understand How Democrats Will Not Save American Democracy on Their Own

Arguably the most important divide in the Democratic primary field isn't by ideology, but between those candidates who understand the obstacles ahead and those who don't. Despite the example of the last 10 years, the centrist candidates are still running as if persuasion and compromise will win the day.

—Jamelle Bouie, *New York Times* opinion columnist[1]

W e've seen how the American electorate was poised to give Democrats a long reign beginning with the 2008 election. But then the empire struck back, and the GOP stormtroopers launched an unprecedented campaign to undermine American democracy. They succeeded. It had unintended consequences.

The old Republican Party is gone. It's now Trump's party.

—Brad Parscale, fired Trump 2020 campaign manager.[2]

Democrats failed us in the 2010 decade. They squandered the presidency of Obama, a leader who could have been transformative. Electing Democrats in November 2020 will not magically fix our problems and save democracy. Understanding some of the limits on Democrats is crucial for keeping us active and persistent after the election. Part of our roles as activated citizens in a democracy is to grasp the challenges within our own party. If we don't face these issues, we could lose this last chance to save American democracy.

Let's start with some obvious questions: Why are you reading for the first time about this coordinated, decade-long attack on our democracy in this book? Why aren't Democratic leaders like Biden, Pelosi, Schumer, and others talking about the Republicans' 4 Weapons Against Democracy every day? Why isn't there a sustained Democratic Party campaign to alert the public about this traitorous attack on our democracy? Why aren't people mad as hell so that we won't take it anymore?

Republicans have acted with impunity for the past decade as they have systematically dismantled free and fair elections. But instead of spending those years explaining to voters that Republicans are trying to effectively end democracy, the Democrats spent most of the decade talking about the cost of health insurance. Considering they lost ten of the twelve federal elections during that time, you can say their strategy failed.

Sometimes the disconnect is so outrageous that you wonder if the Democrats even care about being in the majority. In 2017, there was a pivotal supreme court race in Wisconsin, which is ground zero of GOP tactics to end democracy. The seat was up for grabs. Democrats ignored the race and lost.[3] That allowed the Republicans to maintain a majority on that supreme court. That majority-Republican court then sustained the outrageous gerrymandering, voter suppression, and even antilabor, antiunion laws. This made capturing a majority in the legislature or even 2020 presidential vote in Wisconsin even more difficult.[4]

So what will be the challenges in 2021 if Democrats win the November 2020 election?

Democrats Will Face the Same 4 Weapons That Defeated Them in the 2010 Decade

In the first congressional midterms for President Biden in 2022, the GOP's 4 Weapons will reassert their power to dictate election outcomes. So far, Democrats are not campaigning on effective solutions to these 4 Weapons.

1. **Unlimited dark money:** The Koch network, among other pissed-off billionaires, will increase its campaign funding to $2–3 billion annually against the Democrats starting January 1, 2021. Unfortunately, there

will be little effective policy passed because there are hundreds of millions of dollars loaded into a sniper's rifle and aimed at any Democrat from a less than left-wing district. Any single billionaire can pump millions and millions of dollars into groups that will make Democrats in swing districts pay dearly for any vote that goes against the interests of the rich and powerful.

2. **Gerrymandering and voter suppression:** The Republicans' second weapon will bedevil Biden, Schumer, and Pelosi as much as it did Obama, Reid, and Pelosi. Gerrymandering gives Republicans a seventeen-seat advantage in Congress before the election even starts. With Democrats likely having no legislative victories in 2021–2022 due to the filibuster and Roberts's court, Republicans will find it not too difficult to win back the House. The Senate map is not good for Democrats in 2022, so the hoped-for Democratic advantage in the Senate starting in 2021 will likely disappear. The Supreme Court continually has upheld Republican voter suppression schemes on a 5–4 vote, in four separate cases in 2020 already.[5] It's so bad that the liberal justices published a dissenting opinion accusing the Republican court of a "trend of condoning disenfranchisement."

3. **The GOP's 4 Weapons will not be blamed:** As the Republican diversionary propaganda continues unchecked, the media, political pundits, and Democratic officials will all wrongly analyze the upcoming Democrats' 2022 midterm wipeout. Just like in 2010, they will label it as a huge rebuke for the alleged overreaching of their party. Left out of the analysis will be that this was all inevitable because of the GOP's 4 Weapons Against Democracy reasserting themselves now that Trump is no longer dragging down the Republican brand.

Once Republicans take Congress back in 2022, the White House will be easy pickings in 2024, regardless of whether or not the Democrats are fielding an eighty-two-year-old incumbent named Joe Biden. Republicans will then have another four years of complete control over all government institutions. I guess I will then have to write a sequel entitled *How to Overthrow the American Autocracy* from my treehouse in an undisclosed country.

Democrats will have precious little time to pass legislation to revive democracy so that the GOP's 4 Weapons are neutralized. But it can be done.

Democrats Will Not Face a Humbled GOP in 2021 and Beyond

Maybe the Republicans will prove to be nicer in the minority? If only we could tell based on recent history. Oh, wait. My time travel machine is beeping. Let's go back, way back, to 2019 to see how that worked out.

After Democratic governors and other statewide officers were elected in Wisconsin and Michigan in 2019 and, in 2016, North Carolina, their Republican-dominated legislatures took away the powers of these newly elected Democrats. What was particularly galling about this was that these Republican-dominated legislatures remained Republican despite receiving fewer votes than their Democratic challengers. The Republicans accomplished this through the GOP's second Weapon Against Democracy: gerrymandering. So even though a majority of voters supported a Democratic governor, attorney general, secretary of state, and Democratic legislature, the Republican legislatures stayed in power, then abused that power and:

1.   removed campaign finance oversight from the Democratic secretary of state's office while cutting down early voting and ensuring that the state's board of elections would be controlled by Republicans in election years;
2.   guaranteed the GOP-controlled legislature the right to intervene in any legal battles the Democratic attorney general refused to defend while making the state's judicial system more Republican; and
3.   stripped the Democratic governors' power over cabinet appointments and stopped these governors from changing welfare, health care, and economic development policies.[6]

McConnell did the same to Obama when he neutered the president's constitutional authority to select a Supreme Court justice, nominee Merrick Garland, for an entire year before Obama left office. The rationale then was that it was an election year. Yet in May 2020, McConnell publicly proclaimed that if the impeached Trump were to have a Supreme Court opening in his last few months in office, the Republicans would immediately approve his nominee. Republican senator Joni Ernst went even farther saying Republicans would fill a Supreme Court vacancy in the lame duck session after the election even if Democrats win the White House and the Senate.[7]

No, Republicans won't change in 2021. Democrats need to acknowledge that their opponent has given up on democracy. Only bold action will undue this damage.

Democrats Have Not Explained How They Would Pass Any Legislation after the 2020 Election

Even if Democrats were to storm back into power in November 2020, the Republicans have too much ability to simply veto or overturn or block anything the Democrats want to do. Promoting any issue other than revitalizing democracy, no matter how vital to our people or our planet, is just political posturing. Democrats can't pass anything. It's like whack-a-mole, where if Democrats:

- win the White House, it doesn't matter because the Republicans have the Senate and won't confirm appointees and McConnell has a filibuster veto over everything;
- win the Senate and White House, it doesn't matter because the Republicans have the Supreme Court; or
- win back all of these branches, it doesn't matter because the Democrats are likely to lose votes from their own caucus. Too many vulnerable Democrats will be scared of the tsunami of money they will face if they take strong stands on issues.

Republicans hold a buzz saw against the Democratic majority setting policy.

By ensuring that the majority is ineffectual, the Republicans buy enough time to ride their 4 Weapons back into power in 2022.

The Republicans will always maintain power over one of these four centers of government, and typically will control all four after Trump is gone and no longer on the ballot.

Most Democratic leaders seem to be holding their breath, waiting for a time when the government isn't dominated by authoritarian enablers. They are hope peddlers. They think that if we can just make it through this latest Republican crisis (Trump being just one of many in the past forty years), they will be able to right the boat. It's as if they learn nothing from the days of the 1990s Gingrich House veto, the McConnell/Boehner veto over Obama in the 2010s, or the current Roberts Supreme Court voting against Democrats 5–4 on important issues. It's as if they believe the Republican Party after Trump will be led by John McCain-type figures, not Donald Trump Jr. types. They refuse to acknowledge that they can't pass anything of substance unless Republicans support it.

Democrats rarely discuss the impossibility of getting their policies passed. Nor are they talking about why the Republicans are either always in power or always have a veto. And they certainly don't talk about how they are going to reverse that.

So in the face of this stark reality, after losing the House in the 2010, 2012, 2014, and 2016 elections, then losing to Trump and losing the Senate in the 2012, 2014, and 2016 elections, what did the team of Schumer and Pelosi decide needed to be done to get back in the majority? In July 2017, they "rebranded" the Democratic Party after spending millions on focus groups and polling and called for "A Better Deal."[8] Their new focus would be on three issues: prescription drug prices, jobs, and limiting corporate mergers. In the midst of a budding dictator, instead of resistance, Democrats pledged to get us discounts on drugs, like a political version of GoodRx.

Doesn't it feel like the Democrats are just hapless? They get cheated out of the presidency by dark money—including millions from Putin—and voter suppression. They previously stayed in the minority in the House and numerous states despite getting more votes than Republicans. The entire party collectively gets outspent by dark-money nonprofit super PACs funded by billionaires, corporations, and foreign governments, and no one knows where the money is coming from. Despite all this, the Democrats will somehow overcome the structural disadvantages caused by the GOP's 4 Weapons by focusing on those three issues?

Democrats will point to polls that show people care about prescription prices. I get it. But it doesn't translate into governing majorities.

Democrats never campaign on the truth, which is that we have lost majority-rule democracy in the United States. Democrats leave voters ignorant of what is really happening. So it's a self-fulfilling prophecy: voters don't care about the problems that they have not been told are problems. Thus, Democrats don't focus on fighting back against the Republicans' extremely effective 4 Weapons.

Democrats need to run a messaging campaign that explains to the American public what the Republicans did in the 2010 decade to our democracy and why we need to focus on saving democracy first. And they need to pair this with the solutions in chapters 7–9.

The Democratic Party Needs to Prioritize Protecting Democracy

Imagine this scenario: Democrats are in the minority in government. With a single change in law, Democrats could regain the majority by electing a large number of new Democratic members. If they do that, in this scenario, some existing members would lose their seats due to a fairer distribution of voters in their district. Raise your hand if you think the elected Democrats would support that change in law.

That's the difficulty of fixing issues like gerrymandering. Many Democrats owe their seats to gerrymandering because it created very safe seats for them. If things are changed in how districts are drawn, they fear they may lose. It's also why you never see the Democratic Party spearheading efforts to end gerrymandering through state initiatives in Republican-controlled states like Michigan.

Fixing campaign finance has a similar problem. Every single Democrat that is in Congress has won under the rules—or lack thereof—of *Citizens United*. For the personal careers of these Democrats, *Citizens United* is not a threat. In fact, for some, they won because they were better able to fundraise under those rules than their opponents—whether they are other Democrats in the primaries or their Republican opponents.

Democrats did very little to fix the already broken campaign financing system when they were in power from 2008 to 2010. Are Democratic leaders going to save democracy in 2021 if it may mean they lose their political career with its excellent salary, health and retirement benefits, and staff?

It is possible.

I acknowledge that that's not quite as catchy a slogan as Yes, We Can or *Sí, se puede*.

One of the problems that Hillary Clinton had, and one of the problems that Democrats still have, is people don't really know what we stand for.[9]

—Michael Kazin, Editor of *Dissent* magazine

Democrats need to say that their mission is to protect democracy above everything. Reviving democracy comes above every policy idea and action necessary to fix our country.

But the Democrats are not built to save democracy. We wish they were a special warrior class trained in the art of political warfare. We need them right now to have the courage and wisdom of our greatest political leaders of the past 240 years. Wishing doesn't make it so. Most of them are career politicians—the best fundraisers of their districts. But I don't want to be the downer at the party who everyone avoids talking to. So let me shine the light on what we do have going for us.

There are definitely some elected Democrats who would be okay with losing if it meant an end to GOP domination. They are martyrs, praise be their names. Others would understand that they could compete and thrive inside the new system of rules just like they did with the old set. They are cocky, God bless them. Many would look at the reforms in part 3, see that they would spend significantly less time fundraising, and thus quickly vote aye. These are the pragmatists, may they multiply.

The rest of the Democrats need to be pressured and threatened with political upheaval and being primaried if they don't support the reforms found in part 3. That's where the actions that we can take in the final chapter will help Democrats make the right decision.

Democrats are trained to trust polls. Even in the campaigns I ran at the local level, we invested money into polls. But following polls is not the type of leadership we need right now. Besides, one can legitimately point to a lack of polling on the democracy reform detailed in part 3. You can't poll somebody to ask them how important issue X is if no one ever talks about issue X. More precisely, you can ask them about issue X, but their response won't tell you anything other than their political leaders are not talking about issue X. Meaning, if Democrats aren't talking about the GOP's 4 Weapons Against Democracy, voters are likely to conclude that there is no threat to democracy. Thus, saving democracy may not immediately poll as high as it would if Democrats campaigned on telling the public the truth about what Republicans are doing.

Polling is also a cynical abdication of political leadership. Too many Democrats don't believe the American public is smart enough or interested enough in reviving democracy. Democrats in the 2010s acted like we were past the struggle for democracy, that such a battle was won in the 1960s and there was no need to focus on *that* again.

Republican tactics are instructive here. Republicans set their agenda, and this pushes the polls.

Instead of putting forth a vision, polling just gives the impression that you are listening to what voters want. Most polling is done to find out the right things to say in order to win. Once in power, you do whatever your financial supporters want you to do. What voters actually want are leaders who will make American great again. Oops. Damn. He really did hit the nail on the head with that phrase. At the very least, we are just desperate for bold, visionary leadership.

So let's learn from 2016. Hillary Clinton had hundreds of pages of intricate policy papers built upon millions of dollars of polling during the 2016 election. Trump had a hat. Which vision connected better?

Every once in a while, the Republicans do such a spectacular job showing their hostility toward democracy that the public wakes up, even if the national Democratic Party is not the one sounding the alarm. The 2020 liberal victory in Wisconsin is a fantastic example of this. In an off-year election, in the middle of the novel coronavirus pandemic, the people of Wisconsin overwhelmingly elected a progressive to the Wisconsin Supreme Court against a conservative incumbent. The Republicans were so intent on keeping the turnout low that they fought the Democratic governor's every attempt to make voting safer. Court cases were filed, the Democratic governor blasted back, and it was a high-profile battle.

Everyone in Wisconsin was talking about the GOP's voter suppression drive. And people were pissed off at the Republicans. *Washington Post* columnist Paul Waldman noted, "As important as legal efforts and grass-roots organizing are for Democrats to push back on the GOP's well-funded campaign of suppression and intimidation, the best weapons may be public attention and outrage."[10]

Yes! That's what I'm talking about!

Democrats Must Choose Transformation over Incrementalism and Reasonableness

Way too many Democratic officials think they are in an honorable political struggle of ideas and vision with the Republican Party. They just don't get it. Republicans are trying to destroy Democrats, undermine democracy, and take full control of the government regardless of what the majority in America wants.

Can you see how this difference in analyzing the political climate of the last forty years plays out in real life?

Al Gore gave up on the pressure campaign in Florida after winning the presidential election. He didn't demand all the Florida counties be recounted because he naively thought that asking for only a few counties would make him seem more reasonable to the conservative Supreme Court. The Supreme Court then found a way to rule against him on equal protection grounds blaming it on his failure to ask for a recount in all of the counties.

President Obama naively believed if he acted reasonably, he could bring Republicans to the negotiating table even though Republicans kept attacking him as a Kenyan. In fact, less than 30% of Republicans believed Obama was born in the United States by the end of his eight years as president.[11] Ask Supreme Court justice Merrick Garland how Obama's reasonableness worked out.

Pelosi and Schumer believed that their reasonable policy arguments would sway independent voters in 2010, 2012, 2014, and 2016 elections—all lost by Democrats.

Multiple Democratic senators—including former Senator Biden and current Senators Manchin (D-WV) and Sinema (D-AZ)—think that changing the arbitrary 60% threshold for the version of the filibuster that has only been in practice since 1975 is unreasonable. After all, it is not respectful enough of tradition. Forget about what McConnell has done to the institution—Democrats are concerned about tradition and being reasonable. Their inability to grasp reality is no different than the gullible adherents to the QAnon cult. If Republicans have taught us anything in the past few years, it is that messaging plus action—not reasonableness—is the key to successful politics. Whether it's the Tea Party or the militias against the coronavirus quarantine, action can drive the message, and the message will then drive the policy. It's fair to say that the Republican Party is now the activist and movement party. Yes, it's a repugnant nationalistic, white privilege movement, but it is mobilizing more people than the unclear agenda of Democratic leaders.

The great recent examples of Democratic mobilization are mostly opportunities missed. Republicans purge hundreds of thousands of citizens from the voting rolls with a single stroke of the delete key. These actions occur every year or two in almost every single state controlled by Republicans since 2008. There's not been a single protest of these actions by national Democrats. There have certainly been great organizing efforts in places like Georgia and Wisconsin, but these efforts have been led by local activists.

Another infuriating example is the lack of response by national Democrats to gerrymandering. In Michigan—after suffering eight years under some of the worst gerrymandering in the country—neither state nor national Democrats did a single thing about it. It required a twenty-seven-year-old Michigan woman, political novice Katie Fahey, to organize an all-volunteer Facebook group to create and pass an initiative.[12] That initiative then ended Republican gerrymandering of the state, effective the first election after the new census. So the greatest minds in the Democratic Party failed to protect democracy. A twenty-seven-year-old political novice had to bail them out. Someone should write a book about this. I tap, not me.

Don't get me started on issues like racism and police killings of Black Americans. There's only a few Democrats who rejected the "tough on crime" and mass incarceration approach of Reagan/Bush/Clinton/Bush or the militarization of police departments. These summer 2020 protests are as much against Democratic Party policies as Republican ones.

So what should the Democrats do when Republicans purge hundreds of thousands of voters from the voting rolls? I can't believe I have to explain this to state and national Democrats. But here it goes:

1. Democrats should organize a high-profile protest and march to make sure Republicans don't think they can do this without suffering an anti-Republican mobilization.
2. They should fly in party, activist, and celebrity VIPs from around the country to that march.
3. That march then has two goals:
    a. One is to bring attention to the issue so that it dovetails into the narrative that Republicans are trying to end democracy.
    b. The second is to convert every marcher and supporter of the march into a volunteer to register voters.

No need to award me the Nobel Prize for Organizing. These ideas have been commonplace since the 1920s. How is it that Democratic leaders have lost sight of them? Democratic leaders have converted the party into a fundraising machine, not a political movement for democracy. Sometimes it's hard to walk and chew gum at the same time, especially when you have to raise huge amounts of money from Wall Street and private equity firms to keep up with the GOP.

It's really time to change this.

The 2021 Divide among Democrats Will Determine Whether They Will Help Us Save Democracy

The American empire may never fall, but American democracy is far more precarious. When democracies fall, there are always two players in the tragedy. One player understands that they cannot gain the support of the majority. Instead of creating better policies, they focus on taking power. They do this by dismantling the democratic guardrails and changing the rules so that they become the permanent party in power. In our country, Republicans play this role.

The second player is the opposition. The opposition plays by the rules and be rewarded for being reasonable. But these rules are constantly being changed by the other side. This losing party—in our case, the Democrats—keeps "inexplicably" losing elections.

Hopefully enough elected Democratic officials will wake up in 2021. If they do, they can challenge their party's ineffective strategy from the past decade and not think everything is fine now that we won an election. This will start a great battle between two groups of Democrats:

- Group 1: Democrats who think voters will only keep choosing them if they focus on the pandemic, recession, and maybe police reform
- Group 2: Democrats who understand that they won because the American public rejected the corruption and threat to democracy of Trump and the Republicans

This is an important distinction.

Group 1 will focus on the pandemic and economy. They will depoliticize the pandemic and accompanying recession and the antiracism marches. During the 2021 legislative season they will avoid blaming Trump and the Republicans for these disasters. They will stress their nonpartisan competency, policy, and managerial skills. The messaging from Biden, Schumer, and Pelosi will be about country over party and focusing on digging out of this deep hole, as if we accidentally fell into that hole.

This was President Obama's approach in dealing with the 2008 economic crisis and the fallout from two simultaneous wars. Democrats won't want to appear that they're taking political advantage of these solemn problems. Mommy and Daddy, in the forms of Pelosi and Biden, will now take care of it for us kids.

Of course, they will run into the filibuster of Senate Republicans. So they must water down their reasonable proposals even further. Later, they might halfheartedly try to make changes to health care, immigration, climate change, et cetera. Many of their laws will be struck down by a Republican-dominated court system, but that is—according to this mindset—unavoidable in our allegedly perfect 240-year-old democratic system.

The week after Election Day these Democrats will slyly plant stories about how they are reaching across the aisle to their old friends and colleagues in the Republican Party. Bipartisanship caucuses will be created that will feature an even number of Democrats and Republicans to make sure that Democrats aren't too Democratic. They will act like the past four years—or forty—never happened. They will say they need to find middle ground, reach out and compromise, be reasonable and calm things down.

If your Democratic officials claim they will inspire a return to bipartisanship, mock them loudly. It's the height of arrogance to pretend that their magnificent personalities will undo the Republicans' decade-long drive for ultimate power. If Joe Biden is banking his success on Republicans coming to their senses, he will become a footnote in history as the ineffective Democratic president between Trump Senior and Trump Junior.

Group 2 Democrats will try to save democracy. They will withhold their support for any legislation that is not focused on reviving democracy until democracy is saved.

These Democrats understand that we are running a deficiency in democracy that paralyzes effective action.

But they still need your help because they will not have enough votes to make a real difference. Part 3 of this book is written to help you help them. If they save democracy this will free them to then heal the pandemic and economy properly, and they will then be able to pivot to our other dire needs. After democracy is fixed, Democrats will be able to stay in power—unless their policy solutions fail. Success or failure of policy should be what determines who governs—not unlimited dark money, gerrymandering, voter suppression, or diversionary propaganda.

The solutions in part 3 are the path back to working in a bipartisan manner—something that would be appeal to a Biden administration. But first we must restore democracy. Only then will Republicans understand they can't cheat their way back into power. At that point, they will see that cooperation is the path to relevancy.

Learning from the 2009–2010 Democratic Party Wasted Opportunity

The 2009–2010 trifecta owned by the Democrats achieved remarkably little. President Obama won in a landslide in 2008. He had sixty of the one hundred senators and a seventy-nine-seat majority in the House where Democrats won thirteen million more votes than Republican candidates. The Democrats' first major piece of legislation was to help unions grow their membership though a "card check" where members could join a union by signing a card. This would have reversed the impact of "right-to-work" laws that the conservative Supreme Court had unleashed. Experts predicted union membership would double within a few years of the bill passing. It had close to sixty votes in the Senate, but it failed because forty-one senators, led by McConnell, opposed it.

Maddeningly, Obama was silent on the bill for a long time; too long.[13] Instead of spending his political capital to strengthen his allies, he saved it for the upcoming health care legislation.

It was a massive strategic blunder.

Obama had the opportunity to help the progressive movement create a counterweight to the oversized influence of corporations and their billionaire owners. That opportunity never returned.

Do you see the failure of strategic thinking? Health care reform would have been much easier had this card-check legislation passed and unions grew. If I had given you a pop quiz in 2009 with one question—"What is the best way to get health care reform passed?"—please tell me that your answer would have been to support the card-check bill. Unfortunately, that was not the strategy the Democrats chose.

Politics is not about having the best ideas. It's about understanding how to marshal the resources to get things done. Without increasing his allies in the union movement, the Democrats were unable to counter the 4 Weapons Against Democracy that Republicans were building. Obama's presidency effectively ended in 2010, even though he remained in the White House until 2016. What a lost opportunity to move our country—and the world—forward. It was just like Bill Clinton squandering his presidency over a blow job, though much less seedy.

Almost any other Republican president besides Donald Trump would have navigated the COVID-19 crisis with more empathy and respect—if not competence—and would be coasting to re-election. Meanwhile, the GOP's 4 Weapons would have kept getting stronger and more impossible to dislodge. It would be game over for democracy.

The super-rich would have wielded their control over Congress and our nation's laws more quietly and with better PR rollouts. They would have had their constitutional convention to "fix" whatever laws they disliked. This political reality would simply have been the new normal. Just as family farms were replaced with corporate farming and now most small businesses have been replaced by chains and franchises, we all would just adapt to the new normal.

We accept a new reality—even when it is a change for the worse—as long as it is incremental. In this new normal of American politics, the real debates would be between Republican conservatives and Republican hardliners. No one else's voices would have mattered. Kind of like what happened from 2017 to 2018 before the Democrats won the House back, thanks to Trump. No need to write him a thank-you card, but it is important to understand just how blessed we are to even have another chance to save democracy.

Notes

1.   Jamelle Bouie, "The Presidency Is Not Enough," *New York Times*, 4 Nov. 2019, www.nytimes.com /2019/11/04/opinion/warren-sanders-filibuster.html.

2.   Michael Kranish, "How Brad Parscale, Once a 'Nobody in San Antonio,' Shaped Trump's Combative Politics and Rose to His Inner Circle," *Washington Post*, 9 Nov. 2018, www.washingtonpost.com /politics/how-brad-parscale-once-a-nobody-in-san-antonio-shaped-trumps-combative-politics-and -rose-to-his-inner-circle/2018/11/09/b4257d58-dbb7-11e8-b3f0-62607289efee_story.html.

3.   David Daley, "Democrats Just Blew It in Wisconsin: Elections Likely to Stay Rigged in Favor of GOP." Salon, 28 Apr. 2019, www.salon.com/2019/04/28/democrats-just-blew-it -in-wisconsin-elections-likely-to-stay-rigged-in-favor-of-gop/.

4.   Riley Vetterkind and Wisconsin State Journal. "Brian Hagedorn's Likely Supreme Court Win Cements Conservative Dominance in State," Madison.com, 6 Apr. 2019, madison.com/wsj/news/local /govt-and-politics/brian-hagedorn-s-likely-supreme-court-win-cements-conservative-dominance /article_809805f4-59c4-5087-a453-ca18625744c9.html.

5.   Emmett Witkovsky-Eldred, Nina Totenberg, "As Concerns About Voting Build, The Supreme Court Refuses To Step In," NPR, 25 July 2020, www.npr.org/2020/07/25/895185355/as -concerns-about-voting-build-the-supreme-court-refuses-to-step-in.

6.   Tara Golshan, "How Republicans Are Trying to Strip Power from Democratic Governors-Elect," *Vox*, 4 Dec. 2018, www.vox.com/policy-and-politics/2018/12/4/18123784/gop-legislature-wisconsin -michigan-power-grab-lame-duck.

7.   Evan Brechtel, "GOP Senator Says She'd Support Trump Filling a Supreme Court Vacancy This Year Even If He Loses and the Hypocrisy Is Real," Second Nexus, 22 July 2020, secondnexus.com/joni -ernst-scotus-lame-duck.

8.   Katrina van den Heuvel, "An Even Better Deal," *The Washington Post*, 1 Aug. 2017, www.washingtonpost.com /opinions/an-even-better-deal/2017/08/01/5da6c40e-7633-11e7-8f39-eeb7d3a2d304_story.html.

9.   Michael Kazin, editor of *Dissent* magazine, as cited in Susan B. Glasser et al., "'People Don't Really Know What We Stand For'." *Politico*, 11 Sept. 2017, www.politico.com/magazine/story/2017/09/11/donald -trump-future-of-the-dems-215592.

10. Paul Waldman, "Republicans Are Serious about Voter Suppression. Here's How to Stop Them," *Washington Post*, 18 May 2020, www.washingtonpost.com/opinions/2020/05/18/republicans -are-serious-about-voter-suppression-heres-how-stop-them/.

11. Josh Clinton and Carrie Roush, "Poll: Persistent Partisan Divide Over 'Birther' Question," NBC News, 10 Aug. 2016, www.nbcnews.com/politics/2016-election/poll-persistent-partisan -divide-over-birther-question-n627446.

12. Kevin Grand et al., "One Woman's Facebook Post Leads to Michigan Vote against Gerrymandering," *Bridge Magazine*, 9 Jan. 2020, www.bridgemi.com/michigan-government/one -womans-facebook-post-leads-michigan-vote-against-gerrymandering.

13. Josh Gerstein, "Obama Silent on Card Check Bill," *Politico*, 30 Jan. 2009, www.politico.com/story /2009/01/obama-silent-on-card-check-bill-018231.

CHAPTER 6

We Just Want a Better World; Is That So Difficult?

When I say it's you I like, I'm talking about that part of you that
knows that life is far more than anything you can ever see or hear
or touch. That deep part of you that allows you to stand for those
things without which humankind cannot survive. Love that conquers
hate, peace that rises triumphant over war, and justice that proves
more powerful than greed.

—Mr. (Fred) Rogers[1]

We want the world to be a better place. So we fight for issues and policies that we believe will lift up humanity, protect the vulnerable, save the environment, and bring more peace to a conflict-ridden world. We participate in our democracy as the path to fight for our issues. Yet, because of the Republicans' 4 Weapons, we are currently facing one of the worst threats to democracy our nation has faced in over 240 years. Unless we focus on that first, we cannot make progress on any other issue. Have I mentioned that?

Our democracy will be fully gone after 2022, unless we implement the #DemRevPlan found in the next three chapters.

The battles that we citizen-activists and progressives are waging are important, yet there is an element of futility. If we can't win and govern, how long will it be until Republicans finally just destroy all of the good policies that remain? "The Resistance" cannot stop the damage that a permanent Republican government will unleash. Until we focus on stopping the super-rich from buying state legislatures and Congress, until we stop gerrymandering and voter suppression, and until we neuter diversionary propaganda, we will not make progress on anything that matters. Everything important to progressives and other compassionate Americans will be lost.

Imagine four more years of denying climate change, hating on immigrants, rolling back access health care and birth control, enduring systemic racism and insanely high levels of incarceration of Black Americans, giving tax breaks to the super-rich, engaging in massive military spending and assassinations of our enemies while embracing dictators, and giving green lights for corporations to ignore the consequences of their actions on our health and environment.

Now imagine ten more years of that.

Or twenty-five more years.

Imagine seven Republican-appointed Supreme Court justices.

Or...

Remember that it takes just thirty-four states to call for a constitutional convention to amend the United States Constitution in any way Republicans see fit.

What happens when these Republican policies fail, yet there is no way to vote Republicans out? What happens when the economy goes south, or climate change gets worse, or homelessness continues to spike, disease spreads, and our cities become desolate and violent? Nothing good.

Trump is a Lifeline to Save Our Sinking Democracy.

Trump was the anchor that scuttled the complete takeover of political power for the elite of his party. I hope you have enjoyed this irony as much as I have—it's literally the only "fun" thing about politics since 2016. He has woken up enough Americans by being such a horrid person that a majority of the country wanted him removed from office after the impeachment.[158] His unfavorables average 52%.[159]

Because Trump is not the main problem for democracy in America, our activism doesn't end with removing him. Rather, it begins there. He is a bump on the road for Republicans to achieve full power permanently. If the Democrats take advantage of this second chance—this *Last Chance* (see what I did there?)—then they can restore democracy. Once the GOP can't throw hundreds of thousands off the voting rolls, once they can't gerrymander their way to a majority, once they can't get millions of dollars from dark money sources, and once their diversionary propaganda is neutralized, there's no way the GOP and the Trump crime family will continue to govern.

Yes, We Can. This time that's not just a slogan. And the most important word is the one in the middle: we.

Are you ready to stop this? Are you ready to make life better in the United States? To expand economic and educational opportunities? Expand justice and fairness? Create a more vibrant social net, with smarter help and less dependency? Want to save the planet from climate disaster and our bodies from pollution and toxins?

This is the time. More than 150,000 Americans are already dead from COVID-19 at the time of writing this book, and there is depression-level unemployment. Trump claims his "authority is total" just two weeks after claiming: "I don't take responsibility at all" for the problematic response of his government.160 As of May 2020, he blamed Democratic governors for alleged mismanagement, the media for exaggerating the threat and then for not giving him credit for his response, various inspectors general, the Obama administration, China, the WHO, and even alleged greedy nurses for stealing much-needed equipment.

When protestors fight against systemic racism and police killings, Trump mobilizes the military and paramilitaries against these practitioners of the First Amendment.

Enough. Our government is dysfunctional. The United States is beginning to resemble a failed state. The GOP's political philosophy—if you can tease one out of their contradictory messages—is a disaster yet again, just like in the George W. Bush days. We must demand that Democrats do more than return us to the status quo. It's not good enough to be effective managers for two years.

I said "we" earlier, but more precisely, it's up to *you* to make sure that Democrats focus on the fundamental issue that rules all other issues: Reviving our democracy. Saving our democracy. Expanding our democracy. It's all you, baby, because it's *your* democracy, not the Democrats' democracy.

Are you with me? Will you be a DemRevver?

Premise #1 of the book is that Trump's election gave us one *Last Chance to Save American Democracy*. Premise #2 is that we cannot passively trust that Democrats will come up with an effective strategy to counter the dismantling of democracy by Republicans.

The Democratic Party is not built to save democracy anymore. Trying to appear as the reasonable party, the Democrats start at half a loaf and the Republicans slice that in half. We can't let the Democrats squander our blue tsunami of 2020, like they did our landslide of 2008. Democrats need to dedicate their first one hundred days of their new administration in 2021 to saving our democracy.

Barricade the Doors, Hide the Small Children

So, dear activists, do not push for pandemic, economic, antiracism, or other progressive policies until we have rebuilt our democracy infrastructure. The good news is that it shouldn't take too long to pass the #DemRevPlan. But first we all need to learn this step-by-step plan to save democracy. You know there will be a test at the end of the book—let me know if you need me to make some flash cards.

Because we know that Democrats won't save us, it is vital for *you* to understand how to fix our democracy. The next chapters have the plan. But it's not for light skimming. Each of us needs to be able to debate our ineffective lawmakers on these issues physically—in their offices or at least on Zoom. We need to be able to grill them at a town hall meeting. We need to be able to articulate our plans to the media. Or we need to be able to write them on placards as we occupy DC.

Okay, I'm getting ahead of myself.

My dear patriots of democracy, activists for just causes, lovers of humankind, it's time for *you* to sound the alarm bells in your own groups and networks. Any cause you support is currently being stymied by the Republican blockade on progress. I do not have to tell you that throwing Republicans out in November 2020 is an essential first step in making progress on your goals. But you do need to persuade your fellow activists that reviving democracy is the essential step 2 in making progress on your goals—whatever they may be.

This is the battle immediately after the November 2020 election is finally called.

So here it is, the single most important thing to save American democracy. The shot in the arm of democracy that Republican leaders fear most. The blessing that would ensure that we remain in the 1% of human civilization that has ever lived under democracy. The pushback against old, conservative, white, Christian fundamentalist men with their authoritarian need to make everyone conform to their narrow—and often hypocritical—self-righteous view of the way we all should act.

I pledge to you with all my heart that this is more important than all the issues I most deeply care about and on which I have worked for my entire career: the Green New Deal[2], workers' rights, ending wars, having a humane immigration policy[3], fixing inequalities in the economy, and stopping racism.

Drumroll, please.

Notes

1. "Revisiting Fred Rogers' 2002 Commencement Address," *Dartmouth News*, 11 June 2017, news. dartmouth.edu/news/2018/03/revisiting-fred-rogers-2002-commencement-address.

2. My first book in 1990 was *The Greening of New Zealand*, so... been there, done that.

3. I built a successful immigration law firm, so don't get me started on how shit our immigration policy was and is.

PART 3

Democrats Won't Save Democracy Unless You—the Reader—Organize for It

The biggest divide in the Democratic Party is not between left and center. It's between those who believe once Trump is gone things will go back to normal, and those who believe that our democracy is under a threat that goes beyond Trump.

—Dan Pfeiffer, former Obama advisor, host of *Pod Saves America*[1]

1.   Jacob S. Hacker, "Can Democrats Save Democracy - or Even Their Own Party?" *The Washington Post*, 27 Mar. 2020, www.washingtonpost.com/outlook/can-democrats-save-democracy--or-even-their-own-party/2020/03/27/e9a598ea-5ff1-11ea-b014-4fafa866bb81_story.html.

CHAPTER 7

#DemRevPlan Solutions 1-7:
Let the Majority Govern

Solution #1: Fix the Filibuster

Believe the hype. Fixing the filibuster by implementing Iowa senator Tom Harkin's 2013 filibuster reform plan is the key to everything. *Nothing* gets done without reforming the filibuster. Mind you, I didn't say abolish it. The filibuster is a sensible idea as originally intended: to slow down the majority's ability to steamroll the minority. But the entire future of our democracy is dependent upon Senate Democrats fixing this misunderstood tool to make it work better for all Americans. And no, that's not hyperbole.

Senator Harkin's proposal was to steadily reduce the vote required to stop a bill from being filibustered. The number of votes required would be reduced by three on each vote (e.g., from sixty to fifty-seven to fifty-four to fifty-one) every two days, until a simple majority could finally pass the legislation. Currently the minority party can simply say they have forty-one of the one hundred senators opposed to a bill or motion, and that stops that bill or motion from even being discussed or voted upon.

Three small changes to Harkin's proposal are needed:

1. These numbers should be percentages (i.e., 40% instead of forty senators) due to the #DemRevPlan to add a few senators (see Solution #2).
2. The filibuster should only be available for use on *final* votes on a bill or appointment, not on procedures, amendments, or motions.
3. The filibuster must be a talking filibuster with live bodies instead of a silent or virtual one that does not require the presence of the senators on the floor.

Talking Points: Fix the Filibuster

How to tell your elected representative or media why this fight is so crucial:

The filibuster should be reformed, not ended.

- The minority can use this reformed version of the filibuster to bring attention to and slow down a bill. It gives them eight days to put pressure on the majority to compromise with the minority. That is the primary intention behind the filibuster.
- Seventy former US senators from both parties see the need to reform the filibuster. They recently wrote, "The filibuster and cloture have shut down action on the Senate floor. It is now commonly said that it takes 60 votes to pass anything in the Senate. This is new and obstructionist.... Filibusters are now threatened as a matter of course and are too readily acceded to."[1]

The GOP has corrupted our democracy through its use of the filibuster.

- Mitch McConnell will again weaponize the filibuster to obstruct almost all legislation, block judges, and usurp democracy after 2020. That is exactly what he did to thwart Obama's agenda, even after the majority of the country elected Obama twice! Elections should have consequences. McConnell has personally violated too many Senate norms to reward him with veto power over the next Democratic president. Besides, in 2017, the Republicans eliminated the filibuster for Supreme Court nominees. Progress and reform should be favored over nostalgia and a vain attempt to appear more statesman like.
- Any Democrat who does not support the Harkin filibuster reform will make no progress on immigration reform, take no action on global climate change, be unable to lessen systemic racism, take no steps toward giving Americans a fair tax system, etc. None of those will ever get past McConnell's filibuster veto. McConnell has found a way to give himself a greater power than those who a majority

of Americans select as their representatives. Without filibuster reform, Democrats will have to follow the senator from Kentucky's lead on any issue.

- We couldn't get the Dream Act passed when Democrats and even a few Republicans supported it. Even though it "passed" by fourteen votes, 55–41, in 2010, it was stopped by McConnell's filibuster. How is that majority-rules democracy?

The current version of filibuster goes against the Constitution.

- The filibuster is *not* in the Constitution. The founders were opposed to supermajority voting requirements such as a filibuster except in rare cases.[2] They wanted the majority to rule; you know, democracy. The filibuster was created in the early nineteenth century but was rarely used until the 1960s. The House abolished their filibuster 150 years ago. The current rule of requiring a supermajority of sixty of the one hundred senators to move legislation forward has only been in effect since 1975.
- A 40% minority in the Senate should not be able to stop Congress from passing a law that has majority support in the House, the Senate, and support from the president. This is a direct violation of the Fourteenth Amendment Equal Protection Clause, in spirit if not law.
- The filibuster itself has nothing to do with democracy. It's supposed to be a check on the tyranny of the majority but instead has given the power to forty senators—mostly from small states—to defeat the will of Americans. This reform offers a check on the majority, just not a veto.

Why might your elected Democratic representative hesitate?

Biden said, "[I do] not support ending the filibuster." Some senators might interpret this as meaning it shouldn't even be fixed. Seems to me that the reform proposed above does not end the filibuster, just brings it back to the more common-sense intent of it.

Solution #2: Fair Representation or No Taxation

[R]eproductive rights, same-sex marriage, and other liberties are now at risk because of two justices who were appointed by a president who lost the popular vote and who were confirmed by senators who received far fewer votes than those who were opposed. Is this any way to run a democracy in the twenty-first century?

—Dan Kennedy, associate professor of journalism at Northeastern University and writer for the blog Media Nation.[3]

Neither the Senate nor the House provides for equal representation for American voters, nor do they guarantee that all Americans are represented. We need to provide a check and balance on the antidemocratic trend lines of Congress before population centers shift even more from rural states and into states with large cities like California and Texas.[4]

1.   To partially fix the Senate, we need to immediately:
     a.   add Washington, DC, and Puerto Rico as states so that those senators can be elected before the 2022 midterms;
     b.   begin consultations with Native tribes and the National Congress of American Indians to explore whether they want to retain their sovereignty while being given a special state status for their combined Native American tribal lands—one that would be the ninth-largest state; and
     c.   promote the splitting of our most populous and largest state into a Southern California State and Northern California State.
2.   To fix the House, we need to implement the Wyoming Rule.[5] This will expand the size of the House by allocating representatives by population using the state with the lowest population—Wyoming, as of 2010—as the baseline to receive one representative.

Talking Points: Fair Representation or No Taxation

How to tell your elected representative or media why this fight is so crucial:

Fixing the Senate: By adding four to eight members to the Senate, our current historic unrepresentativeness will be partially fixed.

The scope of the imbalance in the Senate was not imagined at the time of the Constitution's creation.

- The worst imbalance currently is California's 40 million people versus Wyoming's 600,000. Both states have two senators. That makes Wyoming voters sixty-seven times more powerful in the Senate than California voters on a per-person basis. At the time of the first census in 1790, the greatest ratio between largest and smallest states was ten to one,[6] not sixty-seven to one.
- The majority of the US population—164 million out of 330 million—lives in ten states. Yet the fewer than 8 million people who live in the least populous ten states have as many senators as these 164 million people. The people in those ten larger states have only 5% as much voting power for the Senate as the voters in the ten least populous states.
- Electing the majority of the US Senate only requires 18% of the population currently. A law—or nominee—that 82% of the population opposed can still pass. Another way to look at that is that half of the US population is represented by eighty-two senators, the other half by just eighteen senators.

The Senate is minority rule and thus undemocratic.

- In 2014, the forty-six Democratic senators elected in the 2010–2014 elections received 20 million more votes than the fifty-four Republicans but were still the minority party.[7]
- Both of Trump's nominees to the Supreme Court were confirmed by senators who received far fewer votes than the senators who opposed them. The senators who voted to confirm Gorsuch and Kavanaugh had received 54 million votes. The senators who were opposed to them had won more than 73 million. That's a margin of 58 percent to 42 percent against confirmation, yet both were confirmed by the Senate.

We've changed the Senate size thirty-seven times.

- In the first 170 years of our country, a state was added on average every 4.5 years. The Senate has changed its numbers on thirty-seven occasions since the Constitution was created. Adding states, and thus adding two senators, was the norm. But it's been sixty years since the last state was added. So it's time to extend democracy in representation to the final Americans who remain disenfranchised.

Making Puerto Rico a state is a nonpartisan issue.

- The Republican platform in 2016 favored adding Puerto Rico as a state, as did the Democratic Party in 2012.[8] But getting both sides to act—even when they are in agreement—seems impossible. Fortunately, you only need a majority in both the Senate and House to make it happen. We revolted against England when they kept us as a colonial territory. It's a betrayal of American democracy to deny representation to 3.4 million Americans living in Puerto Rico. This is especially true considering that Puerto Rico has more US citizens than twenty other states.

Americans in Washington, DC, are entitled to Senate representation.

- There are 710,000 US citizens in DC with no representation in the Senate and no votes in the House. DC has a larger population than Wyoming, North Dakota, and Vermont.[9] There is no rationale to keep these DC residents without senators.

We've already taken steps for Puerto Rico and DC statehood.

- Puerto Rico and DC have already voted to be added as states. It's simply been the dereliction of Congress that has stopped these additions. The Democrats voted to make DC a state in 2019 in the House of Representatives under H.R. 1. It did not include Puerto Rico, shamefully! Obviously, Mitch McConnell did not even let it get introduced in the Senate.

The Americans of Puerto Rico and DC suffer due to lack of representation.

- Look how Trump abandoned Puerto Rico during its calamities despite every person there being a US citizen. That is wrong. But making Puerto Rico a state may be the only way to make its economy self-sufficient again. It will open tremendous tourism to Puerto Rico, which is good for everyone. People argued that the poor, impoverished Hawaii would be a burden on the United States economy. So far, so good. Hawaii and Alaska averaged double-digit economic growth for more than a decade after admission.[10] DC and Puerto Rico are underfunded and neglected. How can Democratic Party senators not see the justification in giving these US citizens—in our nation's capital and in the Puerto Rican territory—representation?

A Native American nation-state would be one of the largest and most populous states in the United States.

- The Tribal Nations in the United States are more than 6 million members strong in 570 federally recognized tribes, about half of which have reservations. Tribal Nations are considered both sovereign governments and domestic dependent nations. The Supreme Court has consistently ruled that Congress has plenary (complete) authority over Indians. Granting Native tribes the power of a state does not in itself destroy their sovereignty if there is no intention on the part of Congress to do so. If you were to combine the state and federal recognized tribal lands (a.k.a. reservations), Native Americans would have the ninth-largest state by territory, equivalent to the size of Colorado.[11] This Hawaii-like noncontiguous state would be the seventeenth most populated state, just behind Tennessee, as the number of Native Americans is currently estimated at 6.8 million in 2020.[12] In thirty years this number is projected to double.[13] The Navajo Nation reservation alone is geographically larger than the state of West Virginia.
- The US government even recognized making "American Indians" the fifty-first state as an option in the studies of the congressional American Indian Policy Review Commission in 1975–1976. President Ford, however, was too busy pardoning Richard Nixon to push for its addition.

No group has suffered more from lack of representation than Native Americans.

- No one can make the argument that the state or the federal government has effectively represented Native Americans this century or last. It's been a never-ending story of genocide, treaty-breaking, discrimination, and second-class citizenship. Although there are Tribal Nations people in all fifty states, they are the last ones cared for in any of those fifty states. Because of this poor representation, the Tribal Nations have the highest poverty rate, a shorter life expectancy than even the people of Guatemala, just over 50% high school graduation rates, the worst problems of alcoholism and domestic abuse, and highest rates of COVID-19 outbreaks.[14]

- This discrimination continues unabated today:
  a. The states ignored the Tribal Nations when they greenlit the massively controversial Keystone XL Pipeline across the land under control of Native Americans despite Native American yearlong "die-in" protests.
  b. In May 2020, Native American tribes set up checkpoints on the highways in their communities to stop the spread of COVID-19. The five areas with the highest rates of COVID-19 are on reservations areas.[15] The Republican governor of South Dakota gave them an ultimatum to take down the checkpoints immediately.[16]
  c. Trump ordered the disestablishment of a reservation for the Native American Mashpee Wampanoag Tribe, whose descendants were the first to greet the pilgrims.[17] This group's casino was directly competing with the nearby Twin River casino. That casino employs Matt Schlapp, chairman of the American Conservative Union, as a lobbyist. His wife, Mercedes Schlapp, was the White House strategic communications director before working for Trump's re-election campaign. Wow.
  d. The political disenfranchisement of Native Americans has increased since 2008, when they massively swung their support to President Obama. Republican states have consistently suppressed their ability to vote, as documented in the voter suppression section above.[18] This is mostly done by requiring voters to prove their physical address, something most homes on Native American

reservations do not have, and by requiring Native Americans to vote off of their reservations, which requires long trips for many people without the means to make those long trips.[19]

- Would Native American nations vote to unite into one legal state entity and obtain Senate representation? We won't know until we have consultation and dialog. If they did become a state, would their elected senators be Democrats? Who knows? They may form their own party, vote Republican, or send conservative Democrats to the Senate. That's not the point. The point is to provide representation to the original people of this land who have never been adequately represented since the founding of our democracy. It's up to the Democrats to change that—now.

California should divide into two states to improve its inadequate representation.

- With its 40 million residents represented by two senators, California has the same population as the twenty smallest states combined, which have forty senators!
- The two states of North and South Dakota have 1.5 million people between them. Yet they have as many senators as California and New York, which have 60 million people combined. If the Dakotans and Carolinians get four senators and the Virginians get six (Virginia, West Virginia, and Kentucky), then why shouldn't Californians get four senators?
- Amazingly, the two California states would still be the third and fourth most populous states in the union.
- California is the largest state, the most difficult to govern state (just look at our COVID-19 record and our fires), and the most populous state. It is too big. Californians already identify as Southern or Northern Californians. Yes, billionaire and innovative Democrat Tim Draper has twice tried to split up California (into six, then three states) and received no traction. But his splits had no relationship to the identity that Californians feel to Southern California or Northern California. Those are real divides. Just ask anyone from San Francisco their feelings on people from Southern California coming into their hometown!

- Private message to Tom Steyer: Hey, Mr. S., you really want to make a difference? (And we know you do.) Help us get two additional Democratic senators by funding a ballot splitting California into two blue states. When Dianne Feinstein's Senate seat finally opens up, you won't have to run against SoCal notables such as Los Angeles mayor Eric Garcetti, former Los Angeles mayor Antonio Villaraigosa, impeachment hero representative Adam Schiff, former state senate majority leader Kevin DeLeon, or any of the other would-be SoCal candidates.
- Private message to governor Gavin Newsom: Dear Gov., you should lead the charge to split your own state, buddy! When you run for president, you will be a hero to the Democrats for having handed them two additional senators. It will also show that your ego is not dependent on having the biggest…state.

Fixing the House: By adopting the Wyoming Rule[20] for the House, our current historic unrepresentativeness will be partially fixed.

The Wyoming Rule is the easiest and fairest way to fix the lopsided representation in the House.

- The Wyoming Rule reform to the House of Representatives would take the state with the least population after each census (currently Wyoming) and set its population number as the population number per House district. Using 2010 numbers, the House would thus increase to 547 members under the Wyoming Rule. Almost all states would receive a much fairer allocation of House members. California, Texas, New York, and Florida would gain a combined 35 new house members. These four states currently have an average of 9 representatives fewer than they should have if there was a fair allocation of representatives. How is this democratic?
- Under the Wyoming Rule, no state would lose a single House member, so it wouldn't hurt those smaller states. Districts would be rounded up to receive an additional House member at the .5 mark of the Wyoming population number.

Our current allocation of House of Representatives members is not set in the Constitution.

- In 1789, there were fifty-nine house members. For the next 124 years, the House membership grew on average by six members every two years. In 1913, it stopped growing at 435. This was a political decision made by the Republicans who were then in power. There was no constitutional reason for this. At that time, the population of the United States was 95 million. Today the population is 327 million, but the House of Representatives has not grown since 1913.

Why Might Your Elected Democratic Representative Hesitate?

It appears that there is full support to create a state out of Washington, DC, and to call it the Douglass Commonwealth. Excellent name IMHO. So that's part of the way there, I suppose.

Strategically, these reforms make sense overall for the party in that there will possibly be an additional eight Democratic senators. Democrats would definitely increase their majority in the House, considering that these additional one-hundred-plus reps would come from states with large urban populations who would no longer be so underrepresented in Congress. Obviously, if expanding representation in Congress benefited the Republicans, they would have already done it.

I won't repeat chapter 5's critique of the Democrats' failure on strategy. At the end of the day, Democrats who oppose this simply would be doing so out of fear—fear that moneyed interests would gang up on them and fear that the public would think it's overreach. That first fear is neutralized by Solution #4. The second fear is completely overblown. The public will care a lot more about the Democrats' success on policy issues than on whether or not California and Texas get more house members or whether Puerto Rico and DC get senators. If the Democrats go from a 50–50 split to a 58–50 majority, that will enable four Democrats—on any vote—to buck their party and protect themselves with more conservative voters in their purple or red home state. So this actually will help keep those moderate senators in office.

Does it seem weird to include Puerto Rico, DC, Native lands, and Southern California as states? Let's just look back at the last time we let multiple states in at the same time: 1959. Congress admitted Hawaii and Alaska. It's not as if there were great demand to do so. Both of those states were thousands of miles away with tiny populations. Congress did it, and everyone moved on. Senate Democrats need to get over themselves and just pass the #DemRevPlan Solution #2.

Solution #3: Court Reform, Not Court Packing

> Nobody has done more to change the court system in the history of our country than Donald Trump. And Mr. President, we're going to keep on doing it. My motto is: Leave no vacancy behind.
>
> —Mitch McConnell, shouted to an adoring Republican crowd at a November 2019 Trump rally[21]

McConnell has ended the practice of having a fair-minded, deliberative role for the Senate in considering court appointments. McConnell has allowed Trump to pack our federal courts with more judges rated as unqualified by the American Bar Association than the previous four presidents combined.[22] McConnell slow-walked or blocked so many Obama appointees that when President Obama left, over 12% of all of the federal judge seats were vacant, including—most famously—a Supreme Court seat. Trump has now appointed more judges in his three years than Obama did in eight years. Sigh.

Many Democrats want revenge. They want to arbitrarily increase the already arbitrary Supreme Court size from nine to eleven. And while Congress sets the number of Supreme Court members, not the Constitution, randomly adding more justices is pure politics, not reform. What we need is court reform that makes it more difficult for McConnell and future leaders like him to hyperpoliticize the court appointment system. To ensure the changes to the courts benefit both sides equally the court reform legislation should have the following components:

1. Eighteen-year terms: The Constitution tried to take politics out of the courts by allowing judges to continue indefinitely during "good behavior" so they would be immune from the political pressures of the moment. Having one set term of eighteen years, however, achieves the same goal. Thus, Congress should enact a version of Trump Cabinet member Rick Perry's plan to establish a single eighteen-year term for Supreme Court justices but apply it to all levels of the courts. How do we enforce an eighteen-year term limit for justices and other federal judges? There are different paths. The Senate may not take a final vote on the nominee until that nominee submits a letter of resignation during the process. The resignation would be dated eighteen years after the beginning of their term on the court and entered into the federal congressional record, making it irrevocable and permanent. Creating an ad hoc rule like this is inspired by McConnell's ad hoc rule that the Senate can't take up a Supreme Court nomination in the last year of a president's term. Alternatively, Congress simply requires Supreme Court justices and appellate judges to transfer to a lower court level after eighteen years. They remain federal judges in accordance with the Constitution but just serve at a different level. Or, Congress legislates that full retirement benefits are given to any judge or justice who serves eighteen years in the federal judiciary. But the justices forfeit both retirement benefits and their budget for staff if they stay past eighteen years, unless they request a reassignment to a lower court. This is similar to the incentivized retirement system for judges in Arkansas and should ensure the district court judges also leave after eighteen years.

2. Expand the courts, including fifteen appellate circuits and fifteen Supreme Court seats, and mandate geographic diversity: Break up the Ninth Circuit Court of Appeals into three circuits, bringing the total number of circuits to fifteen. Then ensure that the fifteen circuits have approximately equal population totals. Republicans are always demanding that the Ninth Circuit be split up anyway, and rightfully so, since that one circuit covers 20% of the US population. Under this reform, each circuit would then, eventually, have one Supreme Court justice paired to it. Accordingly, all future Supreme Court justices will be required to have lived for no less than fifteen years in the geographic

circuit to which they are assigned. This would create a geographic diversity that we do not currently have in each of the fifteen circuit areas of the United States. Finally, the lower-level federal district and appellate courts should grow by 33%, as recently suggested by conservative Republican commentators.[23] The Democratic-controlled Congress can help alleviate the backlog of cases like they did for George H. W. Bush in 1990.

3. Scheduled appointments: Each president may fill up to—but no more than—four Supreme Court vacancies every four year term. The terms for the appointments would start the court sessions beginning on July 1. Up to four appointments could be made in the first half of the first year of the term as long as the number of justices do not exceed 15. If four do not need to be filled in the first year of the president's term, then a second opportunity to fill the vacancies would occur in the first half of the third year. Thus, the earliest we would reach fifteen Supreme Court justices is likely July 2029, considering there may be at least four additional vacancies in between June 2021 and 2027 from retirements or deaths of current justices. Those vacancies would only be filled in accordance with the scheduling rule above. This next president's first four appointments would start serving on July 1, 2021. No other appointments are permitted, even during vacancies. The number of Supreme Court justices will fluctuate from time to time because vacancies would not be immediately filled but that is not a problem as Republicans showed us when they left eight justices on the court during the entire 2016 year.

4. Full votes: The Senate is required to take a final full Senate vote on whether to confirm a nominee within one hundred days of the presidential nomination.

After this legislative solution, Congress could seek a constitutional amendment for these changes. This would simply be to ensure Republicans don't undo these reforms, even though these reforms benefit each party equally. Republicans would need to capture the trifecta of the White House, Senate, and House again to undo these reforms. If the rest of #DemRevPlan is enacted, the Republicans should never gain the trifecta again which means that they will have to learn to compromise.

Talking Points: Reform Our Courts

How to tell your elected representative or media why this fight is so crucial:

Unless we reform our courts, no Democratic policy priorities will otherwise pass the constitutional hatchet wielded by this 5-4 illegitimate conservative Supreme Court majority.

- Even if the filibuster is reformed and blue states are added to the United States, the Republican-appointed Supreme Court majority is the most politicized the court has ever been. They have declared corporations to be human and thus allowed them to donate unlimited dark money to campaigns.[24] They've said courts can't stop extreme gerrymandering.[25] They ended the congressionally passed Voting Rights Act and thus allowed unchecked voter suppression.[26] They prevented Trump administration officials from testifying to Congress on his abuse of power, like soliciting Russian and Ukrainian interference into our elections.[27] And they blocked the release of parts of the Mueller Report—reflecting the investigation into Russian interference in the 2016 election—until after the 2020 election, to name just a few outrages.
- The Republican Party is now the interpreter of the Constitution, and they do so in a manner aimed at expanding their 4 Weapons Against Democracy. The longer their attacks go unaddressed, the more difficult it will be to fight back.

McConnell has driven a Mack truck though the Constitution's loopholes on judicial selection.

- McConnell bragged about blocking Obama's court picks and expediting those of Trump's.[28] By doing so, he negated Obama's re-election. He swung the ideological leanings of the Supreme Court for a decade by giving that extra appointment to President Trump in disregard of political norms and constitutional guidelines. Ironically, four members of the five-person conservative majority on the Supreme Court were appointed by presidents who lost the popular vote but were still crowned president through the antidemocratic Electoral College or Republican Supreme Court decisions. If Democrats can't now see the dire need for court reform, they never will.

Dark-money groups have captured the courts.

- After *Citizens United* was decided, Leonard Leo, head of the right-wing Federalist Society, helped the Judicial Crisis Network and other conservative legal groups collect $250 million in donations between 2014 and 2017. They used this money to support right-wing attorneys in obtaining lifetime appointments to the federal bench, including the Supreme Court.[29] Most of these donations are hidden from any public knowledge, except of course from the attorneys whose appointments were being supported. As Democratic senator Sheldon Whitehouse from Rhode Island stated, "The American people ought to know who's influencing their court. There is a dark-money campaign by partisan donor interests to capture our judiciary."[30]

- So what do these secretive, large-scale donors want from their paid-for judicial picks? *Gundy v. United States*.[31] This 2019 Supreme Court case has laid the groundwork for the Republican judicial system to invalidate most financial, health, and safety regulations. Had Kavanaugh been seated in time, there would have been a 5–4 majority for the Republican courts in that case to take away one of Congress's main powers: creating agencies to regulate American corporations and industries. This would have eliminated the Environmental Protection Agency's ability to clean the air, Health and Human Services' ability to prevent discrimination by health providers, the US Department of Labor's ability to determine who receives overtime pay, and so on.[32] In essence, there'd be almost no regulations protecting American consumers or the environment.

The number of federal court justices and judges is not in the Constitution.

- Having nine Supreme Court justices was decided by Congress 150 years ago when there were a lot fewer cases, states, citizens, and controversies. That number is not in the Constitution.

- The numbers of federal judges and justices is completely left up to Congress based on caseload. Who thinks we need to expand the courts? Republicans in 2017: "The judiciary desperately needs more federal judges, because the caseload has grown immensely—by about a third in the district courts and nearly half in the circuit courts—since the last bill creating new judgeships was passed in 1990."[33]

The Supreme Court justices should be representative of all Americans.

- Currently, each justice is assigned to one or two of the thirteen federal geographic circuits. But there is no requirement that a justice be from that circuit or otherwise have ever worked in or in any way have a connection with that circuit. Indeed, six of the nine justices come from states to the northeast of Washington, DC. Four justices were born or raised in New York City.[34] This is a lack of diversity that should alarm both parties and is solved by this plan.

Court reform is better than court packing.

- Is this court packing? No. The next president may have four or more appointments anyway. During the next president's first term, the ages of the four oldest justices will be as high as ninety-one, eighty-seven, seventy-seven, and seventy-five. Scalia died in his seventies.
- Because the #DemRevPlan court reform eliminates lifetime appointments, Republicans simply need to win back the presidency in 2024 to "rebalance" the courts in their own image. Republicans could reverse any majority gained by the next Democratic president from 2021 to 2025 as soon as July 2026 if the GOP wins back the White House in 2024.

Why Might Your Elected Democratic Representative Hesitate?

No, I'm not prepared to go on and try to pack the court, because we'll live to rue that day.

—Joe Biden[35]

It's unclear what Biden meant by this. Packing the court simply to give Democrats a temporary majority does seem like a crass political maneuver that will generate legitimate heat on the right. Reforming the court, however, in a manner that benefits future Republican presidents as much as Democratic presidents is the right thing to do. Adding term limits and better geographic distribution among Supreme Court justices is exactly the type of smart reform we need for our dysfunctional system. Plus, we know that voters will not punish Democrats for expanding the Supreme Court.[36]

The great advantage of having eighteen-year term limits is that we can increase the diversity of our Supreme Court Justices. Sixty-four-year-old Yale law graduate Anita Hill would not be considered too old for the Supreme Court, under this plan. Likewise, an ambitious forty-six-year-old Stacey Abrams could serve her term and still be young enough to run for president after her term ends.

Solution #4: Citizens United Vouchers

Congress is at the mercy of the wealthiest in our society, not at the mercy of voters. Polls show that 96% of the country believes big money is the cause of the dysfunction in our government.[37] Of the twelve reforms, this one is the most crucial. This will not become law, however, unless the filibuster is reformed, the Senate is broadened, and the federal courts are reformed. That's why it's fourth.

The terrible, horrible, no-good, very bad decision of *Citizens United* blessedly holds the key to the reform. There is so much money now in our political system that for the first time we can have "publicly funded campaigns" and may not use a single taxpayer dollar. Here's how:

1. Congress passes legislation that places a 50% levy on all contributions over $100 from any person, PAC, union, corporation, 501(c)(4), or other campaign entity, et cetera, received by or paid to any PAC, party, candidate, campaign, issue committee, 501(c)(4), corporate or union political fund, and the like. We can—and should—go

In the last four years, the top Fortune 100 companies spent $2 BILLION lobbying Capital Hill.

They have received $396 BILLION in government grants and contracts.

Figure 10. Source: "In the Last 4 Years, the Top Fortune 100 Companies Spent $2 BILLION Bribing (Aka Lobbying) America's Politicians. These Same Companies Later Received $396 BILLION in Government Grants and Contracts! Yes, Bribing Politicians Is Profitable for America's Corporations." *9GAG*, 26 Sept. 2019, 9gag.com/gag/a5RZgXo.

even a step further and put the levy on all money paid to registered congressional lobbyists under the Lobbying Disclosure Act (LDA) of 1995—you know, people like lobbyist Jack Abramoff, who was convicted on twenty-one counts of corruption. Now that would drain the swamp! Since *Citizens United* is still law, corporations and individuals can continue to contribute millions if they choose. (See Figure 10.)

2. The money collected by the levy is then evenly distributed to the voters in vouchers each year at tax time. To keep it simple, only voters who voted in the prior presidential election—and others who have registered for the first time since then—can receive the voucher. To use the vouchers, voters give them to any candidate, PAC, 501(c)(4), or party of their choice, as long as that candidate or entity does not accept contributions over $100.

Let's please call this campaign funding mechanism "Citizens United vouchers." We can put Chief Justice Roberts's frowning face on the vouchers!

Any voucher not contributed and deposited by March 15 of the next year would expire. That money would then be rolled up in the pool of money to be distributed after April 15. The distribution could be digital, and voters could pick vendors like ActBlue and WinRed, which are the primary contribution technologies for the respective parties. Or the IRS can distribute the vouchers with its tax refunds. Congress can legislate the same Citizens United levy to cover contributions to state and local campaigns.

Speaker Pelosi shepherded some other campaign finance legislation, H.R. 1, through the House in 2019. McConnell killed it in the Senate, of course. Those reforms were good starts but did not have the Citizens United levy or the vouchers. The H.R. 1 reforms could be added to this Citizens United voucher system. From the summary of the legislation:

> H.R. 1. amplified small-dollar donations through public financing, encouraged small-dollar donations through tax incentives, eliminated "dark money" by requiring disclosure of all political spending (including online ads), cut off cooperation between candidates and super PACs, and empowered the Federal Election Commission to truly enforce campaign finance law. Corporations, labor unions, super PACs and other groups would be required to have their top official appear in and take responsibility for the ads, and the top five donors to a group would have to be listed in the ads.

These are good starts. But they really don't fix the Weapon #1 attacking democracy: the buying of federal and state legislative bodies. H.R. 1 called for a constitutional amendment to address the big money unleashed by *Citizens United*. Waiting for a constitutional amendment is just pie-in-the-sky thinking. Worse, it's just so disingenuous, an excuse to do nothing. A copout. #DemRevPlan has no constitutional amendment. The Citizens United voucher is a much better way to deal with the grotesque amount of money currently contributed by corporations and billionaires—and deal with it right now.

None of the three previous #DemRevPlan reforms matter much if the super-rich can continue to buy Congress or state legislatures. The rich people are getting richer, so the buying of Congress takes less of their wealth percentagewise. For rich people, Congress is now like the 99-cent store: bargains everywhere relative to the size of their bank accounts. Not to pick on poor former mayor of New York Mike Bloomberg, but if not for the massive increase of wealth he experienced in the ten years before running for president—going from $18 billion to $60 billion—he would not have been able to spend $1 billion (!) on his three-month campaign for the Democratic nomination. Since 2010, his wealth has increased by $1 billion approximately every three months.[38, 39] So he likely did not lose $1 of his wealth during that campaign despite spending $1 billion. That's a little different than my campaign for Congress!

When your wealth increases by a billion dollars or more every three months, why not plunk down money to help grease the congressional machinery that enables your accumulation of wealth? Not talking about you personally, Mike.

This is why we have bad laws. There are people who make lots and lots of money from those bad laws, and they take a small portion of their ill-gotten gains and invest in the purchasing of your local politician or party.

Money is like water. Eventually it can break down any mountain into a canyon. Meaning that we could have all the Democratic reforms we can think of, but if we continue to allow money to buy elections, those reforms will be washed away. Unlimited money from the super-rich is just too destructive to democracy.

Talking Points: Citizens United Vouchers Make Campaign Financing Fair

How to tell your elected representative or media why this fight is so crucial:

The Democrats' plan for matching public funds does not do enough to stop the buying of Congress.

- Joe Biden has pledged to "enact legislation to provide voluntary matching public funds for federal candidates receiving small dollar donations."[40] That's a good start. But it doesn't do enough to stop the buying of Congress. For instance, how would it have stopped Republican Jeb Hensarling of Texas from raising $10.1 million, half of it from finance, insurance, and real estate interests, immediately after the mortgage crisis? Jeb was the representative *in charge* of regulating those industries as the chair of the House Financial Services Committee. He then transferred almost $9 million of that to other Republicans. Interesting fact: all Jebs are Republicans, I've heard.

- Much of activism today does not protest the real source of the problems: money in politics. Want gun control? The NRA is only a part of the problem. The real problem is the gun manufacturers who make massive political expenditures to the NRA PAC—who then send it to their favorite politicians. Concerned about the environment? Republicans are only a part of the problem. The real problem is the oil companies and car manufacturers who make massive political contributions to stop sensible climate policy. Citizen United vouchers will empower everyday voters with half of the tidal wave of money currently in our campaign and lobbying system.

- It was Citizens United in 2010 that began the Republicans' decade-long assault on democracy. If it was not for the Republicans unleashing unlimited dark money, they would have been out of power this entire decade. Instead of going backward on so many issues and in so many ways, our country and our world would have made the progress that we all longed for. Without the Citizens United vouchers, billionaires will reassert themselves and politicians will adhere slavishly to their agenda. And Republicans will reign once again.

The Citizens United vouchers return the focus of politicians onto their voters.

- With the Citizens United vouchers, candidates, parties and political PACs would all be scrambling to reach voters so they could obtain those vouchers. Imagine—politicians catering to and soliciting voters. We're so far from that system that it seems radical that politicians would care as much about an average voter as they do a millionaire donor.

- Providing all voters with these vouchers should also increase the participation in elections. It gives these voters a stake in the elections. With a voucher at their disposal, they know they can actually affect the outcome of elections. You no longer have to be rich to make a difference in this democracy. Perhaps then we wouldn't have such a depressing difference in voting based on wealth: the richest 20% in the United States regularly have voter turnout of over 60%; the poorest 20% only have voter turnout at about 20%.[41]

- Politicians would welcome not having to fundraise all the time to solicit high donor contributions. It certainly would push them to get in front of as many voters as possible, considering every voter can make a campaign contribution that won't cost that voter a penny.

A Constitutional amendment to overturn Citizens United is a cynical excuse for inaction.

- There are simply not enough states with Democrats—let alone reform-minded Democrats—to pass a constitutional amendment for *anything*. By claiming that we need a constitutional amendment for campaign finance reform, Democratic leaders preserve the status quo, a status quo on which they have built their careers. Instead, the Democrats need to reform the courts and, with a new Democratic-appointed majority on the Supreme Court, let the Citizens United vouchers be challenged. Republicans will likely find their interpretation of the Constitution is no longer a veto on all Democratic policy.

Why Might Your Elected Democratic Representative Hesitate?

It's possible that this reform will dry up giant campaign contributions. That means politicians would have to survive on small contributions from many people and spend their time meeting their constituents and holding events instead of fundraising with rich people. Now that's a revolution! It's unclear if politicians would prefer spending time with voters instead of at cocktail parties with rich donors. I've heard rich people smell better than the rest of us.

Every elected politician in the country was elected under the rules of *Citizens United*. This might seem threatening to them professionally. Of course, elected politicians all have the advantage of incumbency. But at the end of the day, protecting our democracy is not one of the responsibilities of our elected representatives. It is solely our responsibility. As we pressure our electeds to adopt this, remember, DemRevvers, we are demanding, not requesting.

The real fight here is the people of the United States versus the politicians. Let's win one for our team.

Solution #5: Eliminate Gerrymandering through Instant Runoff+

The US uses a winner-take-all, single-member district system. Those districts are often drawn in a way to privilege one party over another—which is called gerrymandering. So if you're a Democrat living in a district drawn to include a huge number of Republican voters, your vote is purposely drowned out (and vice versa). And the winner-take-all system means that if you want to vote for a third party, your vote will often be "wasted," as two parties compete to get the most votes and other votes are considered inconsequential to the outcome.

—Zaid Jilani, journalist with the *Intercept*[42]

Congressional races are less and less competitive. In 2016, less than 9% of the House races—37 of the 435—were considered competitive.

97% of Congressional incumbents won re-election in 2016, even though the overall congressional job approval rating was less than 20%.[43]

Gerrymandering makes most political districts safe from competition. They are drawn in such a way as to ensure a particular party will always be elected. And while this is mostly a Republican abuse, Democrats in Maryland have done egregious gerrymandering as well. "We the People" cannot hold them accountable, so they can be as extreme—or corrupt—as they want.

There are two parts to the instant runoff+ solution:

1. All political boundaries—for local, state, and federal office—should be drawn by independent, nonpartisan commissions; and
2. All elections have instant-runoff voting along with either multimember districts or proportional representation.

I am happy to report that Speaker Pelosi won a vote in the House in 2019 to pass the first part of this #DemRevPlan solution. The legislation was called H.R. 1, which I referenced in Solution #3. Since Democrats inexplicably have done so little to promote this legislation before or after passing it, I thought I'd give it a shout out. McConnell, of course, killed it in the Senate. It was—maybe—a great start. For a true democracy revival, we need both parts of this #DemRevPlan solution. Here's what House Democrats passed:

H.R. 1 required all states to use independent citizen commissions to draw congressional districts. Strong conflict of interest rules would prevent lobbyists from serving on the commission, and screening processes would ensure that qualified commissioners are selected. All proposed maps would need to win support from all groups on the Commission. The public would have a minimum of 30 days to review and submit comments on the plan. The commission would be required to issue a final report responding to comments. The public would also be able to watch commission proceedings via digital livestreams.[44]

You know my twins and I will be watching those livestreams! There are two problems here: first, H.R. 1 doesn't go far enough to really end gerrymandering; second, it's unclear if Democrats want it to become law.

I have three #DemRevPlan additions to H.R. 1 that eliminate the GOP's gerrymandering weapon while ensuring a more democratic system for all.

First, nonpartisan commissions must be required for the 2021 redrawing. The H.R. 1 legislation needs to be implemented for the redrawing of the maps currently slated for the end of summer 2021. These are the maps that will determine whether we have a democracy or not over the next ten years. If it does not include this cycle of redistricting, then H.R. 1 is simply political theater not meant to make any changes but only to satisfy some critics or partisans. If Democrats do not pass the #DemRevPlan, then the likely 2024 Republican trifecta will just undo this gerrymandering reform before it ever changes how districts are drawn. So this will all be for naught.

Second, nonpartisan commissions must be required for state legislative districts. H.R. 1 needs to be expanded based on Fourteenth Amendment requirements to encompass the way the states draw boundaries for their own legislative seats, not just congressional ones. We already know how the Republicans will attack the law as outlined in appendix 9: they cry "overreach," *Fox and Friends* hosts melt down, and the GOP claims Tenth Amendment protections. Democrats won't win any points by unilaterally embracing defeat and allowing Republicans to continue controlling states in which they are the political minority. Democrats need to include this in the legislation and let Republicans sue to stop it.

In order to pass Solution #5 to eliminate gerrymandering, the Democrats will have to have ended the filibuster (Solution #1) and reformed the courts (Solution #3) in time for the July 1, 2021, Supreme Court session. If they've done this, then we should have a Supreme Court that will hold that prohibiting politicians from picking their own voters at the local, state, and federal levels is constitutional.

And third, to win an election, candidates must have majority support. H.R. 1 should require that in order for a candidate to win at the local, state, or federal level, a majority of voters must vote for them. This is to be implemented through an instant-runoff+ system.

Multiple large US cities, the state of Maine, and other democracies like Ireland and Australia already have instant runoff. Some Democrats with marbles in their mouths call this "ranked-choice voting" because they have forgotten how to communicate with voters. So what is instant runoff? Here is an example of what could have happened if we had had the instant runoff in the 2000 election:

> Let's say 45 people voted for Bush, 44 voted for Gore, and 11 voted for Ralph Nader. No one received 50%+1 of the votes. Nader is statistically eliminated from being able to garner a majority. We then look to see who was the second preference of the 11 Nader votes. If 8 were for Gore and 3 for Bush, then Gore wins the election with 52 votes to Bush's 48.

Basically, this ensures that the winner is the candidate who would receive a majority of the votes because only two candidates are eligible for the final vote transferring of the instant runoff. But instead of having multiple elections to determine this, there's just one election. Voters can rank their preference all at once so that it becomes an instant runoff.

In this third change to H.R. 1, Congress should require states to choose between these two instant runoff+ options.

Option A: Instant-Runoff Elections Plus Multimember Districts

As a means to defeat gerrymandering and create better representation for *all* voters in a district, the brilliant representative Don Beyer, a Democrat from Florida, proposed larger districts in which multiple congressional members would be elected.[45] Under this plan:

- in states with six or more congressional representatives, the state would establish districts such that three to five representatives are elected from each district;
- states entitled to fewer than six representatives would elect all representatives on an at-large basis, which means there's only one district, but between one and five representatives elected to that district (states such as Wyoming already have this); and,
- all state elections would require instant runoff.

These changes would ensure that as many voters as possible have a representative who reflects their views. For instance, if these multimember districts had three representatives, and the vote was two-thirds Republican, one-third Democrat, then two Republicans and one Democrat would be elected. Under our current system, Republicans could gerrymander these seats so that three Republicans win, but no Democrats do, thus shutting out one-third of the voters. Instant runoff+ multimember districts guarantee that every voter would have an elected representative (or more) who advocates for their views.

Option B: Instant-Runoff Elections with Proportional Representation

More than ninety countries use proportional representation for elections, some for a hundred years now.[46] Proportional representation ensures that the number of elected officials from each party actually represents the proportion of votes they each get. Simply put, if Democrats get 50% of the votes and there are ten House seats, Democrats would get five of those seats. There's a variety of different ways of doing this, including multimember districts in option A above. But there's only one way to do this that preserves the current single-member districts. I call it: single district proportional representation.

The primaries for each geographic district (a.k.a. seat) would use instant-runoff voting as explained above. Each party would then have a single candidate in that district that runs in the general election. In the general election, however, voters would select the party they want to represent them in Congress (or state senate or assembly), not a specific candidate.

For example, say that in the general election statewide, Democrats receive 50% of the votes, Republicans receive 29%, and the Libertarian and Green Parties receive 11% and 10% respectively. Remarkably, as seen in Weapon #2 of chapter 4, under today's rules in Michigan, Wisconsin, and almost a dozen other states, Republicans might win the majority of seats with 29% of the vote. Under this reform, using single district proportional representation, Democrats—as the largest vote-getters—get the first seat allocated to them based on which district had the highest percentage of votes for Democrats. Then Republicans get a seat allocated to them based on which of the remaining districts had the highest percentage of voters selecting Republicans to represent them; then the Libertarian Party receives a seat, and then finally the Green Party receives a seat. Then it goes back to the Democrats and then the Republicans. If there were 10 seats statewide in this election neither the Libertarian nor the Green Party receive a second seat because they didn't get enough votes.

At the end of the allocation system, if there were ten seats available, Democrats would have five seats, Republicans three seats, and both the Libertarian Party and Green Party would have one seat each. All voters would have their voice in the state and Congress represented in proportion to their numbers.

The primary advantage to this system is that it maintains having one representative per district. In order for a state to choose this option B for House races, it should have no fewer than four congressional House districts. There are thirty-five states that currently qualify. The other states should stick with option A.

Talking Points: Eliminate Gerrymandering through Instant Runoff + and Nonpartisan Commissions

How to tell your elected representative or media why this fight is so crucial:

Ending gerrymandering removes one of the worst of the 4 Weapons Republicans wield against democracy.

- The United States is the only democracy in the world that allows its politicians to decide the boundaries of their districts. Courtesy of Republican-controlled gerrymandering in the thirty-plus states they control, Republican politicians now literally get to pick their voters, instead of the other way around.
- Because of gerrymandering, Democrats have to win by at least 6% nationwide in order to have a majority in Congress as shown in chapter 4.

- Gerrymandering creates a second problem. The intense polarization of our body politic comes directly from gerrymandering. By creating super solid Republican seats—or super blue Democratic seats—the candidates emerging from these races, on average, are more extreme in their views or corrupt in their conduct.

Instant runoff+ expands representation to all voters and ensures majorities elect their representatives.

- Instant runoff means that a candidate is only elected if they have support from a majority of the voters. But instead of having multiple elections to determine this, it's all done at once. Very efficient.
- If you're part of the 48% minority who lost the election, as an example, who represents you? Congratulations, you have no one to represent your interests because at this point the other party sees you as the enemy. Instant runoff+ ensures that all voters have a representative either because it is a multimember district or because their vote counts toward the statewide proportional allocation of seats by party support.
- Single district proportional representation might mean that you have a candidate who represents your views even if they received overall much less than 50% of the vote to serve your district. This prioritizes fairness for all voters on a statewide basis, not just the plurality of voters in each district, as is done currently. Under our current system, Republicans can win 45% in each district, Democrats 40%, and third parties a combined 15%, and the Republicans can still win *all* the seats. This denies representation to the voices of the 55% majority of the state. Who wants this system (besides Republicans)?
- Republican-appointed Justice Roberts allowed the extremely partisan gerrymandering in Wisconsin to continue unabated. He wrote that it was up to Congress—not the judicial branch—to make such determinations. So even instant runoff+ should pass constitutional muster as it is a political and legislative, not judicial, issue. As Republican Chief Justice Roberts says: "We conclude that partisan gerrymandering claims present political questions beyond the reach of the federal courts."[47]

Why Might Your Elected Democratic Representative Hesitate?

In this reform, districts would be drawn by citizens, not by politicians. Every Democrat elected to Congress was elected under the current gerrymandered rules. It works fine for them individually. Who knows what will happen if the system is made fair? Of course, with a redistricting set to take place before the 2022 midterm election, who knows if their seats will be safe anyway? This is the time to fix the system.

The Democrats will gain a larger percentage of the seats once gerrymandering is prohibited. It's just sometimes those seats will be redrawn so that you have two Democrats facing each other in the same district. But as long as the Democrats do away with gerrymandering and also support the Wyoming Rule (see Solution #2), they will gain up to ninety seats in the House of Representatives—more than enough to go around.

We currently have a winner-take-all system, except "winner" does not mean 50%+1. The winner doesn't even have to come close to getting a majority of the votes. This really makes no sense. In a three-person race, we are okay with letting someone "win" with just 34% support. For instance, if two conservative candidates run for office and one progressive does, chances are the conservatives will split their vote and the progressive wins the race, even if the overall district is conservative. This leaves too many voters voiceless and unrepresented.

In the 240 years since our Founding Fathers came up with our election system, many other countries have come up with more democratic and sensible ways of electing their representatives. But change is difficult when those who control the change are the ones elected under the inferior system. That equation, however, has changed somewhat. More people understand now that Republicans have brutalized our democracy with their weaponized gerrymandering—among other weapons. More people connect their corrupt leadership with their bungled COVID-19 response that has cost so many more lives than necessary. They are alarmed that Republicans can be so brazen as to attack Americans with the military in order for the president to get a photo op in front of a church. This is the time for activists—including you—to demand that Democrats make reforms to protect democracy even if it is potentially at the expense of their own self-interests.

Solution #6: Our Power, Our Vote

> Voter suppression works by instilling such an acute sense of dread
> in those trying to vote—about the hours and resources and effort it
> will take—that they don't or even can't make the attempt.
>
> —Ja'han Jones, *HuffPost* reporter[48]

At some point, everything got turned upside down and inside out in our democracy. Politicians started to think that they gave citizens the right to vote. Trump exemplified this aristocratic view of voting best when he attacked Democrats' attempt to pass a national requirement for both fifteen days of early voting and no-excuse absentee vote by mail: "The things they had in there were crazy. They had levels of voting, that if you ever agreed to it, you'd never have a Republican elected in this country again."[49]

The "right to vote" is actually a misnomer. It suggests that we can be denied our right to vote by the very politicians who are in positions of authority because we elected them. We don't have just a right to vote—*our vote is our power.* It's a power that we use to shape our country and our lives. That power comes from democracy, not the politicians we temporarily elect. Having the power to vote is the fundamental underpinning of living in American democracy. Future president Biden came closer to articulating the sacredness of voting: "We've got to make it easier—not harder—for Americans to exercise their right to vote, regardless of their zip code or the color of their skin, and make sure we count every voter's voice equally."[50]

Solution #6 recognizes that voting is our power, not merely a right. It cannot be abridged, interfered with, suppressed, or taken away, at least not without due process. Accordingly, Congress needs a voting power bill that removes any obstacles that politicians use to take away our power to vote:

- Every American should be automatically registered to vote.
- Every American should be able to vote at home.
- The votes that are cast should be handled and counted transparently.

Pelosi's H.R. 1 bill had a lot of what we need:

Automatic voter registration for any citizen that interacts with government agencies; Same-day registration; Restoring the Voting Rights Act; Protecting against improper purging of voter rolls; Requiring states to upgrade and secure their election systems; Restoring voting rights to those with past criminal convictions; and, Providing adequate early voting opportunities.

Here are the eight vital tweaks to H.R. 1 from our "Our Power, Our Vote" reform:

1. Timing and logistics: Automatic voter registration must be in place before the 2022 midterms; otherwise, the GOP will simply cancel it once they regain their trifecta regardless of the money invested in it. Government agencies participating in automatic voter registration should include public high schools and colleges and should conduct preregistration for seventeen-year-olds.

2. Vote at home: Send all voters a vote-at-home (a.k.a. "absentee") ballot for local, state, and federal elections that can be mailed in at no cost, collected by nonprofit agencies certified for ballot handling, or turned in at polling locations or in vote lock boxes, up to and including on Election Day.

3. Every vote counted: Use the sophisticated software already in use in states like Colorado to match signatures on file. If there is a mismatch or any other problem with their vote, voters are notified and have several days to solve the problem. Use ballot tracking for the entire journey of the ballot to allow a voter to see where his or her ballot is at any given time — including when it is mailed to them, received by the state, and counted — and notify them if there is a problem so that they can correct it instead of the government just trashing the vote.[51] This technology is already in use in multiple states.

4. Transparency on handling and counting of the votes: All ballots have intelligent ballot tracking and barcodes that are scanned

to prevent duplicates. Remove machines—all of which can be hacked—from the vote count and replace them with paid humans to do a hand count. Voters can watch ballots being counted and verified by signature on a live Internet feed. Make the paper ballots open for inspection immediately after an election and before the result is finalized to let citizens verify counts where needed. Tracked not hacked.

5. Reform voter purges: The government may not purge any voters except in case of a death certificate. It is the state agency's responsibility to transfer the voter registration to any new address of the voter, even if it is out of state.

6. Reform voter ID laws: Repeal all voter ID laws unless the state can prove that it has issued the required IDs to all its citizens at no cost.

7. Penalties: Create draconian penalties for both people engaging in voter fraud or attempting to deny citizens the vote. Penalties include a lifetime ban on voting and participation in any political career.

8. Don't let the GOP confuse voters: There must be uniform requirements about font size, instructions, and such so that Republicans cannot make fonts very small or instructions so confusing that the vote-at-home ballots will all be thrown out. Okay. That sounds paranoid. Except that it just happened:

> Because of a rise in its Latino population, Gwinnett County in Georgia had to mail out absentee ballots with information in both English and Spanish in 2018. The result was chaos. The county accommodated the increased text by printing it in 6.5-point font, making each letter smaller than a sesame seed. Many voters were confused by the instructions. Gwinnett rejected 595 absentee ballots, a third of all those tossed in Georgia, often without notifying the spurned voters.[52]

Great job, illegitimate governor Brian Kemp. That's almost as incompetent as your COVID-19 response.

Talking Points: Voting at Home Protects Our Power, Our Vote

How to tell your elected representative or media why this fight is so crucial:

Voting at home best safeguards our power to vote.

- Oregon, Colorado, and Washington already hold their elections using this system. These three states are all in the top seven states for voter participation.[53] The voter turnout of these three states is almost two-thirds, compared to less than half nationwide.[54] Vote at home is credited with a 9% increase of voters (fourteen million) for a presidential election.[55] Republican-run Utah also has this system, and it has the eighth-highest turnout among red states. Hawaii and California have adopted this for the 2020 election, although the Republican National Committee is suing to get those laws overturned, of course. I would have taken that bet! Worse, while the coronavirus pandemic is raging, Oklahoma Republicans passed a law in May 2020 requiring would-be vote-at-home voters to have their request *notarized*.[56] Arrogant asses. It's our power, not theirs.
- Vote at home lowers costs to run elections by 40%.[57] And voters—both Democrats (85%) and Republicans (76%)—love it.[58] Already 25% of all votes nationwide are done by voting at home. In Denver, after they implemented voting at home, election costs went down from $6.51 to $4.15 per voter. Vote at home also improves accuracy and efficiency: In 2016 in Denver, there were just 340 provisional ballots cast by voters whose eligibility or registration was questioned, down dramatically from 10,721 in 2012, which was before they implemented universal voting at home.
- Ebola, coronavirus, and future pandemics have no effect on vote-by-mail programs. Election day goes on! Not enough polling stations or volunteers, or are the voting machines too slow and the lines too long? None of that happens with vote by mail. Republicans can't suppress the vote!

Eliminate voting machines from counting.

- A Harvard cybersecurity expert, Bruce Schneier, said it best: "The problem we have is that voting security doesn't matter until something happens, and then after something happens, there's a group of people who don't want the security, because whatever happened, happened in their favor. That makes it a very hard security problem, unlike your bank account."[59] When we use humans to count, we eliminate that threat and not even Russia can hack the paper ballots of vote by mail counted by hand. Sorry Vladimir.

The GOP suppresses voters, even in their own states.

- It really is no surprise that ten of the twelve states with the lowest voter participation are solid-red states.[60]
- Sixteen states have already passed a form of this automatic voter registration. Not surprisingly, almost 90% of those states are blue states.
- Democrats (84%) say that voting should be made as easy as possible for citizens. Only 35% of Republicans favor making voting as easy as possible, despite loving vote at home when their states allow that.[61]

Automatic voting registration

- Studies have shown that automatic voter registration keeps rolls more accurate, with a constant stream of updates between registration agencies and election officials. This reduces errors, eliminates duplicates, and lowers costs.[62]
- Democrats would control the White House forever if they could capture Texas. Right now, one-third of eligible voters in Texas are Latinos, but they only make up 14% of registered voters.[63, 64] With automatic registration and vote at home, Texas flips blue overnight. Florida and Arizona have similar percentages of unregistered Latino US citizens of voting age and will likewise turn blue.
- As Jason Kander, Missouri secretary of state, said, "Automatic voter registration is one of the easiest ways to get young people involved and make sure they stay involved in the electoral process. We know that when folks start voting early, they keep voting throughout their lives. The easier it is to register, the easier it is to vote."[65]

Reforming voter purges

- Wisconsin's Democratic governor Tony Evers stated it best when the Republicans who controlled his state did their annual voter purge: "I won the race for governor by less than 30,000 votes. This move pushed by Republicans to remove 200,000 Wisconsinites from the voter rolls is just another attempt at overriding the will of the people and stifling the democratic process."[66] Automatic voter registration eliminates voter purges. Sorry, Republicans.

Reforming voter ID laws

- 10% of Americans who are fully eligible to vote don't have the right form of identification to satisfy new voter ID laws. Voter ID laws shift the power of voting away from citizens and let politicians arbitrarily interfere with that power.

Hand counting ballots

- Remember that war we talked about earlier, in Afghanistan? The one that cost $1 billion per week (and one US soldier fatality every three days) for 988 weeks (and counting)?[67] One day's worth of that total would pay for counting the entire federal election while paying workers $15 per hour. Other countries—like Germany, the Netherlands, Norway, and Ireland—have already returned to hand counting in the face of Russian cyberthreats.

The Putin problem

- According to the National Security Agency in its report on May 5, 2017, Russian General Staff Main Intelligence Directorate executed a cyberattack on at least one US voting software supplier in August 2016. After successfully infiltrating their system, the Russian hacking may have breached at least some elements of the voting system with unknown results.[68, 69] Trump responded to the report by defunding the agency that coordinates the fight against Russian interference in our elections.
- Even as recently as August 2019, white-hat hackers at DEF CON hacked into one hundred of the one hundred voting machines given to them

to test.[70] Waiting until we uncover the Russian changing of votes is not acceptable. We must prevent it. The submission and counting of the ballots is where Russians can most easily change the outcome of elections. Imagine if this were discovered a few months after the election. First, the entire Republican Party apparatus would seek to cover it up, suppress it, attack those who were making the claims, and obviously reject it. Look no further than the sham trial in the Senate when Trump was impeached to get a taste of the diversionary propaganda Republicans would wield. Second, do you think the Trump family would exit the White House even if such irregularities were uncovered in a few key states? Never going to happen.

This is the time to revive our democracy.
- Democrats need to be bold. No need to poll on these changes. Americans want strong, principled leadership. Making it easier to vote, increasing voter participation, making the vote Russian-hacker proof, and lowering the costs of elections are no-brainers. This will be embraced by 80% of the electorate, and the other 20% believe the Earth was created 4,000 years ago, so it's kind of hard to cater to everyone.
- It is difficult for many people to take time off work to vote on Election Day or get a legally acceptable form of ID—especially when COVID-19 has shuttered so many government agencies. Republicans use any crisis to try to suppress voters, COVID-19 being the latest. Let's stop their ability to do this, once and for all.

Why Might Your Elected Democratic Representative Hesitate?

Maybe some Democrats will be squeamish about losing the American tradition of voting at polling locations—or the tradition of disenfranchising felons. Unfortunately, those traditions come with an equally long tradition of voter suppression—as resurrected by Republicans. We need to confront Democrats about their quaint little excuse for inaction by claiming they want to preserve "traditions." It reminds one of Southerners claiming that the Confederacy racism is their tradition. Democrats need to admit that they have failed at protecting our power to vote. We are way past the time to whine about the loss of a Normal Rockwell image that some head-in-the-ground Democratic congress members have about what voting should look like.

That being said, Congress can still provide the option of voters turning in their ballots at designated locations if voters don't mind risking infectious diseases.

Solution #7: A Representative Electoral College

The Electoral College cannot be changed? Don't believe the hype. There is a legislative solution to the Electoral College—right now! It does not require a constitutional amendment. Nor must we wait for that never-to-be-reached moment when Democrats capture the trifecta in enough states to enact the otherwise sensible National Popular Vote Interstate Compact. There's so little prospect of that happening that I refuse to even explain what that compact is.

No Democrat needs to be told that the Electoral College interferes with the majority's wishes. It was built for a different time in American politics. The Electoral College was a failed effort to keep the country united by making sure less populous states didn't bolt the Union. The fact that we had a civil war demonstrates that Union soldiers were far more effective in keeping the country united than the Electoral College.

The will of the majority of voters should determine the election of the president. That's Democracy 101. The obvious flaw in the Electoral College is that it allows candidates with a minority of voter support to beat the candidate with majority of voter support. There's no constitutional rationale for that outcome.

To get a representative Electoral College, Congress fixes the Electoral College system by passing proportionate elector legislation. Congress amends 3 U.S.C. § 6, Credentials of Electors, and requires states to apportion the Electoral College electors directly in proportion to the vote of the people of that state for president; otherwise, the electors cannot be credentialed. Any other form of apportionment is declared unconstitutional by Congress because it violates the Fourteenth Amendment and *Gore v. Bush*.

How does representative Electoral College reform work? Let's take Colorado, with its nine electoral votes. If the Democrat receives 55% of the vote and the Republican receives 45%, currently all nine electors are pledged to the Democrats. That's just stupid. If only there was something that helped us figure out a more fair and sensible allocation of electors...oh, wait. There is. It's called math. Under the representative Electoral College plan—using math—five electors would be chosen to represent Democrats and four to represent Republicans. Problem solved, and all voters are fairly represented in the Electoral College.

The counter to this argument is that states can allocate their electors any way they see fit. Really? So Colorado can allocate eight of its nine electors to voters who live in the residence of the governor and give the rest of the state just one elector? That is legal under the Constitution—or it was, before the Fourteenth Amendment equal protection clause.

Talking Points: Representative Electoral College

How to tell your elected representative or media why this fight is so crucial:

The winner-take-all allocation for the Electoral College unconstitutionally values votes differently.

- The Fourteenth Amendment (which I cover in appendix 9) and the more recent *Gore v. Bush* decision compel Congress to safeguard the constitutional requirement to have votes count equally. The winner-take-all approach of allocating all electors to the person with the most votes in a state is thus unconstitutional. Such an unconstitutional approach treats the votes for president in a state differently. The 51% of voters supporting Candidate A get their votes basically doubled. The 49% of voters supporting Candidate B diminishes those votes to zero. That's unconstitutional; even my ConLaw professor should agree—refer to appendix 9 for our disagreements!
- The beauty of the representative Electoral College approach is that Republicans will be on the defensive. They will be the ones who have to go to the courts to stop this. Democrats have countless

cases—most notably the *Gore v. Bush* travesty of 2000—that support the constitutionality of representative Electoral College reform. In *Gore v. Bush*, the Supreme Court stopped the recount in Florida that would have given Gore the presidency. Then–Chief Justice Rehnquist, a Republican appointee, claimed in his decision that Gore's request to recount in *some* counties but not all would give "disparate treatment" to some voters versus others in the state.[71] This violated the Equal Protection Clause of the Fourteenth Amendment: "[h]aving once granted the right to vote on equal terms, the State may not, by later arbitrary and disparate treatment, value one person's vote over that of another."[72] Yep, that's all we need to know to move forward on this reform.

The Constitution and Supreme Court cases support a representative Electoral College allocation.

- Besides the *Gore v. Bush* case, the Supreme Court applied the Equal Protection Clause of the Fourteenth Amendment in *Reynolds v. Sims* in 1964. In that case, the court declared malapportioned state legislatures unconstitutional and a violation of the "one-person, one-vote" standard. The Supreme Court had previously reached a similar decision invalidating a state's election scheme because it weighed one citizen's vote differently than another citizen's vote.[73] The precedent is there, we just need a new case—and a new Supreme Court—to extend the protection of one-person, one-vote to the Electoral College.

- Republicans will say that Article V and the Tenth Amendment stop Congress from passing such legislation. Wrong. The voting rights amendments were adopted after both Article V and the Tenth Amendment. These voting rights amendments clearly and repeatedly authorize Congress to protect "the right of citizens of the United States to vote" against any abridgement "by the United States." The current Electoral College apportionment restricts the voting rights of citizens whose votes are not being apportioned to electors. The 32% Republican vote in California and the 43% Democratic vote in Texas are both just thrown out. This kind of inequality is within the delegated power of Congress to address.

- The US Constitution does not mandate that states allocate their Electoral College votes on a winner-take-all basis. It's just state laws that do that. We don't need to list the hundreds of state laws that have been on the books for decades or even centuries that are later ruled unconstitutional.

- The only thing the Constitution says about the Electoral College is that the states retain all manners of authority in appointing electors to the Electoral College. This is pretty ambiguous. But regardless of the ambiguity, no state has the authority to violate the other constitutional protections. Accordingly, a Democratic-appointed majority on the Supreme Court should find that yes, the states retain authority to make a whole bunch of decisions regarding the electors. But they don't have the authority to diminish one person's voting strength compared to another. Just like the states couldn't say that African Americans only count three-fifths as much as white Americans *despite* it being written into the Constitution. So while the states do have some authority, they can't violate other provisions of the Constitution.[74]

Legislation around representative Electoral College reform is a political question and should not be addressed by the court.

- It's not hard to find Supreme Court cases under the current Republican-appointed majority that declare that courts should not enter the "political thicket." This constitutional principle was newly invigorated by this Republican-appointed Supreme Court to allow Republicans to gerrymander and suppress voters without constraint. Accordingly, Congress is the branch of government that should make the decisions on elections and voting. That principle suggests that the Republican-appointed majority Supreme Court would not get involved in this dispute. Consistency in constitutional interpretation, however, is not something favored by conservatives.

- The Supreme Court usually decides cases based on political leanings versus straightforward application of the law. Accordingly, for this reform to be upheld as constitutional, Democrats will need to have passed Solution #3, "Court Reform, Not Court Packing," to swing the Supreme Court back to majority Democrats. That's how you get a Democratic reform to be something declared constitutional. Praise be to McConnell for teaching Democrats that. Let's hope they learned.

Congress needs to make representative Electoral College reform because states cannot make this reform on their own.

- So why do forty-eight states use this unconstitutional winner-take-all approach? States can't make representative Electoral College reform on their own. If either red states or blue states were to stop the winner-takes-all system, their side would always lose the Electoral College because, you know, math. Imagine if California and New York made the reform and all of a sudden gave 40% of their electors to the GOP candidate. Madness. So the states need to be reformed at the same time. That's where the national Congress steps in.

- Some states love the Electoral College *because* it violates one-person, one-vote. We have a one-person, .27 vote instead of one-person, one-vote happening for Wyoming compared to California voters. Wyoming gets 3 electoral votes with a population of 578,000. California gets 55 electoral votes with a population of forty million. So even though California has a population that is sixty-nine times greater than Wyoming's, it only gets eighteen times the Electoral College votes. California should receive 207—not 55—electoral votes if Wyoming receives 3. Accordingly, California voters have 27% of the voting power in deciding the presidency compared to Americans in Wyoming. Representative Electoral College reform is at least a partial corrective to this disparity.

A winner-take-all Electoral College removes 80% of the country from the presidential election.

- Since the 1988 election, Republicans have only received more votes for president than the Democratic candidate one time (50.7% in 2004). Yet we have had a Republican president for more than 40% of that time. If George W. Bush and Donald Trump are your ideas of what presidents should be like, then please don't change the Electoral College.

- The current Electoral College system turns our national presidential election into an election in a few states. A political problem with the Electoral College is that 99% of presidential campaign spending in 2016 was in just fourteen swing states.[75] Two-thirds of all of the campaign events occurred just in the key states of Pennsylvania, Michigan, Ohio, Florida, North Carolina and Virginia.
- Representative Electoral College reform should impact elections in two positive ways. First, there will no longer be presidents elected with a minority of the vote. Second, there will be a significantly larger turnout in votes for the presidency. The United States has one of the smallest voter turnouts for presidential elections in the world. This is due in part to the winner-takes-all method of allocating electors; it renders the vast majority of states as irrelevant to the election. After this reform, candidates will be traveling all over the country, not just in a few states, inspiring involvement and participation. Republican voters in California will now be just as important as Democratic ones in Texas.
- If Democrats hesitate in pulling the trigger on this reform, they will be 100% responsible for the election of Donald Trump Jr. in 2024.

Why Might Your Elected Democratic Representative Hesitate?

Democrats simply may not be brave enough to do the right thing. They can probably understand the logic of my argument on solving the problem of the unconstitutionality of the winner-take-all Electoral College. It's just a courage thing for them to take that first legislative step.

Another argument that timid Democrats might make is that surely this reform can't be constitutional because it's upending a two-hundred-year-old tradition. Only someone who hasn't been paying attention to the Supreme Court in the twenty-first century could say such a thing. This Republican-appointed Supreme Court has overturned so many long-established laws that no Democrat can believe there is one constitutional standard applied throughout the centuries. There is a simple explanation as to why this winner-takes-all scheme has never been ruled unconstitutional: no one has brought forward a case challenging winner-takes-all when the majority of the Supreme Court justices were appointed by Democrats. It's just like how *Citizens United* upended the entire campaign finance structure that had been in place forever. Republicans recognized that their conservative majority on the court would do them a solid, so they challenged the law and won. That's how constitutionality is decided now. You dig?

Party bigwigs may oppose this reform because it would seem to increase the viability of third parties. The first presidential election using the Equal Protection Clause of the Fourteenth Amendment approach to electors would be in 2024. It's possible that neither of the main two parties would receive a majority vote. Instead, third-party and independent candidates could hold the key to deciding how their few but important electoral votes are cast. This will certainly give voters a wider choice and make for perhaps the most exciting presidential election in a long time. Ironically, this is what might finally prompt a constitutional amendment to get rid of the Electoral College. Republicans and Democrats will see that third parties are gaining relevancy and the two mainstream parties are losing voters. At that point you can certainly envision two-thirds of Congress and three-quarters of the states supporting a constitutional amendment to letting the popular vote decide presidential elections. Hopefully such a constitutional amendment would include an instant-runoff procedure.

Notes

1. "70 Former U.S. Senators: The Senate Is Failing to Perform Its Constitutional Duties," *Washington Post*, 25 Feb. 2020, www.washingtonpost.com/opinions/former-us-senators-the-senate-is-failing-to-perform -its-constitutional-duties/2020/02/25/b9bdd22a-5743-11ea-9000-f3cffee23036_story.html.

2. David RePass, "Why the 'Silent' Filibuster Is Unconstitutional," *The Atlantic*, 4 Jan. 2011, www .theatlantic.com/politics/archive/2011/01/why-the-silent-filibuster-is-unconstitutional/68825/.

3. Dan Kennedy, "Minority Rule: Why Our Undemocratic Republic Must Give Way To Something Else," WGBH, 10 Oct. 2018, www.wgbh.org/news/commentary/2018/10/10/minority-rule-why -our-undemocratic-republic-must-give-way-to-something-else.

4. Todd Tucker, "Fixing the Senate: Equitable and Full Representation for the 21st Century," The Roosevelt Institute, March 2019, https://rooseveltinstitute.org/wp-content/uploads/2019/03 /RI_Fixing-The-Senate_report-201903.pdf.

5. "Implementing the 'Wyoming Rule,'" *Daily Kos*, 5 Jul 2018, https://www.dailykos.com/stories /2018/7/5/1778149/-Implementing-the-Wyoming-Rule.

6. "Free white males over 16."

7. Dylan Matthews, "The Senate's 46 Democrats Got 20 Million More Votes than Its 54 Republicans," *Vox*, 3 Jan. 2015, www.vox.com/2015/1/3/7482635/senate-small-states.

8. "Statehood Movement in Puerto Rico," Wikipedia, 21 Apr. 2020, en.wikipedia.org/wiki/Statehood_movement_in_P

9. Congress could add to the D.C. or Puerto Rico state the four other territories and their almost 400,000 disenfranchised U.S. citizens: Guam, American Samoa & the Northern Minerals and U.S. Virgin Islands. That wouldn't increase the number of Senators above two, but it would bring almost all stateless Americans into a state. Those territories could petition later to be added to one of the states.

10. Cesar Conda et al., "Why Washington Should Finally Make Puerto Rico a State," *Politico*, 18 Oct. 2017, www.politico.com/agenda/story/2017/10/18/puerto-rico-hurricane-maria-statehood-000552/.

11. The American Indian Digest, Appendix D: Indian Nations, https://www.fs.fed.us/people/tribal/tribexd.pdf and Esri GeoInquiries Collection for U.S. History, "Native American lands, 1819-2015," https://www.esri.com/content/dam/esrisites/en-us/media/pdf/geoinquiries/history/7-nativeamlands-ushistory-geoinquiry.pdf.

12. *Native American Population 2020*, worldpopulationreview.com/states/native-american-population/and https://www.census.gov/history/pdf/c2010br-10.pdf

13. "Native Americans By the Numbers." Infoplease, www.infoplease.com/history/native-american-heritage/native-americans-by-the-numbers.

14. Nikolas Kristof, "The Top US Coronavirus Hotspots Are All Indian Lands," *New York Times*, https://www.nytimes.com/2020/05/30/opinion/sunday/coronavirus-native-americans.html.

15. UCLA American Indian Studies Center, https://www.aisc.ucla.edu/news/akee_indiancountrytoday.aspx.

16. Chris Boyette and Deanna Hackney, "Sioux Tribe Rejects South Dakota Governor Request to Remove Covid-19 Checkpoints," CNN, 10 May 2020, www.cnn.com/2020/05/09/us/south-dakota-sioux-tribes/.

17. Marc Fisher, "Derailment of Mass. Casino Spotlights Trump's R.I., Twin River Connections," The Providence Journal14 May 2019, www.providencejournal.com/news/20190513/derailment-of-mass-casino-spotlights-trumps-ri-twin-river-connections.

18. Julian Brave NoiseCat, "Republicans Wanted to Suppress the Native American Vote. It's Working," *The Guardian*, 26 Oct. 2018, www.theguardian.com/us-news/2018/oct/26/the-real-reason-for-voter-id-laws-to-prevent-native-americans-from-voting.

19. Massoud Hayoun, "Native American Rights Groups Are Targeting Six States to Fight Voter Suppression in 2020," *Pacific Standard*, 14 Feb. 2019, psmag.com/social-justice/native-american-rights-groups-are-gearing-up-to-fight-voter-suppression-in-2020.

20. "Representation in the House: The Wyoming Rule," *Outside the Beltway*, 14 Dec. 2010, www.outsidethebeltway.com/representation-in-the-house-the-wyoming-rule/.

21. "Mitch McConnel Praises Trump for 'Changing the Federal Courts Forever,'" *The Week*, 4 Nov 2019, https://theweek.com/speedreads/876359/mitch-mcconnell-praises-trump-changing-federal-courts-forever.

22. "Trump Picks More 'Not Qualified' Judges (1)." Bloomberg BNA News, news.bloomberglaw.com/us-law-week/trump-picks-more-not-qualified-judges-1.

23. In 2017, the conservative National Review demanded that it was necessary to expand the judiciary by 33% to reduce the backlog of cases they uncovered. Steven G. Calabresi, "The Federal Courts Are Overworked and Need to Be Expanded," *National Review*, 30 Nov. 2017, www.nationalreview.com/2017/11/federal-court-expansion-republicans-courts/.

24. *Citizens United v. Federal Election Commission*, 558 U.S. 310 (2010).

25. *Rucho v. Common Cause*, No. 18-422, 588 U.S. ___ (2019), and *Lamone v. Benisek*, No. 18-726 (2019).

26. *Shelby County v. Holder*, 570 U.S. 529 (2013)

27. Actually, this was the DC Court of Appeals on a two-to-one vote with both Republican appointees voting to protect the President's secrets about Russia in the case Committee on the Judiciary of the United States House of Representatives versus Donald McGahn (2020).

28. Ed Mazza, "Mitch McConnell Brags About Blocking Obama for 2 Years, Then Laughs About It," HuffPost, 13 Dec. 2019, www.huffpost.com/entry/mitch-mcconnell-blocks-obama -laughs_n_5df32430e4b0deb78b517322.

29. Ephrat Livni, "Senators Demand Records Illuminating Dark Money Ties to Supreme Court Appointments," Quartz, 12 Mar. 2020, qz.com/1816542/senators-demand-records -on-dark-money-ties-to-court-appointments/

30. Ehprat Livni, "Senators Demand Records Illuminating Dark Money Ties to Supreme Court Appointments," Quartz, 12 Mar 2020, https://qz.com/1816542/senators-demand -records-on-dark-money-ties-to-court-appointments/.

31. Gundy v. United States, 139 S. Ct. 2116 (2019), https://www.supremecourt.gov/opinions/18pdf /17-6086_2b8e.pdf.

32. Ian Millhiser, "Justice Alito Just Wrote the Most Terrifying Sentence to Appear in a Supreme Court Opinion in Years," ThinkProgress, 20 June 2019, thinkprogress.org/justice-alito-just-wrote-the-most-terrifying -sentence-to-appear-in-a-supreme-court-opinion-in-years-83a535d3ce58/ .

33. Steven G Calabresi, "Republicans Should Expand the Federal Courts," National Review, 16 Nov. 2017, www.nationalreview.com/2017/11/gop-tax-bill-should-expand-federal-courts/.

34. "Demographics of the Supreme Court of the United States," Wikipedia, 18 Apr. 2020, en.wikipedia .org/wiki/Demographics_of_the_Supreme_Court_of_the_United_States.

35. Naomi Jagoda, "Biden Says He Opposes Expanding the Supreme Court," The Hill, 4 Jul 2019, https: //thehill.com/homenews/campaign/451778-biden-says-he-opposes-expanding-the-supreme -court.

36. Daniel Marans, "Embracing Supreme Court Expansion Carries No Political Cost, Study Says." HuffPost, 18 Feb. 2020, www.huffpost.com/entry/expand-supreme-court-no-political-cost-democrats -take-back-the-court_n_5e4a1652c5b64d860fccca4b.

37. "'It's Just Messed up': Most Think Political Divisions as Bad as Vietnam Era, New Poll Shows," Washington Post, www.washingtonpost.com/graphics/2017/national/democracy-poll/.

38. "Forbes Rich List 2010: World's 100 Wealthiest," This Is Money, 10 June 2011, https://www.thisismoney .co.uk/money/news/article-1690636/Forbes-Rich-List-2010-Worlds-100-wealthiest.html.

39. Luisa Kroll and Kerry A. Dolan, "The Forbes 400: The Definitive Ranking of the Wealthiest Americans," Forbes, 2 Oct 2019, https://www.forbes.com/forbes-400/#428143c07e2f.

40. "The Biden Plan to Guarantee Government Works for the People," Joe Biden presidential campaign, https://joebiden.com/governmentreform/.

41. "The Politics of Financial Insecurity." Pew Research Center - U.S. Politics & Policy, Pew Research Center, 30 May 2020, www.pewresearch.org/politics/2015/01/08/the-politics-of -financial-insecurity-a-democratic-tilt-undercut-by-low-participation/.

42. Zaid Jilani, "New House Bill Would Kill Gerrymandering and Could Move America Away from Two- Party Dominance," The Intercept, 5 Jul 2017, https://theintercept.com/2017/07/05/new-house-bill -would-kill-gerrymandering-and-could-move-america-away-from-two-party-dominance/.

43. "Reelection Rates Over the Years," OpenSecrets.org, www.opensecrets.org/overview/reele& Gallup. "Congress and the Public," Gallup, 13 Apr. 2020, news.gallup.com/poll/1600/congress-public.aspx.

44. Michael Li, "Five Ways H.R. 1 Would Transform Redistricting," Brennan Center for Justice, 19 June 2019, www.brennancenter.org/our-work/analysis-opinion/five-ways-hr-1-would-transform-redistricting.

45. H.R.4000 from July 2019 Fair Representation Act.

46. "Proportional Representation." Wikipedia, 15 Apr. 2020, en.wikipedia.org/wiki/Proportional _representation.

47. "Supreme Court Rules Partisan Gerrymandering Is Beyond the Reach of Federal Courts," NPR, 27 Jun, 2019, https://www.npr.org/2019/06/27/731847977/supreme-court-rules-partisan -gerrymandering-is-beyond-the-reach-of-federal-court.

48. Jones, "Texas Officials Want to Suppress Democratic Voters," HuffPost.

49.   Aaron Blake, "Analysis | Trump Just Comes out and Says It: The GOP Is Hurt When It's Easier to Vote." *Washington Post*, 30 Mar. 2020, www.washingtonpost.com/politics/2020/03/30/trump-voting-republicans/.

50.   "Joe Biden's Views," Equal Citizens, https://equalcitizens.us/joe-biden-views/.

51.   Ballot Scout or BallotTrax are two such off-the-shelf complete solutions.

52.   Jessica Huseman, "Voting by Mail Would Reduce Coronavirus Transmission but It Has Other Risks," *ProPublica*, 24 March 2020, www.propublica.org/article/voting-by-mail-would-reduce-coronavirus-transmission-but-it-has-other-risks.

53.   "Full 50 State 2018 Turnout Ranking and Voting Policy," *Nonprofit Vote*, 16 Apr. 2019, www.nonprofitvote.org/full-50-state-2018-turnout-ranking-voting-policy/.

54.   Brad Tuttle, "How Much Election Day Costs the Country-and Voters," *Money*, 8 Nov. 2016, money.com/election-day-2016-costs-country-voters/.

55.   Charlotte Hill et al., "We Should Never Have to Vote in Person Again," *New York Times*, 4 May 2020, www.nytimes.com/2020/05/04/opinion/coronavirus-vote-by-mail.html.

56.   Zack Budryk, "Oklahoma House Republicans Vote to Reverse Court Ruling on Absentee Ballots, Require Them to Be Notarized," *The Hill*, 7 May 2020, thehill.com/homenews/state-watch/496512-oklahoma-house-republicans-vote-to-reverse-court-ruling-on-absentee.

57.   "Colorado Voting Reforms: Early Results," The Pew Charitable Trusts, 22 March 2016, www.pewtrusts.org/en/research-and-analysis/issue-briefs/2016/03/colorado-voting-reforms-early-results.

58.   "Vote-by-Mail: Voter Preferences and Self-Reported Voting Behavior in the State of Oregon," ResearchGate, www.researchgate.net/publication/308014394_Vote-by-Mail_Voter_Preferences_and_Self-Reported_Voting_Behavior_in_the_State_of_Oregon.

59.   Matthew Cole, Richard Esposito, Sam Biddle, and Ryan Grim, "Top-Secret NSA Report Details Russian Hacking Effort Days before 2016 Election," *The Intercept*, 5 Jun 2017, https://theintercept.com/2017/06/05/top-secret-nsa-report-details-russian-hacking-effort-days-before-2016-election/.

60.   "Full 50 State 2018 Turnout Ranking and Voting Policy," *Nonprofit Vote*, 16 Apr. 2019, www.nonprofitvote.org/full-50-state-2018-turnout-ranking-voting-policy/.

61.   "Public Supports Aim of Making It 'Easy' for All Citizens to Vote," Pew Research Center - U.S. Politics & Policy, 30 May 2020, www.people-press.org/2017/06/28/public-supports-aim-of-making-it-easy-for-all-citizens-to-vote/.

62.   "Automatic Voter Registration, a Summary." Brennan Center for Justice, 10 July 2019, www.brennancenter.org/our-work/research-reports/automatic-voter-registration-summary.

63.   US Census Bureau, "Population and Voting Rates for Congressional Districts: 2018," The United States Census Bureau, 3 Feb. 2020, www.census.gov/data/tables/time-series/demo/voting-and-registration/congressional-voting-tables.html

64.   John C. Moritz, "Hispanic Vote Share Rises in Texas during 2018 Midterm Elections," *Corpus Christi Caller*, 19 May 2019, www.caller.com/story/news/local/texas/state-bureau/2019/05/14/hispanic-vote-share-rises-texas-during-2018-midterm-elections/1120993001/.

65.   Sam Levine, "Amid an Assault on Voting Rights, Here's Where Advocates See Some Hope," *HuffPost*, 9 Jun 2017, https://www.huffpost.com/entry/automatic-voter-registration-n_593a97d7e4b0c5a35c9e9d7a.

66.   Victoria Bekiempis, "Wisconsin Judge's Ruling Could Purge 200,000 Voters from Rolls," *The Guardian*, 14 Dec 2019, https://www.theguardian.com/us-news/2019/dec/14/wisconsin-purge-voter-rolls-judge-ruling.

67.   Sophia A McClennen, "The Real Outrage of the Afghanistan War Papers That No One Wants to Talk About," *Salon*, 13 Dec. 2019, www.salon.com/2019/12/14/the-bombshell-revelations-in-the-afghanistan-war-papers-no-one-wants-to-talk-about/.

68.   A.J. Vicens, "Researchers Assembled over 100 Voting Machines. Hackers Broke into Every Single One," *Mother Jones*, 16 Dec. 2019, www.motherjones.com/politics/2019/09/defcon-2019-hacking-village/.

69.   Richard Esposito et al, "Top-Secret NSA Report Details Russian Hacking Effort Days Before 2016 Election," *The Intercept*, 5 June 2017, theintercept.com/2017/06/05/top-secret-nsa-report-details-russian-hacking-effort-days-before-2016-election/.

70.   Vicens, AJ. "Researchers Assembled over 100 Voting Machines. Hackers Broke into Every Single One." *Mother Jones*, 27 Sept. 2019, www.motherjones.com/politics/2019/09/defcon-2019-hacking-village/.

71.   *Bush v. Gore*, 531 U.S. 98 (2000)

72.   *Bush*, 531 U.S. at 104– 05.

73.   *Gray vs Sanders*, 372 U.S. 368 (1963).

74.   *Williams v. Rhodes*, 393 U.S. 23, 89 S. Ct. 5, 21 L.Ed.2d 24 (1968).

75.   "Equal Votes," Equal Citizens, https://equalcitizens.us/equal-votes/.

CHAPTER 8

#DemRevPlan Solutions 8-9:
Fulfilling Democracy's Promise to Those Hurt in the GOP Attacks Against Democracy

Democratic voters must adjust their thinking. This is no longer a game in which everyone behaves according to the rules. This is a slow-motion civil war in which the GOP is taking advantage of the liberal preference for fair play. Democrats see Republicans as mere opponents—or worse, as potential partners in compromise. The GOP, however, sees the Democrats as *the enemy*. Enemies must be destroyed.

—John Stoehr, editorial board of AlterNet[1]

PRODUCT ADVISORY WARNING:

These next measures are aimed at leveling the playing field by undoing the damage that Republican attacks did to certain Democratic Party constituencies in an aim to weaken the Democrats. Those constituencies are immigrants, unions and Democratic coalition voters. The power of these members of the Democratic coalition must be restored. Thus, this is more about democracy revival than a mere progressive wish-list.

Solution #8: Welcome Citizen Dreamers

Don't give up. Don't allow it to happen. If there's a concrete wall in front of you, go through it. Go over it. Go around it. But get to the other side of that wall.

—Donald Trump[2]

What is another way to help Democrats regain power so that they may revitalize democracy in the United States? Add to the number of people voting Democrat. There is no better way to do that than to provide the power to vote to 700,000 people who are American citizens in every way other than birthplace.

Since 2000, politicians have disappointed very few groups more than the Dreamers, the children brought over to the United States by their parents as young kids. Democrats—and obviously Republicans—have failed to provide them with a path to citizenship. President Obama gave them some relief in the form of a legal limbo called the Deferred Action for Childhood Arrivals (DACA) program. Trump then took away that little protection. Then the courts restored it. Then the program was stopped. It's just a mess.

Time for America to step up and offer a hearty embrace to the stepchildren of our American family:

1. With the addition of only a few words to the law, we can create fast-track citizenship for any of the 700,000 DACA recipients who have held DACA status for three years.[3]
2. In addition, Congress should allow anyone who has held the U status for immigrants or the Violence Against Women Act (VAWA) status for three years to apply for citizenship immediately while removing the yearly cap on how many immigrants can benefit from these programs. Both of these groups are immigrants who came to the United States and who were abused and otherwise victimized. Most have helped government agencies such as the police arrest the criminals who have hurt them.
3. Finally, US Citizenship and Immigration Services (USCIS) should be required to adjudicate naturalization, U status, and VAWA applications within ninety days instead of the years and years it is now taking.

Talking Points: Help Dreamers and Victims of Crime Have a Fast Path for Citizenship

How to tell your elected representative or media why this fight is so crucial:

Congress has already fast-tracked certain groups for citizenship.

- Congress already allows this three-year fast track to citizenship—instead of the normal five years—to spouses of US citizens. In my experience leading an immigration law firm in Los Angeles, those foreign spouses have generally been in the United States for less than two years. They often have limited English. On the other hand, Dreamers average twenty-five years in the United States, and all have a high school degrees from US schools. Many have attended college here as well. Which group has *earned* fast track more?

- The DACA, U, and VAWA recipients would still need to pass the moral character requirement like all other naturalization applicants.

- Naturalization applications under Obama were often adjudicated within four months. Under Trump they have extended to eighteen months or more. Congress and the executive branch can direct the Department of Homeland Security to use its enormous resources to streamline this final part of the American Dream journey and adjudicate naturalization, U status, and VAWA applications all within ninety days.

Dreamers have already been abused enough; it's time to embrace them.

- Politicians have psychologically tortured DACA recipients and hurt them financially and educationally. U and VAWA recipients have been victimized by fellow Americans or residents. Let's fix this once and for all and give them an immediate path to citizenship. Welcome to America, we value you, we love you, and we expect great things from you. So register to vote and make sure no Republicans are ever elected in your district again. This should be an easy reform to get done.

- Approving a three-year fast track to citizenship for DACA recipients and U visa/VAWA holders creates almost a million new citizens in 2021. Hate to bring politics into this, but these highly motivated individuals will not be voting Republican. There are enough new voters here to flip states like Texas, Florida, Arizona, and Georgia blue. Why do you think Republicans have fought so hard against creating a path toward citizenship for immigrants, even just these Dreamers? Well, yes, racism. But really, it's about control. Imagine if the Republican Party lost those four states. Yeah, keep smiling. #DemRevPlan just gets better and better.

Why Might Your Elected Democratic Representative Hesitate?

Is this the immigration reform our country needs? No, not even close. The immigration system was terrible before President Obama, and it has gotten worse under Trump. Kids in cages. It's just awful and so un-American, whatever that means nowadays. But we must save democracy first if any real meaningful immigration reform will happen. So this is just a small step toward that. This should be separate and before any immigration reform bill that is contemplated after the saving of democracy.

On the Democrats' side, the biggest obstacle is likely fear, not racism. Without the #DemRevPlan reforms, this doesn't pass. If the other #DemRevPlan reforms have already been passed, this too will pass. McConnell can't filibuster it, tens of millions of dollars can't attack the Democrats that support it, and the Democrats will not have to fear they will lose the majority because gerrymandering and vote suppression are a thing of the past. Finally, with Republican-appointed justices on the Supreme Court in a minority, the court would not stop this either.

Solution #9: Clean Slate to Revitalize Unions

Any employer intent on resisting workers' self-organization can drag out legal proceedings for years, fearing little more than an order to post a written notice in the workplace promising not to repeat unlawful conduct...Many employers have come to view remedies like back pay for workers fired because of union activity as routine costs of doing business, well worth it to get rid of organizing leaders and derail workers' organizing efforts.

—Human Rights Watch report on the lack of worker rights in the US[4]

Obama's presidency effectively ended in 2009—the first year of his first term—when he abandoned the fight to help workers unionize as explained in chapter 5. McConnell's filibuster killed the bill—the Employee Free Choice Act (EFCA)—despite fifty-four of one hundred senators supporting it. Instead of helping workers gain greater job security and benefits, Obama was done in by the corporate control of a few Democratic senators who received massive amounts of campaign contributions from antiunion corporations and lobbyists. Obama then pivoted to fighting for health care reforms and never got back to the union fight.

This was a fatal strategic blunder. Instead of using his massive capital—remember, he had just won by a landslide—to bring in the last few Democratic senators to support the EFCA, Obama remained mostly silent about the law. Democracy would have gained millions of more union activists. Instead, Republicans passed more right-to-work (for less) laws in six newly captured state legislatures. They then crippled workers' ability to unionize and unions' ability to spend money in political campaigns.[5]

The next president must do what Democrats failed to do in 2009: help workers join unions to protect their collective interests. Solution #9 includes a series of reforms called the Clean Slate created by Obama's former National Labor Relations Board member Sharon Block.[6] These reforms go past the updated EFCA passed by the House in 2020, which was dead on arrival to the Senate. Solution #9 Clean Slate reforms:

1.   Make it easier for workers to organize themselves and take collective actions and thus help slow down economic inequality.
2.   Eliminate right-to-work laws.
3.   Give farmworkers and domestic workers rights to unionize.
4.   Allow workers to choose a union without interference from their employer.

Under these reforms, workers can, for the first time, sign up to be a part of a union just like they can sign up for a credit card, a political party, or a fantasy sports team.

The one tweak that Solution #9 needs is that small businesses under $2 million in revenue, nonprofits, and start-ups in their first three years should be exempted.

Talking Points: Revitalize Our Unions through Clean Slate

How to tell your elected representative or media why this fight is so crucial:

Unions are critical allies in saving our democracy.

- The Clean Slate reforms secure allies for democracy. These laws will increase union membership, which will help supply volunteers, logistics, and support to the democracy movement for the next generation. Indeed, this is what unions have done for democracy for a hundred years.

Before our economy irreversibly cements inequality, we need revitalized unions to strengthen the middle class.

- After the 2008 recession, our economy grew considerably but in completely inequitable ways. The top 1% in the United States captured half of all real income growth between 2009 and 2017.[7] People in the top 1% have had their income grow four times as fast as those of the bottom 99% since the Great Recession ended. According to the *Atlantic*, "Millions of young families who tried to save for a home were unable to purchase one, sapped by the toxic combination of high rents and a lack of stock. Throw in sky-high childcare prices, spiraling out-of-pocket health care fees, and heavy educational debt loads, and the 2010s crushed a whole generation as it entered its prime earning years."[8]
- Unions played a major role in reducing income inequality in the midtwentieth century. Their decline since the 1960s contributed significantly to the widening gap between rich and poor.[9] As unions have been decimated, the ability of employers to steal wages from employees has increased unchecked; wage theft is now estimated at over $3 billion annually.[10] Yet the Supreme Court has crippled workers' ability to collectively regain those stolen wages in decision after decision.[11]
- The Clean Slate proposal is one of the few economic proposals that will claw back some of that inequity. The 1% earn their money in hedge funds that own stock in corporations. Once those corporations have to start paying workers more from their profits, the boats of the middle class will be lifted.

US workers who make up the Democratic Party already owe unions.

- Clean Slate eliminates the GOP's right-to-work laws. Not only have these laws hurt workers by lowering wages and benefits, they also hurt voter turnout for Democrats. Democratic presidential, Senate, House, and governor vote shares decrease by 3.5% when Republican states pass these antiunion laws.[12]

- Elected officials may think that they do not have much connection to unions. But millions of workers—long before our current crop of Democrats were born—fought for rights and benefits that we all take for granted. Many of them died in these battles because the corporate overseers in the early twentieth century regularly used violence against workers with impunity.

- Do Democrats like not working weekends? That's because of unions. Paid vacations? Unions. Family medical leave? Oh yeah, that's all unions. Lunch breaks and other rest periods during the working day? Corporations didn't give that willingly. Sick leave, paid holiday, military leave, disability leave, and even the forty-hour workweek are all due to union negotiations and pressure campaigns. It's a simple equation. When workers can unite to protect their interests, we all benefit. This is because almost all of us are workers.

Small businesses, start-ups, and nonprofits are our allies against giant corporations and should be exempt from Clean Slate requirements.

- Corporations and monopolies demand government subsidies, get loopholes so they don't pay taxes, warp our political process and pollute the environment and our bodies. They need to be checked through unions. But Democrats should understand that small businesses, nonprofits, and start-ups are actually their allies against these large corporations. These small businesses politically align with Republicans now only because Democrats have not sought to divide and conquer. Having an economy full of small businesses, start-ups, nonprofits, and unionized corporations should be the goal. Does it make any sense to treat the local mom-and-pop nonprofit bookstore the same as Walmart? Perversely, it's easier to organize at a nonprofit bookstore than at large corporations like Walmart.

- It's time for Democrats to align with entrepreneurs and small businesses against the giant corporations. It's a natural alliance. It's also great politics. Sort of like bringing family farmers back into the Democratic fold if you treat them with preference over agribusiness. Of course, once Solution #4 is implemented and we have our Citizens United vouchers, Democrats can remove economic obstacles for family farmers and small businesses while closing tax loopholes and subsidies for their monopolistic behemoth brethren.

Why Might Your Elected Democratic Representative Hesitate?

Pro-union reforms did not pass the Senate in 2009 when Democrats had sixty senators and Republicans had only forty. At least five Democratic senators did not support the bill. In 2021, Democrats will be lucky if they have fifty or fifty-one senators. Chuck Schumer will have his hands full trying to keep every senator on his side in support of this legislation. He will also have to have already passed filibuster reform, among other #DemRevPlan solutions.

Notes

1. John Stoehr, "Republicans Act as Though Being a Democrat Is a Crime - and the Party Needs to Start Fighting Back," Alternet.org, 10 Feb. 2020, www.alternet.org/2020/02/republicans-are-treating-democratic-partisanship-as-a-crime-and-the-party-needs-to-start-fighting-back/.

2. Meagan Flynn, "'If There's a Concrete Wall in Front of You, Go through It,' Trump Said in 2004 Speech," *Washington Post*, 10 Jan. 2019, www.washingtonpost.com/nation/2019/01/10/if-theres-concrete-wall-front-you-go-through-it-trump-said-unearthed-commencement-speech/.

3. Immigration Naturalization Act (INA) section 319(a) (8 U.S.C. §1430)

4. "Unfair Advantage." Human Rights Watch, 29 Apr. 2015, www.hrw.org/report/2000/10/05/unfair-advantage#.

5. Sean McElwee, "How the Right's War on Unions Is Killing the Democratic Party," *The Nation*, 23 Jan. 2018, www.thenation.com/article/archive/right-to-work-laws-are-killing-democrats-at-the-ballot-box/.

6. "Clean Slate for Worker Power," www.cleanslateworkerpower.org/.

7. Sarah Donovan, "The U.S. Income Distribution: Trends and Issues," Congressional Research Service, 8 Dec. 2016, https://fas.org/sgp/crs/misc/R44705.pdf

8. Annie Lowrey, "The Decade in Which Everything Was Great But Felt Terrible," *The Atlantic*, 2 Jan. 2020, www.theatlantic.com/ideas/archive/2019/12/road-late-capitalism/603769/ .

9.   Henry S. Farber et al., "Unions and Inequality Over the Twentieth Century: New Evidence from Survey Data 1," Nat'l Bureau of Econ. Research, Working Paper No. 24587, 2018, https://www.nber.org/papers/w24587.

10.   David G. Savage, "Supreme Court Upholds Arbitration that Bans Workers from Joining Forces Over Lost Wages," *Los Angeles Times*, May 21, 2018, http://www.latimes.com/politics/la-na-pol-court-workers-20180521-story.html.

11.   Most notably in the 2018 decisions: *Janus v. American Federation of State, County and Municipal Employees*, 585 U.S. ___ (2018) and *Epic Systems v. Lewis*, 584 U.S. ___ (2018).

12.   James Feigenbaum and Alexander Hertel-Fernandez, "From the Bargaining Table to the Ballot Box: Political Effects of Right to Work Laws," 20 Jan. 2018, https://jamesfeigenbaum.github.io/research/pdf/fhw_rtw_jan2018.pdf.

CHAPTER 9

#DemRevPlan Solutions 10–12:
Democracy Needs Truth

S olutions #10 through #12 are about fighting for the truth and against diversionary propaganda. While Fox News will always continue its campaign of lies to elect Republicans, these solutions help bolster democracy in the face of the war against truth.

Solution #10: Citizen-Run, Citizen-Owned Media

I do it to discredit you all and demean you all, so when you write negative stories about me, no one will believe you.

—Donald Trump to CBS *60 Minutes* correspondent Lesley Stahl about why he persisted in going after journalists[1]

Mainstream media are "for-profit" subsidiaries of the largest corporations in the world. These media outlets are mostly owned by major corporations like Comcast cable or billionaires like the Fox News Murdoch family or Amazon's Jeff Bezos. Their powerful corporate sponsors give them lots of money to advertise on their networks. If you were designing ideal protectors of democracy, would this be them?

The Public Broadcasting Service (PBS) and National Public Radio (NPR) are our alternative to corporate-owned media outlets, but they are poorly funded and limited in their reach. They aren't even in the top forty broadcasters nationwide, and PBS has less than a 1% audience share.[2]

PBS and NPR are also subject to government control in that they rely on the federal government for funding. Trump slashed the funding for these two entities to zero in his budget. But worse, the president appoints the members of the board that oversee NPR and PBS. At what point will Republicans begin using these entities in their cultural war?

The people's media should not be at risk of funding cuts if the party in power does not like their truth-telling. As Thomas Jefferson said: "Our liberty depends on the freedom of the press, and that cannot be limited without being lost."[3]

We need a media source that is not tied to the government or to giant corporations. Congress can make this happen. With Solution #10, Congress converts the Corporation for Public Broadcasting (CPB), NPR, and PBS into a nonprofit consumer cooperative, like a credit union—or the outdoor company REI.[4] This shifts ownership to the already existing base of subscribing members. These members would then elect the leadership subject to certain constraints: a majority of the board must be journalists, and no members of the board can come from either government or for-profit corporations that might seek to bias its reporting.

Congress should apportion the amount of funding it would have otherwise provided to CPB, NPR, and PBS over the next two generations and allocate that as a one-time contribution to their endowment. This endowment would now be controlled by the newly constituted consumer cooperative. This *final* contribution by the government would make NPR and PBS financially sustainable, strengthen their reach, and allow them to keep an independent voice. The interest from the enhanced endowment should be enough to replace the 18% of NPR's budget that currently comes from government sources and, ideally, the money that comes from for-profit corporations.

The National Endowment for the Arts and the National Endowment for the Humanities could be included as part of this new public-owned entity. This is especially true considering Republicans continually try to zero out their budgets as well.

Talking Points: Citizen-Run and Citizen-Owned Media to Defend Democracy

How to tell your elected representative or media why this fight is so crucial:

Corporate media is insufficient to defend democracy.

- There is nothing more important to a functioning democracy than having a free press. The problem is that our democracy is only protected to the extent that the corporate media can make a profit off of its coverage. This is why the corporate-controlled media failed us in 2016. They elevated the candidacy of the great con man and huckster Donald Trump because he boosted their ratings and thus profits. Instead of the media covering his opponents' critiques of Trump, they just gave free rein to the much more watchable Trump show. An independent NPR and PBS will not have to pursue such short-term profits over responsible journalism.

- In total, the corporate media covered the supposed scandal of Hillary Clinton's emails 40% more than they covered all of Trump's scandals combined.[5] Fair and balanced? They normalized Trump's scandals by making it appear Clinton was just as scandal prone as Trump. Overall, the media gave more positive coverage to Trump in the campaign than they did to Clinton. Even more disturbing is the sophisticated and all-encompassing right-wing echo chamber of Fox News and Breitbart and so many other conservative media companies. They have locked in 40% of the American electorate into this upside-down world built exclusively of diversionary propaganda. So when the Trump administration completely fails at handling a true crisis like the coronavirus pandemic, 40% of the country still thinks Trump is doing a great job and that 150,000 Americans dead from COVID-19 is, somehow, a hoax.[6] We need an alternative that people can believe in that isn't controlled by the government or for-profit corporations with their own agenda.

- Want to heal global climate change and social inequality? What's the plan to get corporate-owned media to provide better focus and better information on these issues? A publicly owned nonprofit media entity that is well funded with a nationwide reach is the antidote to Fox and Facebook news. It must be able to both focus on investigative journalism and help us understand the complex long-term problems we face, not just the most sensationalistic story of the day. The First Amendment was the gift of our Founding Fathers to the American public. A member-owned CPB, NPR, and PBS will be the gift of our current leaders to the First Amendment.

Right-wing attacks on media show the importance of an
alternative news source.

- Giant corporations like Facebook, Twitter, and other social media
  are the new alternative to corporate media. But they are easily ma-
  nipulated by outside forces like Russian president Putin and his
  bots—although stay tuned, there is a solution for that coming up
  next. There's really only one place to turn right now in our media
  landscape that is not a corporate-controlled, right-wing or left-wing
  echo chamber: public radio (and TV). But it's currently at the mercy of
  President Trump and Republican budget chairs in Congress. Giving
  NPR and PBS to the American public protects its independence from
  government.

- It's hard to remember every scandal of this president's administration, but there was one in January 2020 that is directly relevant to
  NPR and PBS. An NPR reporter was pressing secretary of state Mike
  Pompeo on an issue when Pompeo went ballistic on the reporter,
  cursing her out. When the reporter revealed to the public what had
  happened, the president retweeted a Fox News tweet asking, "Why
  does NPR still exist?"[7] In each of his budgets, Trump zeroed out all
  funding for NPR and PBS. Congress restored it, but barely. It's just a
  matter of time before either the funding is ended—like Republican
  president Ronald Reagan almost achieved in the early 1980s—or
  Trump-appointed CPB board members so co-opt NPR and PBS that
  it's just an extension of Fox News and government propaganda. If you
  think that won't happen, then you haven't read the previous eight
  chapters of this book—caught you!

- Trump and associates are not just aiming at PBS. In 2017, Matthew
  Boyle, *Breitbart News*'s Washington political editor, gave a speech at
  the Heritage Foundation in Washington explaining the right-wing's
  goals: "The goal eventually is the full destruction and elimination
  of the entire mainstream media. We envision a day when CNN is
  no longer in business. We envision a day when the *New York Times*
  closes its doors. I think that day is possible."[8] An NPR and PBS with
  a well-funded endowment is the means to create a bulwark of media
  independence.

- Much of the conservative media has as their goal to spread their diversionary propaganda in order to achieve their own policy goals. They play on the anti-intellectualism of many of their followers by design. Much of the conservative movement—especially Christian fundamentalists—oppose education. Education fosters critical thinking, critical thinking challenges authority, and challenging authority is not appreciated in conservative religious or political environments. An independent NPR and PBS can foster critical thinking and media literacy as part of their mission to their members.
- The more difficult it is for people to distinguish the truth from misinformation, the easier it is for autocrats to inject their "certainty" into their followers. Putin's goal is to convince people that "the truth is unknowable" and that the only sensible choice is "to follow a strong leader."[9] Citizen-run and citizen-owned media finally is a reform that Democrats can make to counter Putin and Fox News' diversionary propaganda.

Why Might Your Elected Democratic Representative Hesitate?

Imagine the difference in our media landscape if we could have better-funded, more muscular, completely independent, citizen-owned PBS and NPR and related media entities. There is not a single reform that anyone can dream up that gets us a better-informed electorate. This would be a popular issue if ever presented to the American public.

Nevertheless, the current public understanding of the need for this reform is nonexistent. The reform might not be popular with the CPB folks if they are afraid of change. The editorial boards of those for-profit mainstream media entities will not champion this reform. And the right-wing media echo chamber will certainly call the new ownership model "communistic" because who can trust Americans to own anything together?

But the recurring question is, will the Democrats do the right thing even if the corporate-owned media or polls aren't clamoring for it?

Solution # 11: Unmasking Trolls

Our adversaries want to undermine our democratic institutions, influence public sentiment and affect government policies. Russia, China, Iran, and other foreign malicious actors all will seek to interfere in the voting process or influence voter perceptions. Adversaries may try to accomplish their goals through a variety of means, including social media campaigns, directing disinformation operations or conducting disruptive or destructive cyber-attacks on state and local infrastructure.

—Joint statement from attorney general William Barr, November 5, 2019[10]

Online discourse is appalling. Go to almost any place on Reddit, the comments section of Breitbart, the public posts on Facebook, YouTube and Twitter, and feel the ick. Death threats and very personal abuse is the price that too many people must pay to dissent—or to speak the truth.

In 1996, section 230(c) of the Communications Decency Act gave online companies broad immunity from liability for content created by their users. It was a smart policy until Russian and troll bots took over our political Internet. Now online companies allow fake and anonymous sources to spread libel, abuse, conspiracies and false attacks but remain protected by section 230(c), as ironically President Trump started pointing out in June 2020.

The solution is simple: unmask the trolls. Amend section 230(c) to require media companies to validate the city and identity of its users. All postings—including paid political ads—must have a valid human being's name and city. To the extent the companies do this, they will remain protected from liability for the content created by those validated users. If foreign actors, bots, or anonymous individuals, however, continue to post or buy political ads interfering in our elections, then the online media companies can be held liable.

Of course, draconian policies for the foreign actors interfering with American elections need to be implemented as well. There can also be provisions about the companies' policing of online bullying, but such trolling should be significantly diminished once anonymity and bots are removed from these platforms.

Congress will also need to require these companies to put a disclaimer on any foreign account that has not been verified. The ability to share, like, retweet, or in any way amplify the posts from those unverified sources should be disabled.

Talking Points: Unmasking Trolls Reform

How to tell your elected representative or media why this fight is so crucial.

Bots and Russians should not be able to drown out the First Amendment rights of Americans.

- Imagine an online world where people share posts and have to have their names on it. No more anonymous trolls. No more bots. No more Russian teenagers posing as a farmer from Tennessee. Imagine all paid-for political speech exposed to the sunlight so that we can see who is paying for what lies and disinformation. That's a public square that any politician should be proud of helping to safeguard.
- Anyone on social media by now has felt the burn from the bots. They are "robots" with preset scripts that can post comments anywhere and everywhere. With AI and machine learning, these bots can actually write entire articles and have consistent "personalities" over hundreds of posts, making them appear human.
- Our Founding Fathers could not anticipate that a teenage troll in Russia could have his lies read more in one week than Thomas Paine's *Common Sense* was read during its entire publication run in pre-Revolutionary America. Nor could the Congress of 1996 have anticipated that section 230(c) would have paved the way for so much diversionary propaganda.

This is easily solved.

- Banks have had to verify the IDs of users online for more than a decade. That is why drug traffickers and other criminals can't use them freely. Even government online agencies do this. Zuck can figure this out for Facebook, too.

- In 1996, these online companies might not have had the resources or technology to police their own product. Now, however, six of the seven largest companies in the world are online tech companies. Bigger than any bank in the world. You will be relieved to know that they can afford to fix this problem, so no need to start a bake sale for Facebook or Google. Trust not in Google; we need reform to unmask trolls. Unmasking trolls will make for a kinder America where free speech is not punished.

Russia currently has carte blanche approval to spend money on Facebook campaigns for Republicans.

- Unmasking trolls will end Russia's ability to create such social media pages dedicated to diversionary propaganda.
- Under Trump, the Federal Elections Committee (FEC) refused to enforce the law or implement new policies even after it was discovered that the Russian government paid for online political ads in rubles. In defending their position, the FEC stated, "We are concerned about protecting First Amendment rights to participate in the political process."[11] The First Amendment doesn't apply to Russians, but what do I know?
- For this entire 2020 election cycle at the time of writing, the FEC has been unable to meet because President Trump left them with so many vacancies that they have no quorum![12] So no one can enforce any election law right now. I just had to mention that.
- Trump has so paralyzed the FEC from enforcing any election law that even the weak penalties that the United States could issue against foreign actors is nullified. This provides no incentive for Russia to stay out of politics, especially considering that Trump openly solicits their assistance, and Republicans make sure he is not punished for doing so.

Why Might Your Elected Democratic Representative Hesitate?

While this reform may seem trivial in comparison with some of the difficult tasks the Democrats have ahead, it is critical in the long run. Unmasking trolls helps prevent the further spread of diversionary propaganda and helps protect our elections and democracy. Would the NRA let liberal or foreign groups flood the American bullet market with fake bullets? No. They'd get Congress to ban fake bullets right quick. Surely, we can act to protect the First Amendment and democracy as well.

Solution #12: Pardons for Truth

The Trump administration and Republicans in government have committed brazen corruption, fraud, and abuse of power. But to date, there have been zero consequences for their corruption and lies. Those who have been prosecuted but remain loyal to Republicans are likely to receive a Trump pardon. The Mueller process of investigating Trump's constitutional violations behind closed doors failed to alert the American public to what was going on. Worse, the Mueller investigation's failure to educate the public emboldened Trump to double down on his corruption. Trump committed the high crime that got him impeached the *very next day* after Mueller testified to Congress regarding the non-confidential parts of his report. Then there's Trump family's buying of business favors using government foreign policy, tax evasion, campaign finance violations, the emoluments clause violations, bribery, witness tampering, and a whole host of other crime-family-level antics that have yet to be investigated. Or maybe they have been investigated but were suppressed by Trump's sycophants.

We need to bring out the truth behind Trump's lies and corruption in a transparent manner and hold people accountable. Democracy can be drowned by lies. By the time this book is published, President Trump himself will have committed over 20,000 lies.[13]

But it's not all Trump. The past ten years have seen the highest level of corruption to our political system than at any point in our nation's modern history. Hidden and illegal campaign contributions, voter suppression, gerrymandering, and collusion with Russia all predate Trump to varying degrees. The American public needs to be enlightened *and* confronted on the corruption that has taken place in the last decade. We need a much better process to openly investigate this. Secretive grand juries would be just as bad as sweeping it under the rug.

Solution #12 creates a Truth and Reconciliation Joint Committee composed of leading members of the House of Representatives and Senate. South Africa created such a commission at the end of apartheid. We must also create a committee to understand what the heck just happened this past decade in our state and federal governments.

There is no better process to uncover illegal activities and hold elected officials accountable than such a committee. Here's why: such a committee gives witnesses and those who committed the crimes an incredibly strong incentive to come forward. If Person A discloses all of the abuses and crimes that they committed or witnessed against our democracy in the past decade, then Congress recommends a presidential pardon. If someone else provides information about a crime that Person A was involved with, but Person A did not disclose that to the committee, then Person A may be prosecuted with that evidence.

Further, depending on the severity of the crime, in exchange for the presidential pardon, the witness must sign a plea agreement. The plea agreement prohibits them from engaging in politics, elections, government jobs, or contracting with or lobbying of the government. Perhaps it strips them of their power to vote—that could make it popular for Republicans. Meaning that they retire to private life, but they face no prison time or fines. The pardon would be taken away if other people's testimony or other investigations find that the witness did not admit to all the crimes in which they participated or had knowledge of.

The only exception for this "pardons for truth" deal should be for elected officials and their family members. There should be no pardons for anyone who was entrusted by the American people as an elected representative—or their family—who has committed abuses or crimes.

There should be a set period during which witnesses may confidentially inform the committee that they will be disclosing information. After that period, the public hearings begin. All of the disclosures will then be public, televised, and streamed. It can be reported on without spin by a better-funded PBS and NPR. Perhaps historian David McCullough and Ken Burns can be contracted to write and film the definitive version of it all. Finally, the committee should send a summary of its findings to every American voter. Get the popcorn ready, this will be must-see TV.

Talking Points: Create the Joint Truth/Reconciliation Committee

How to tell your elected representative or media why this fight is so crucial:

The GOP needs to be held publicly accountable for the sake of our democracy.

- When Trump clings to power through diversionary propaganda, there must be a response. Certainly, the citizen-run, citizen-owned reforms of NPR and PBS mentioned in Solution #10 aim at that. So too does unmasking trolls in Solution #11. But without pardons for truth, Republicans will literally get away with a decades-long attack on democracy. And that's unfair to…Republicans.
- A prodemocracy GOP is crucial for our country to move forward. The antidemocracy ideologies in the GOP, however, still control the party. If they are not held accountable, they will continue to control it. That puts the prodemocracy Republicans at a great disadvantage. Exposing the Republicans who attacked democracy and branding them with the truth is the only way to inspire regime change within the GOP. Honorable Republicans like the Lincoln Project. Mitt Romney and the "Republican Voters Against Trump" group are begging the Democrats to hold the GOP accountable. Will Democrats comply?
- Canada recently used a truth and reconciliation commission to understand the extent of its genocide and discrimination against its First Peoples. The United States has not ever used this despite having done worse to our Tribal Nations and having committed slavery for centuries. The attacks on democracy warrant such a commission and could lead to other such commissions in the future.

The committee witnesses will mostly be Republicans telling the truth about other Republicans.

- Pressure mounts to cooperate with the Truth and Reconciliation Committee every time someone commits to cooperate. Because if they reveal criminality—and are pardoned for it—but implicate you, then you are now subject to prosecution...unless you cooperate with the committee. So we will see dozens of Republican operatives, volunteers, and staff spilling their guts, knowing that the only path to a recommended pardon is through telling the truth to the committee. Imagine the line of Trump administration officials waiting to get a chance at a pardon for truth. Even Fox News would have a hard time spinning those Republican-admitted truth bombs.

- Let's see an example of how this works. Let's say Mitch McConnell ordered a trusted staff member to coordinate millions in illegal monetary contributions from Russia into American political campaigns. Let's say they laundered the money through the NRA. Perhaps a handful of people were involved, and the federal intelligence community has heard rumors of it. Without this committee, it's very unlikely Democrats will go after McConnell. It's very unlikely that anyone involved will suddenly blow the whistle. In other words, everyone will get away with the crime, and no one will be held accountable. Americans will never learn what happened. But if the people involved knew they would only receive a pardon if they came forward—and if they didn't come forward but someone else did, then they would be prosecuted—there's suddenly an irresistible incentive to disclose this information to the committee. If one of these direct witnesses were to publicly disclose this information, then the committee could refer McConnell to prosecution. Okay, now I'm getting excited. Such a public disclosure is much more difficult for Republicans to reject than if it were done behind closed doors in a grand jury by secret witnesses.

- For supporters of Trump, the Trump administration will finally have its day "in court." No one will block testimony of witnesses, no one will hold back "exonerating" documents or evidence. Republicans will even be on the committee. It will bring sunlight to a very dark and confusing time in American history.

Other democracies must understand the threats our democracy just survived.

- The Steve Bannon–Putin alliance of interests will not stop just because Trump is defeated in 2020. Bannon has already taken his noxious white nationalism to multiple countries. Putin obviously is operating in dozens of countries concurrently. Our allies have to see that the antidemocracy schemes of Bannon, the Koch network, and Putin's tactics can be exposed and defeated.

Why Might Your Elected Democratic Representative Hesitate?

There will be a (large) segment in the Democratic Party that just wants to move on from the Trump era. These are the same people who wanted to move on from the Bush era. They gave the Republican Party a pass on the two wars Bush started, despite the fact that we entered into them based on criminally doctored evidence. Likewise, no one was ever held accountable for the Great Recession that devastated our country in 2007. No branding, no blame, no education, no accountability, no jail time, and frankly the public was never informed of how it all went so wrong.

Once the Democrats ousted the incompetent Bush and team, Democrats naively thought that governing in a sane, bipartisan manner would defeat the Karl Rove/Rush Limbaugh/Fox News wing of the Republican Party. Of course, they were comically wrong. Instead we got Steve Bannon, Sean Hannity, Breitbart, and the Trumps. Allowing Republicans to escape accountability facilitated the GOP roaring back into power two years later and Trump six years after that. The one possibility of changing the hearts and minds of enough voters to encourage Republicans to reform themselves is an open and transparent investigation.

Some Democrats would want to make this a bipartisan effort. It's unclear if Republicans would participate. While you might think the GOP would be humbled by a 2020 loss, history suggests they will just be more vitriolic and militant. Would it even be possible to find Republicans to put on such a committee? Perhaps Elizabeth Warren and Mitt Romney or Alaska's Lisa Murkowski can be the Senate cochairs? Democrat Val Demings of Florida and Republican Jeff Van Drew of New Jersey in the House, or maybe a retiring member. Or maybe Democrats could bring in a few retired Republicans who are appalled at what has happened over the past decade but who are willing to represent the Republican Party.

One can easily picture Republican senator Lindsay Graham trying to prop up false criminal charges against the son of his former close friend, Joe

Biden. It's hard to imagine Democrats, however, investigating their fellow Republicans no matter how legitimate the investigation. The impeachment took place as quickly as it did in order to produce as little fuss as possible. Pelosi allowed the impeachment despite desperately not wanting to do it. Democrats would need to change their minds about their nonpolitical approach to the Republican Party. Democrats don't brand. The question is, can we at least get them to encourage the truth to be told?

Notes

1. "Lesley Stahl: Trump Admitted Mission to 'Discredit' Press." CBS News, 23 May 2018, www.cbsnews.com /news/lesley-stahl-donald-trump-said-attacking-press-to-discredit-negative-stories/.

2. Nellie Andreeva, "Cable Ratings 2019: Fox News Tops Total Viewers, ESPN Wins 18-49 Demo As Entertainment Networks Slide," *Deadline*, 27 Dec. 2019, deadline.com/2019/12/cable -ratings-2019-list-fox-news-total-viewers-espn-18-49-demo-1202817561/.

3. "Founders Online: From Thomas Jefferson to James Currie, 28 January 1786." National Archives and Records Administration, founders.archives.gov/documents/Jefferson/01-09-02-0209.

4. REI, by the way, is ten times larger than NPR. "Recreational Equipment, Inc.," Wikipedia, 3 Apr. 2020, en.wikipedia.org/wiki/Recreational_Equipment,_Inc.

5. "Don't Blame the Election on Fake News. Blame It on the Media," *Columbia Journalism Review*, www .cjr.org/analysis/fake-news-media-election-trump.php.

6. "Poll: Voters Split on Trump's Handling of Coronavirus Outbreak," *Politico*, 15 March 2020, www .politico.com/news/2020/03/15/poll-voters-coronavirus-outbreak-130033.

7. Justine Coleman, "Trump Questions Why NPR Exists after Pompeo Clashes with Reporter," *The Hill*, 26 Jan 2020, https://thehill.com/homenews/administration/479977 -trump-questions-why-npr-exists-after-pompeo-clashes-with-reporter

8. Alex Clark, "Breitbart's Boyle: Our Goal Is the 'Elimination of the Entire Mainstream Media,'" *Breitbart*, 19 Jul 2017, https://www.breitbart.com/the-media/2017/07/19/breitbarts -boyle-goal-elimination-entire-mainstream-media/.

9. Sean Illing, "'Flood the Zone with Shit': How Misinformation Overwhelmed Our Democracy," *Vox*, 16 Jan. 2020, www.vox.com/policy-and-politics/2020/1/16/20991816/impeachment -trial-trump-bannon-misinformation.

10. Other signatories: Secretary of Defense Mark Esper, Acting Secretary of Homeland Security Kevin McAleenan, Acting Director of National Intelligence Joseph Maguire, FBI Director Christopher Wray, U.S. Cyber Command Commander and NSA Director Gen. Paul Nakasone, and CISA Director Christopher Krebs.

11. Ann Ravel et al., "How the FEC Turned a Blind Eye to Foreign Meddling," *Politico*, 18 Sept. 2017, www.politico.com/magazine/story/2017/09/18/fec-foreign-meddling-russia-facebook-215619.

12. Maggie Miller, "FEC Commissioner Resigns, Leaving Agency without a Quorum Again," *The Hill*, 26 June 2020, thehill.com/policy/cybersecurity/504767-fec-commissioner-resigns-leaving-agency -without-a-quorum-again.

13. "Tracking All of President Trump's False or Misleading Claims," *Washington Post*, 4 Apr. 2020, www .washingtonpost.com/graphics/politics/trump-claims-database/?itid=lk_inline_manual_2.

CHAPTER 10

Plan B: Balance of Power Party

> If a consistent partisan majority ever united to take control of the government, it would use its power to oppress the minority. The fragile consent of the governed would break down, and violence and authoritarianism would follow. This was how previous republics had fallen into civil wars, and the Framers were intent on learning from history, not repeating its mistakes.... The future of American democracy depends on heeding the warning of the past. The country must break the binary hyper-partisanship so at odds with its governing institutions, and so dangerous for self-governance. It must become a multiparty democracy.
>
> —Lee Drutman, author of *Breaking the Two-Party Doom Loop*[1]

What if the 2020 election does not deliver the trifecta for Democrats? What if the Democrats don't take the Senate in 2020? Or—Armageddon levels of panic here—what if Trump and the Republicans maintain control of both the White House and the Senate again?

Deep breath.

If Biden wins but the Democrats don't retake the Senate, McConnell as majority leader wrecks the new president, blocks judicial nominations, and ensures the House flips to the Republicans in 2022 and the White House in 2024 to Donald Trump Jr. If Trump is re-elected and McConnell stays as the majority leader, those two will finish packing the courts, continue to disgrace the country, and all but invite Putin to control the levers of our campaigns.

My #DemRevPlan has a Plan B in case either of these happen. Plan B creates a balance of power party—a.k.a. the "Moderate Party," "American Centrists," or the "Checks and Balances Party." For now, let's call it the "Common Sense Party."

Here's how this lever can move the entire world of American politics. The Common Sense Party will be a party of four to six senators. They will immediately have more power than either the Democratic or Republican parties in the Senate—because neither the Republicans or the Democrats will be able to pass legislation without the four to six votes of the Common Sense Party.

This is how it happens: Mitt Romney, Lisa Murkowski, and maybe one other Republican join with an equal number of moderate-to-conservative Democrats in the Senate, leave their parties, and form the Common Sense Party.

They will then hold all the power in the Senate.

The Common Sense Party makes Romney or Murkowski the senate majority leader by adding the Common Sense Party's four to six votes to the remaining forty-seven or so Democratic senators' votes. This makes Romney (or Murkowski) the second most powerful person in government. The Common Sense Party appoints their members to lead the committees and then appoints an equal number of Democrats and Republicans to fill out the committees. Accordingly, the Common Sense Party will hold the balance of power and be the decisive vote on *every* committee. They can decide—on any issue—with which party they will align. Sometimes they will have a coalition with Democrats and sometimes a coalition with Republicans.

Or the Common Sense Party can recruit one of the two other parties to legislation originating from the Common Sense Party. Common Sense makes sure the best ideas and policies of both parties are implemented. Common Sense is immune to any of the normal tribalistic allegiances currently found in Democrat and Republican parties. Maybe they'll even be able to cobble together coalitions that are half-Democrat half-Republican. Doubtful, but it doesn't really matter. Common Sense wins every vote. Every time. On any issue.

Maybe Mike Bloomberg pledges a fraction of his wealth—or just three months' income—to support the new party. Surely, he would invest another billion to create a veto on Trump or to take away McConnell's veto on the next Democratic president. Perhaps it's a different billionaire. Considering that the #DemRevPlan would be put on hold if Trump or McConnell stay in power, big-money billionaires can provide the funding for this overnight without the Citizens United vouchers from Solution #4 screwing it up for the super-rich.

As Common Sense governs with the best ideas from the left and the right, the voters will follow. It won't just be four or six senators, but there will be millions of voters flocking to this party. Or not. It doesn't really matter. It's set up to stop Trump and stop McConnell and buy a little more time for our democracy until I can write a sequel to this book. Spare me that nightmare, please.

In exchange for this role the new party will play, Democrats agree not to run any candidates against the initial Senate members of the Common Sense Party. In the states with Common Sense senators (that does sound like an oxymoron, no?), the Common Sense incumbent would only face a Republican challenger. With this electoral map division, the Common Sense Party and their candidate have a good shot at winning, considering Democrats, disaffected Republicans, and newly found fans of this party will all potentially vote for them.

Who might join? For the Democrats: Manchin [D-WV], Tester [D-MT], Jones [D-AL] (if he survives 2020), Peters [D-MI], and Sinema [D-AZ] are all on the moderate side and are from moderate or conservative states. For Republicans, Romney [R-UT], Sasse [R-NE], Portman [R-OH], Murkowski [R-AK], or Collins [R-ME] might join, though Collins will hopefully be out of the Senate after 2020.

If the Republicans only have fifty-one senators but Biden wins, Romney could do this on his own with the Democratic vice president breaking the tie. But surely Lisa Murkowski would join him—Trump has already very publicly tweeted that he will be opposing her in her 2022 primary. So what does she have to lose? Most of those senators listed are currently back-benchers with no power or authority in the Senate or in their own caucus, relatively speaking. Joining the Common Sense Party immediately makes them the premier power brokers in Washington, DC.

Once in power, the Common Sense Party may decide that some of these #DemRevPlan solutions work for their new party and implement them as part of the price they extract from Democrats. Or maybe they just implement them because they're common-sense reforms and good for democracy.

But at the end, just having a third party with power in the United States will help save democracy. No longer will one party be able to dismantle democracy so that they can stay in power without the popular will. It would take two parties to do this, and such an antidemocracy coalition is a lot harder to put together.

Note

1.   Lee Drutman, "America Is Now the Divided Republic the Framers Feared," The Atlantic, 2 Jan. 2020, www.theatlantic.com/ideas/archive/2020/01/two-party-system-broke-constitution/604213/.

CHAPTER 11

Understand What You Must Do in 2020-2021
Since It's Up to You to Save Democracy

The problem with the progressives and liberals right now is that they are still treating this situation like we are in a state of normalcy...We have got to mobilize...When this nation was built out of my city, Philadelphia, the odds were simple. They win or they hang. And now it's simple again. We win or we lose American democracy. We lose it forever, and I don't think we'll come back from autocracy.

—Malcolm Nance, career intelligence and counterterrorism officer for the United States government

What is it worth to you to live in a country that has no Trump as president? One in which Democrats can govern, if that's what the majority wants? Where compassion and science are respected, and all people have more opportunities? Where our freedoms aren't trampled on by rich, old white conservative men like Mitch McConnell?

How much are you willing to work for a future where our country is united in addressing important issues like curing cancer, Alzheimer's, or COVID-19; where people have access to clean air, food, and water; where discrimination and racism are not tolerated; where health care is available to all and schools are well funded; and where problems are solved and we have a feeling that we are all in this together?

All of this is possible. In fact, it's kind of crazy that we don't have this. Let's get our act together, people. You see, like suckers, we let the super-rich change tax law through their control of Congress so they could concentrate wealth and power into their own hands. Many nonrich Americans were misled to favor these changes, starting in the 1980s. Branding by the Republicans strikes again! This created problems, as this book has identified. Fortunately, I have provided the solutions to those problems in the previous four chapters of this book. What we are missing, however, is the most important part of the solution: you.

Democracy requires participation, otherwise it just devolves into an oligarchy.

There is no massive organization funded by billionaires supporting this movement, just a lot of volunteer hours. When writing this book, sometimes it felt like it was just me at a coffeehouse, headphones on, drinking black coffee and wondering if I was doing enough.

The great asset we all have in 2020 is that we are more connected than ever, so we never have to go it alone. When George Floyd was murdered, we all saw it, we felt it, and hundreds of thousands marched in the streets, all over the world, within days of the murder. The GOP's 4 Weapons Against Democracy are not as visible—thanks to Democrats' failures—as that tragedy. Nevertheless, these 4 Weapons block the oxygen that democracy gives to us all just as surely as that criminal blocked Mr. Floyd from breathing.

Building a movement for a democracy revival is what we owe to every activist, protestor, soldier, agitator, and patriot that has ever fought for democracy and against the concentration of wealth and power in our world. The great thing about movements is that it only takes the few to open the eyes of the many and force change.

- The antiracism protestors in June 2020 have already set in motion dozens of reforms throughout the country.
- The Occupy movement, with just a few thousand protestors, forced many Democrats to reassess their coziness with Wall Street.
- Only 14% of voters were strong supporters of the Tea Party at its height in 2011.[1] Yet those 14% dominated the GOP for three election cycles.

- The minority LGBTQ community forced Democrats—and the country—to accept marriage equality even though Obama was not for it during the first term of his presidency.
- Fearless African Americans in the south in the 1960s forced Democrats and Republicans to embrace civil rights.
- Women activists forced Democrats to protect choice and end all-male presidential tickets.
- And don't forget the improbable movement of the people to elect Obama and (almost) Bernie Sanders, neither of whom were likely figures to gain massive support so quickly.

None of these were a product of Democratic Party leadership. Indeed, most were opposed or ignored by those Democratic leaders. But the grassroots forced bold priorities onto the Democrats, and the Democrats—to their credit—changed.

So now you have three options. Option 1: Don't do anything. You read the book (though that counts for something!), and you hope that others will take care of this whole democracy-in-crisis problem. Option 2: You say heck no, we won't be the last generation to experience free and fair elections in the United States of America. You go through the organizing plan below and begin to build the movement. Option 3: You do Option 2 *and* you become a leader in the movement. That's right, you have a sneaking suspicion you could just do great things if given the chance. Well, here it is—your chance. The not-for-profit, Common Sense Democracy, responsible for this book is volunteer powered and ready to accept your leadership skills. Tell us what you can do and become an official leader on our team. Find us at CommonSenseDem.org

> Unfortunately, the last year has shown that we need to fight for our democracy. "Freedom is not free" is a pithy phrase that usually refers to the sacrifices of our military against external threats. It turns out that the same slogan can be applied to challenges which are closer to home.
>
> —Marie Yovanovitch, ambassador fired by Trump[2]

Organizing Plan

The rest of this chapter outlines the different goals for each of the five phases of our organizing plan, and how to explore your assets, build your team, and pick your targets. The appendices have additional organizing tips.

Phase 1: Before the November 3, 2020, election
Phase 2: November 3, 2020, Election Day!
Phase 3: November 5, 2020–January 16, 2021
Phase 4: January 17–January 23, 2021: Inauguration Week/Democracy Revival Camp
Phase 5: January 24, 2021–April 30, 2021: First one hundred days of Biden's administration

Phase 1: Before the November 3, 2020, Election

The uncertainty is almost paralyzing! Will Trump win again? Will McConnell continue controlling the Senate? Will there be strife on Election Day or in the aftermath? On the day I am writing this, Election Day is in five months. At this point, it appears that Biden will beat Trump handily. A big enough win will render the Republicans' voter suppression efforts useless; Trump's cry of a "rigged election" will be drowned out in the celebrations; Putin will be impotent; and even the gun-toting militias will have no reason to terrorize anyone.

Of course, by the time you read this, the election is probably looking a lot closer. You might not share the confidence that I am enjoying in early June 2020.

So let's get to work.

A healthy turnout will swing the election to the Democrats. Alternatively, with enough voter suppression and blocking absentee voting, Republicans will maintain their ill-gotten control of government.

Goals for Phase 1: Primary: Turn out the vote for 11/3/20. Secondary: Build capacity for the #DemRevPlan.

Primary Goal: Turnout. We start with your network and assets, focusing on those in certain groups and/or in certain states.

Key Voter Groups: Trump is losing to Biden among these voter groups:[3]

1. African Americans by 78%
2. [Your friends by 60%+ (that's just a guess)]
3. Latinos by 36%
4. Asians by 28%
5. Under the age of thirty by 24%
6. Women by 19%

Key States: These are the key states that will decide the White House and the Senate and/or have critical state houses up for grabs: Arizona, Florida, Georgia, Iowa, Michigan, North Carolina, Pennsylvania, Texas, and Wisconsin.

Your Assets: Tier 1 Targets. If you know people in the six key voter groups above who are also in any of the nine key states above, these are your Tier 1 targets. Think of it like this: you are a safety captain. There are now some very unsafe conditions in our democracy. You are responsible for organizing the people in your list to take safety precautions: (a) register to vote now; (b) request a vote-at-home, a.k.a. absentee or mail-in, ballot immediately; (c) send in the vote-at-home ballot early, at least ten days before the election; and (d) volunteer to save democracy.

Your organizing steps for our primary goal to increase turnout:

1. To keep track of your Tier 1 targets, use our "Team Member Survey" tool at CommonSenseDem.org/organize or create a spreadsheet. Also see "My Network" under the Teams and Assets Tips in appendix 1.
2. Start filling in the information of your Tier 1 targets into our survey tool or in the spreadsheet you created. See "Teams and Assets Tips" in appendix 1 to help broaden your targets. This is your work from now until Election Day. If you don't have enough people in those nine key states, then you can either go after people in the other forty-one states

or join an allies program. See appendix 2 for "Allies Program Tips." Not sure what to say to people? Check the "Scripts Tips" in appendix 3.

3. Keep following up with people until you have a yes that they requested an absentee ballot and a yes that they already voted. See "Allies Program Tips" in appendix 2 to help your list vote-at-home targets.

4. Consider being a poll worker for this election. Republicans plan an unprecedented 50,000-person vote challenger operation in fifteen states to slow voting down on November 3, 2020.[4] This militia of vote suppressors needs to be met by DemRevvers supporting the logistics of voting. Call your county clerk or registrar office *now* to find out how you can serve as a poll worker. Don't forget your face mask. Alternatively, Democratic groups are organizing poll watch observers to make sure the GOP vote challengers don't steal the election. More on our website at: CommonSenseDem.org/election.

5. In all of your communications about the election, remind people to ask for a vote-at-home ballot *early* and send in their completed ballot ASAP. Remind them to fill everything out, sign carefully, and use a stamp. Inform your targets that over 10% of vote-at-home ballots are illegally thrown out each election because of minor errors. So they need to be careful! If you are making public posts, always add our #DemRevPlan hashtag and our book title.

Secondary Goal: Building #DemRevPlan Capacity. Most Democrat officials and candidates will be focused exclusively on Election Day 2020. Despite this, it is still important to push them on reviving democracy through the #DemRevPlan. So for every hour you might work to get the vote out, add fifteen minutes to get the #DemRevPlan out.

Your organizing steps to the secondary goal to Build #DemRevPlan Capacity:

1. Leave a review of the book on Amazon. That really does help.

2. Post our #DemRevPlan hashtag onto every item you post or tweet in social media between now and the end of Phase 5. See "Scripts Tips" in appendix 3 for ideas on how to best do this.

3. Are you part of any prodemocracy groups on Facebook like Indivisible, Swing Left, Our Revolution or any other Bernie groups, Democratic clubs, MoveOn, or League of Women Voters? Talk about the #DemRevPlan there every few days or so, especially if you can link it to a current issue or story and use our hashtag #DemRevPlan. See "Scripts Tips" in appendix 3 for ideas on how to do this.

4. You or any group you belong to can partner with us in getting the word out on this book. Our nonprofit, Common Sense Democracy (CSD), is all volunteer. No one at CSD earns any money from our revenue or donations. Contact us at partners@commonsensedem.org to make this happen for any group with which you are affiliated. We will share 50% of profits on book sales with any prodemocracy group partner.

Watch for: Be on the lookout for any opportunity to get this book in front of any elected Democrat, especially any in Congress—or their staff members. Give us their names and we will send them a copy of this book, gratis. Best if you have a copy of this book with you in case you suddenly find yourself adjacent to a Democratic candidate—like, say, Joe Biden. Slip it to them, and we will replace your copy. Practice your downward-inflecting late-night FM DJ voice and tell them that this book will help them save our democracy. Note that when candidates or elected officials—like the president—are at an event but are unreachable, they always have aides. Ask around until someone can point you out to the unassuming, eager-to-please aide. Then give them a copy of the book, get their phone number, and tell them you want to meet to talk about this soon. Feel free to share what magic words you plan to use on our Facebook.com/CommonSenseDem page!

> Those who profess to favor freedom, yet deprecate agitation, are men who want crops without plowing up the ground. They want rain without thunder and lightning. They want the ocean without the awful roar of its many waters. This struggle may be a moral one; or it may be a physical one; or it may be both moral and physical; but it must be a struggle. Power concedes nothing without a demand. It never did and it never will.
>
> —Frederick Douglass[5]

Phase 2: November 3, 2020, Election Day OMG!

Goal: Turnout. Today is all about turnout. You should still have the list that you created above while organizing to increase turnout, and at least every single person you know in those nine states has voted. Maybe you are serving as a poll worker. Or maybe you are volunteering with Democrats to make sure that the Republicans' vote challengers aren't making it too hellish on voters on Election Day. Alternatively, look at the Allies Programs Tips in appendix 2 for more volunteer options for Election Day.

Watch for: Voting. I once ran a Los Angeles County–wide campaign and was so busy on Election Day that I didn't have time to vote. Please don't tell anyone that, and more importantly, don't make my mistake. Besides, voting absentee at ten days before the election is the safest way to vote this election!

Phase 3: November 5, 2020, to January 17, 2021

Goals for Phase 3: Primary: Congressional buy-in for the plan. Secondary: Get Democrats in Congress to cosponsor the #DemRevPlan; build support for the #DemRevPlan; build awareness of the #DemRevPlan; mobilize for Democracy Revival Camp.

Are you okay? I ask because you must have partied very hard last night celebrating Trump being trounced, Democrats winning back the Senate, and Nancy Pelosi remaining as speaker. It might take weeks (and lawsuits) for many races to be officially called. I know I won't be able to sleep that night (or the night before the election for that matter). Oh, the sweet relief of winning. Revel in it. High-five strangers—using appropriate social distance—frame the *New York Times* front page, make up with any estranged family members, eat an edible, take a bike ride, get a massage, laugh, cry, and shout!

You get one day.

The day after the "November 4 National Holiday Celebration, Party, and Gratitude Day"—November 5, 2020—is the key moment for the #DemRevPlan. That's the day to continue to push forward and do your part to save democracy. Otherwise, you run the risk of being infected by the Democratic Party's tendency to push a fake "Reset Button." The Reset Button symbolizes the Democrats happy thoughts that their opponents will finally behave and that everything will be okay now.[6]

Don't make me remind you that the Koch network won't be giving up. Nor will Steve Bannon, or Donald Trump Jr., or their friend Vladimir Putin. Fox News won't be prodemocracy all of a sudden, nor will the Mercer or DeVos families. Billions of dollars are being readied to undermine the new president and take back the House and Senate in 2022 for the GOP. Remember, Democrats are demons in their eyes, and Biden is a usurper who only gets four years. Republican states will gerrymander voters to hell, voter suppression tactics will make voting a puzzle to solve and...well, you know the rest. Just wanted to make sure you do not let any Democratic friends forget or engage in any unwarranted triumphalism or naïve Resets.

Primary Goal of Phase 3: Get Democrats in Congress to cosponsor the #DemRevPlan. *What not to do*: phone calls, letters, and emails to Congress members. (Though, see the "Teams and Assets" section in appendix 1 on "How to Make What Doesn't Work, Work.") Sorry. It would be great if we could have a vibrant democracy simply by sending out an email or reposting a tweet or signing an online petition. It sure would make things easier for the tens of thousands of youth in Hong Kong currently protesting for their basic rights. Heck, I guess even Thomas Jefferson tried to send the equivalent of an email to King George III. Subject: Declaration of Independence. Apparently, the king claimed he didn't see it—darn spam filter—and the whole war was just a misunderstanding. At least that's how they teach it in England.

We have to do more. It's time for a road trip. Yeah, road trip! We simply don't get the same amount of road trip invites as we used to—especially in COVID-19 times. No one wants to see us anymore. (I am assuming it's not just me.) Accordingly, I am happy to give you this invite. You are welcome. Get some snacks, bring your cell phone charger, wear your mask, take your hand sanitizer, and bring some lozenges just in case you end up yelling a lot. You never know.

Where are we going? To find some Democratic members of Congress in their native habitat: their offices. It's your choice whether you are going to travel to the great state of the Douglass Commonwealth (DC) or to the local field office closest to your home. Or whether you push for a virtual Zoom meeting. See "Meeting Congressional Democrats" in appendix 4 on the failproof steps to get your meeting with your member of Congress.

I might not have room for you in my car for this road trip, so I suggest you carpool with friends. As you will see in the "Meeting Congressional Democrats" section in appendix 4, it's much better if you have a few fellow prodemocracy folks with you for this meeting.

A quick note: if you only have Republican members of Congress (house members and senators), then go down a rung. County supervisor? State senator? State assembly? City council? School board? If there are simply no Democrats, then I gotta ask you to run for something. Jeez. Or just hit us up for other volunteer opportunities at volunteers@CommonSenseDem. org. Or just keep reading.

All of the secondary goals in Phase 3 are to build capacity for the primary goal of getting Democrats to cosponsor the #DemRevPlan. If you have your group of people to meet with your local Democratic congressperson, you are all set. If you need to recruit more volunteers to support the #DemRevPlan, read on.

Your organizing steps to build support for the #DemRevPlan: Because of the inspiring Black Lives Matter protests of early June 2020 (while this is being written), people are understanding that there is a lot of pent-up frustration in the United States. It's not just about blue-on-Black violence, it's a whole host of terrible policies creating generational inequities and structural racism that are undermining the social fabric of our country. This is a time for activism and bold change. So not only has there never been a greater need for the #DemRevPlan, there have never been as many people open to push for it and politicians scared enough to embrace it. So let's look at three ways to build support for the #DemRevPlan.

1.   Hosting DemRev Parties: These can be at your house, house of worship, the local VFW club, parks and recreation space, the donated office space of a friend or supporter, or via Zoom or other virtual meeting space. These are fun. You put the invite out to your friends and the people you have uncovered on your "Teams and Assets" from Phase 1. If you

have any friends who are active in politics or political organizations, don't forget to invite them. They come over (or log on). Your goal is six people—more than that is gravy. You have salsa and chips. Get this book out. Find an article or two on a topical issue that relates back to the issues of this book. Have a reading from the book (a favorite passage or something relevant to the other articles you have clipped). Then go around the room and ask your guests to share the issue that is most important to them and how it connects to the GOP's 4 Weapons Against Democracy and/or the #DemRevPlan solutions. Then, it's a push to make progress on the agenda. See "Hosting DemRev Parties Tips" in appendix 6 for more information on the agenda of the parties.

2. City or County Support for the Reforms: Next is to get your local Democratic city council or other governing body to pass a proclamation in support of the #DemRevPlan. Find your most progressive member—or the one with the reputation for being most active on issues—and let her know Common Sense Democracy will be sending her a copy of the book. (Make sure you tell us so we can send it out.) Schedule a meeting with her (see "Meeting Congressional Democrats" in appendix 4 for tips on getting meetings with elected officials). For big cities, you might have to work through staff. Get the chief of staff or scheduler on the phone, then get us the address to send them a copy of the book. For most cities, there is no staff, and the council person is extremely accessible. For that reason, if you invite them to your DemRev party and tell them you will have at least five friends there, they will likely show up. We have a sample city proclamation at CommonSenseDem.org/Proclamation ready for their submission. This is an oddly easy step. Cities are constantly making proclamations in support of one thing or another. There will not likely be any controversy on the #DemRevPlan during Phase 3 because it simply will not be well-known enough. I guess that is the good news and the bad news. But what you're doing is making it known, so march on! Please keep us updated on your efforts. As you get your local council, board, or even individual elected official(s) to support the #DemRevPlan, let your team, your local Congress member, your local newspaper, and all of us know.

3. Newspaper and Social Media: Getting your local newspaper editorial board to endorse the #DemRevPlan will likely be harder than getting

your Democratic city council to support it. Because, contrary to the diversionary propaganda of the claim of #fakenews, most newspapers are controlled by conservative media conglomerates. So if your newspaper endorsed Romney in 2012 or Trump, don't even bother. The newspaper website should have the contact information for the publisher, editor, or opinion writers or instructions on how to write your own letter. In our "Scripts Tips" section in appendix 3, we offer ideas on how to approach these folks. Most papers have editorials, opinions, and letters to the editor. What's the difference? Editorials are the official voice from the paper—usually a group of leaders of the paper plus the publisher. The next rung down is an opinion piece from a member of the editorial board who could not get the backing of the publisher. Or it can be a local resident who has a relationship with the publisher or editor and is allowed to write occasional opinion pieces. Focus on someone who has advocated for issues that need the #DemRevPlan passed in order to accomplish their goals. You can certainly write a letter to the editor but trying to get an editorial or opinion piece first is best. See "Scripts Tips" in appendix 3 for ideas on this.

Your organizing steps to build awareness of the #DemRevPlan: Got a favorite podcast? Are you a member or host of a Facebook group? Subscribe to a particular YouTube channel? These are all great forums that always need content, guests, or new ideas to explore. Do a favor for these hosts by introducing them to *Last Chance to Save American Democracy* and the #DemRevPlan. You may not know this, but these folks dream of getting communications from their audience. As a former podcaster and YouTube content creator, I can tell you there is nothing we want more than to hear from our fans. (Well, I guess wanting to have fans in the first place is the higher desire.)

Most of these people provide their email or at least Instagram or Twitter handle. At other times, you just have to leave comments under that episode or on the iTunes pages (if it's a podcast), the Facebook group page, or the YouTube episode page. If you go that route, make sure you tag their name, usually just by putting @ before their full name, no space. Use our hashtag #DemRevPlan. Feel free to use the ideas from "Scripts Tips" in appendix 3 to contact them.

Spreading the message from our social media: CommonSenseDem.org has a whole set of TikTok, Instagram, YouTube, and Facebook videos on the #DemRevPlan. It's called DemRevU. On Instagram, TikTok, and YouTube look for DemRevU; on Facebook look for CommonSenseDem. Sharing these videos and posts is a good way to build awareness—but please always include a sentence or two about why this is important to you! And use our hashtag #DemRevPlan.

Sharing on Facebook is best done by creating a group aimed at your member of Congress. Then you invite your friends, family, and all others you are in contact with, obviously including anyone who you made sure voted. Our goal is for each Democrat in Congress to have one Facebook group created by DemRevvers like you. If you can't find the Facebook group for your Democratic congressperson, create your own. It's free. Thanks, Zuck. But please follow this naming protocol: the name should be LastChance-[last name of Democratic member of Congress]. So for my congress members, it would be facebook.com/LastChance-Bass (for representative Karen Bass), LastChance-Harris (for senator Kamala Harris), and LastChance-Feinstein (for senator Diane Feinstein). If any Democrats have the same last name, just add the district number after their last name. See CommonSenseDem. org/organize for more information on how to do this and whom to invite to join. We also have Instagram, TikTok, and other social media tips there.

Mobilize for Democracy Revival Camp: Remember that road trip at the beginning of Phase 3? Let's call that a trial run. The real road trip is inauguration week. It involves camping, making lots of new friends, getting out of your comfort zone, and being part of history. This will be one of the stories you pass down to your grandchildren or at least talk about for the rest of your life. Phase 4 will be camp time. There's a tips section in appendix 5 to give you more ideas. It's just something we need to do, a box to check off our to-do list. Perhaps even an item on our bucket list.

Here's the preview for Phase 4: We are going to get some attention from our Democratic friends. Camp involves walking to our congressperson's office every day and asking for a meeting. It involves finding anyone with a microphone or camera and explaining why #DemRevPlan is important to you. It involves educating other activists about what the #DemRevPlan is and inviting them to camp out as well. The camps will be in DC and at the local office in the forty-four states (as of summer 2020) that have Democrats in Congress.

So one important Phase 3 activity is trying to get your team together for Democracy Revival Camp. Aim for six people, and welcome as many as you can find. Look at both the Teams and Assets Tips and Democracy Revival Camp Tips sections in appendices 1 and 5 for help on this.

Watch for: connections. Your friends, family, and new DemRevvers may have a way to get the word out about this book and the #DemRevPlan. Someone, somewhere knows the people who curate Oprah's "Favorite Things" list, am I right? Or maybe more importantly, they may know Democrats in Congress or their staff. Always ask that extra question about who they know. You may be the person who activates the person who gets us the final vote we need to pass the #DemRevPlan. Or *you* might be that person.

> The point of protest is to raise public awareness, to put a spotlight on injustice, and to make the powers that be uncomfortable;... it's only in response to protest that the political system has even paid attention to marginalized communities. But eventually, aspirations have to be translated into specific laws and institutional practices.
>
> —Barack Obama[7]

Phase 4: January 18 to January 22, 2021: Democracy Revival Camp

Time for camp! Our goal is to force Democrats to meet or have video calls with us so that we can ask them to cosponsor the #DemRevPlan. It sure would be nice if Congress could have votes on a few of the #DemRevPlan priorities during camp. While we pursue these goals, we are likely to have a very fun and lively camp time. There are some highly creative, hypercharged fun folk who should guide the camp to meaning, action, and delight. Expect music, theater, songs, marches, knocking on the doors of the capitol, you know, usual camp stuff. This should work for everyone from eighteen-year-olds to eighty-year-olds.

The work of lobbying and pressuring our Democratic reps during Phase 3 will hopefully yield us a sponsor or two hundred for the legislation. They can then get actual bills written. There will be more Democracy Revival Camp resources and assistance on CommonSenseDem.org/camp.

Will this turn into an Occupy Wall Street or Occupy DC situation? Will it be as lively as the Black Lives Matter protests? The Occupy movement of 2011 came after the GOP swept back into power in 2010, taking the House and a whole bunch of states. BLM came as Trump continued to extend his authoritarian grip on US institutions. It was no surprise that both police and some protestors resorted to violence during these marches. Inauguration Week 2021 should be a party. Democrats are likely to order the authorities to stand down and not to escalate the protests. Regardless, wear your mask!

The stakes, however, are higher than the Occupy or even the BLM protests. It's been ten years since Occupy, and everything is worse. The super-rich control more. Republicans have almost become the permanent government, except for brief respites. Republicans will never allow the policies we need to end mass incarceration, discrimination and racism toward Black Americans. What both movements need more than anything is more democracy. To all the activists who are tired of fighting Trump for four years and who thought they won on November 3, 2020: our next battle is here—and it's the mother of all battles.

Phase 5: January 23, 2021, to April 30, 2021: First One Hundred Days

By now, the new president has been sworn in. There are a thousand issues and people competing for his attention. Racial injustices will continue to demand attention and change, as will the pandemic. The economy ain't too grand. Climate change and fires are worse. Russia is as aggressive as ever, disrupting democracies and making its presence felt in international affairs. A new round of gerrymandering is about to happen when the census count is released. Millions of dollars are already being spent attacking any hint of Medicare for All, an estate tax or a wealth tax, and so on.

Where to start? Don't worry. I know you now know the answer to this. But our poor friends in the Democratic caucus do not know. They are confused while being pulled in many directions. They are getting conflicting messages from every constituency that supports Democrats. They are hearing ominous warnings from those who oppose Democrats. They are reacting out of fear and forever attracted to shiny objects. They are desirous of riding the wave of outrage on whatever is the current issue covered by the corporate media. As always, they are being tripped up by the challenges that we explored in chapter 5 that Democrats inevitably experience.

But the first hundred days after the January 20 inauguration is our best shot to get the #DemRevPlan passed. Many of the strategies and tactics spelled out in the phases above and in the appendices will continue through this period. Directly lobbying your Democratic members of Congress is the most important step we should be taking in Phase 5. Don't give up until you have had face- or Zoom time with them. After that, you can continue to spread awareness and build support.

Lobbying them during Phase 5 might be the easiest task of all. They will likely have passed a whole bunch of neato policies in the House just to see them stall in the Senate. If they manage to get through the Senate, then well-funded billionaires will have already begun the litigation to get injunctions and eventually the laws ruled unconstitutional by the Republican-appointed Supreme Court justices. You should have a receptive group of frustrated Democratic officials when you ask them to cosponsor the #DemRevPlan.

Notes

1. Lydia Saad, "Tea Party Sparks More Antipathy Than Passion," Gallup, August 10, 2011, news.gallup .com/poll/148940/tea-party-sparks-antipathy-passion.aspx.

2. Melissa Quinn, "Yovanovitch Says Trump Administration Has 'Undermined Our Democratic Institutions.'" CBS News, 6 Feb. 2020, www.cbsnews.com/news/marie-yovanovitch-trump -administration-undermine-democratic-institutions/.

3. This is as of early June 2020. Now you see why Republicans have targeted these groups—other than white women—for voter suppression.

4. Michael Wines, "Freed by Court Ruling, Republicans Step Up Effort to Patrol Voting," *New York Times*, 18 May 2020, www.nytimes.com/2020/05/18/us/Voting-republicans-trump.html.

5. Frederick Douglass, "If There Is No Struggle, There Is No Progress," Black Past, 8 Aug. 2019, www.blackpast .org/african-american-history/1857-frederick-douglass-if-there-no-struggle-there-no-progress/.

6. Taylor, Adam. "The Failure of the U.S.-Russia Reset in 9 Photos." *The Washington Post*, WP Company, 18 Mar. 2014, www.washingtonpost.com/news/worldviews/wp/2014/03/17/the-failure-of -the-u-s-russia-reset-in-9-photos/.

7. Barack Obama, "How to Make This Moment the Turning Point for Real Change," *Medium*, 1 June 2020, medium.com/@BarackObama/how-to-make-this-moment-the-turning-point -for-real-change-9fa209806067.

APPENDICES

APPENDIX 1

Teams and Assets Tips

Updated each week at CommonSenseDem.org/organize
To be used during Phases 1 and 3-5

You have assets and connections that will help revive democracy in America. I guarantee it. If you live in a big blue city, it might seem like the potential allies are limitless even if you don't think you are connected to any of them. In a small red town, it might feel like you are by yourself. You are not. Here are three steps to create your assets map which will show you have more connections—and targets—than you would think.

1. Your Network

The first step is to identify the people you already know or the groups you can target. We normally put these in a spreadsheet, but if you are fancy, you can use Customer Relationship Management (CRM) software like Salesforce. CommonSenseDem.org/organize has a Team Member Survey tool you can use as well. Your network will include:

- All the people you know who might vote against Trump or vote for democracy
- Your wedding, holiday, or birthday cards/email lists
- Your social media connections, even if it is just an email or text group
- Cell phone contacts list or old-fashioned address book where you have the names and contact information of people you know

Remember, if it is still the Phase 1 time period (before November 3, 2020), you are taking your network and running them through the Phase 1 tasks, such as registering to vote as an absentee and sending in their ballot at least ten days early. Bonus points for those in your network that are in the key voter groups or key states (see Phase 1 in chapter 11 for this list).

You can go past your own network and recruit voters from your community. Here are some groups and locations where you can find—or advertise for—potential DemRevvers:

- Political, activist, and community benefit groups—there's probably even a lefty group if you search hard enough
- Colleges and universities and their student activist groups
- Facebook groups or meetup.com groups operating around you
- Teachers or nurses or other unions working nearby

Lots of different ideas can be found appendix 3 in the Scripts Tips for what to say when making contact with any of the groups or when using the methods above. A good first word: Hi! Next sentence: "So Trump sucks, but there is even a bigger battle happening right now..."

2. Information to Obtain

The second step is to find out what connections, skills, gifts, and resources your network or your community assets have. We usually do this through a survey. Go to CommonSenseDem.org/organize for our Team Member Survey tool. Note this survey tool is combined with your Phase 1 tasks in chapter 11. Alternatively, you can make your own. Relevant questions are:

- Name
- Cell phone #
- Email
- Facebook, Instagram, Twitter accounts
- Registered to vote as an absentee?
- Already voted?
- Part of which voter group targets?
- Potential volunteer?

- Confirmed volunteer? If so, continue:
  - o Do you or someone you know have any connections with any elected Democrats? If so, who?
  - o Do you have any connections with any political or other community groups (like Swing Left, Indivisible, MoveOn, political Facebook groups, or ethnic, youth, or women's groups)? If so which?
  - o Do you have a sizable following in social media? How big and on which platform?
  - o What skills or resources do you have related to getting a message out to a wider public?
  - o Who do you know that could help get our message out to a wider public or to Democratic officials?

If you are making your own spreadsheet or survey, then your next step is to copy that spreadsheet into nine new tabs, naming each one for one of the nine key states from Phase 1 (also listed below) and then a tenth tab for the other forty-one less important states.

Key States: Arizona, Florida, Georgia, Iowa, Michigan, North Carolina, Pennsylvania, Texas, Wisconsin

Key Voter Groups: African Americans, Your Friends, Latinos, Asians, Under the Age of 30, and Women.

3. The Right Approach

The third step is just having the right mindset. You are not asking anyone for favors. As you recruit people to your teams, remember: you are doing them a favor. You are giving them an opportunity to be part of the movement to save democracy. They probably missed the civil rights movement of the 1960s, didn't fight Nazis in World War II, definitely missed the suffragette movement, and missed the war to end slavery and the one to get rid of that obnoxious English king. It would suck for them if they missed out on this—just like it would suck for all of us if we lost democracy. So don't be selfish. Who are you to decide for someone that they would not want to be part of this historic campaign to revive democracy? Best of all, they can do it in the time it would take to watch one mediocre Netflix miniseries.

The heart of recruiting team members is to have conversations, not texts or emails. Real talk where you are vulnerable about how agitated you are with the Republican regime we've suffered under this past decade. Then get them to open up about how they feel things are going and really deeply listen to their distress or frustration or even cynicism. That two-way share opens a world of possibilities:

- What can we do about it? (Join our volunteer team.)
- How can this be solved? (Get the #DemRevPlan passed into law.)
- What steps can I take right now? (Depends on the date or phase right now.)

Meanwhile, keep track of your team members and volunteers (and their assets) by using the "Team Member Survey" tool at CommonSenseDem. org/organize or your own spreadsheet. If you have a Facebook group (See Phase 3 in chapter 11), you will be able to share messages more easily with your team and really facilitate the conversations.

How to Make What Doesn't Work, Work

Calling, mailing, or emailing your representative doesn't work on an issue like this. To illustrate, Senator Feinstein reported receiving 35,000–210,000 contacts per week, including emails, calls, and letters.[1] So more emails, calls, and petitions are just noise. Letters are just more junk as well, but if you want to write a letter, make sure it is noticed. I'd recommend writing it on giant kraft paper. Use wide markers and large print. Get a few different people to sign it. I would recommend doing this only if your request for a meeting has been ignored. Try it and let me know how it goes. Don't put glitter on it, though, or we will be cursed for the next week by everyone in the office who can't get the microplastics off of their skin.

Posting on Twitter, Facebook, TikTok, et cetera, will not get the attention of your congressperson in 99% of the cases. What it can do is to help others refocus. As folks complain about some stupid Trump tweet, some crisis, or some dumb Republican policy or statement, use something like this: "Great point! But we need to start focusing #Democrats & @____ (handle of your local congressperson) or @JoeBiden on saving our democracy. I hope you support #DemRevPlan from the *Last Chance to Save American Democracy* book."

Note

1.   "Congressional Offices Are Overwhelmed by Constituent Calls and Lawmakers Are Changing to Handle the Influx." WRAL, 17 Apr. 2020, www.wral.com/congressional-offices-are-overwhelmed -by-constituent-calls-and-lawmakers-are-changing-to-handle-the-influx/19060682/?version=amp.

APPENDIX 2

Allies Programs Tips

Updated each week at CommonSenseDem.org/organize
To be used during Phases 1-2

I f it is still Phase 1 or 2 (before or on Election Day 2020):

- Use iwillvote.com to help your network check to see if they are registered to vote, and if not, to register. This should help them to vote as absentees: votefwd.org.
- Has everyone in your network voted, and you are looking for additional volunteer opportunities?
  - Target voters in key states to help defeat vulnerable Republican senators: paybackproject.org
  - Want to send postcards to Democrat voters in important races to remind them to vote? Then text JOIN to the Democratic Party at 484-275-2229
  - Want to send letters to key voting group voters in key states to remind them to register to vote as absentees? Go to votefwd.org.
  - Other great groups for Phase 1:
    - whenweallvote.org
    - rockthevote.org

Remember, all your communications about the election should remind people to ask for a vote-at-home or absentee ballot *early* and send in their completed ballot ASAP. Remind them to fill everything out, sign carefully, and use a stamp.

APPENDIX 3

Scripts Tips

Updated each week at CommonSenseDem.org/organize
To be used during Phases 1 and 3-5

First things first: legal stuff. I hereby give you permission in line with the Creative Commons license to use anything from this book as long as you mention the source (our book title), use "#DemRevPlan," and tag your Democratic congressperson.

This tips sheet has some ideas on things you can write or say. You will be in conversations (verbal or written) with people who are concerned about other issues, not just the state of our democracy: pandemics, racism, global climate change, et cetera. We need to help them understand how to successfully move forward with their issues.

Syllogism Time

Here is the syllogism to help them understand the connection between their issues and this issue of reviving democracy:

1. Our problems are mostly due to poor policy. We need a democracy revival so that the interests of the super-rich don't block better policies.
2. In order to have a democracy revival, we need to (a) win the November 2020 election and oust Republicans from government and then (b) force Democrats to pass the #DemRevPlan.
3. Then we can fix the problems that are plaguing us by having a majority elected that understands the need for better policy.

If you get that, deep down, then you really don't need any Script Tips. Nevertheless, I wrote them, so I will share anyway.

Voter Turnout

As you approach potential voters in your network to try to get them to vote, let them know you've read the *Last Chance to Save American Democracy* book. Go ahead and talk about the book for a few hours if you must! (Or am I the only one that does that?) Tell them that you are worried about more than just Trump. You want a democracy revival, and to get that we need to vote Republicans out on November 3, 2020. You are contacting them to make sure they do their part. You also want to make sure that they:

- Don't get sick: Don't let them waste time in voting lines, which would expose them and other people to sick people, so vote at home.
- Don't get cheated: Tell them to get their absentee ballot early, send it with a stamp ASAP, and be extremely careful when filling it out and particularly when signing it so that it is counted.

You can then tell them you are conducting a little survey and ask them what the most important issue is facing our country is right now. Whatever their answer is, you know that the syllogism above is a great response. As you help make them aware of this, provide them with the life-changing opportunity to volunteer to help save our democracy.

Volunteer Recruitment

Once people understand what you are doing, they're probably gonna be a little impressed that you are doing this. Of course, if they are Fox News fans, they will think you are a total nutter. But for all others, people will see that you are taking our current crises seriously and are willing to do something about it. You are also giving them a chance to get involved because so many people just simply don't know how to do so. Once you note that they are in the slightest way concerned about our democracy, that's when you ask them to commit to making sure *their* network votes. If we can raise voting levels to three out of every five US citizens in this election, Democrats win big.

Once you get people "volunteer curious," what you recruit them for will depend on what phase we are at. Reading this book is not a prerequisite to volunteer, though you can certainly encourage them to do so to get a deep understanding of today's political crisis. The first step is to do the "Team Member Survey" tool with them at CommonSenseDem.org/organize or onto the spreadsheet you created (see "My Network" under the Teams and Assets Tips above). Then match them to the priorities of our current phase.

Cheat sheet on the best volunteer opportunities in each phase:

Phase 1: Increasing voter turnout of their Tier 1 targets through November 3, 2020
Phase 2: Being a poll worker or Democratic Party poll observer on November 3, 2020
Phase 3: Joining you for meeting with your Democratic rep from November 5, 2020–January 17, 2021
Phase 4: Bringing the s'mores to the Democracy Revival Camp from January 18–22, 2021
Phase 5: Getting Democratic cosponsors for #DemRevPlan from January 23–April 30, 2021

If they have read the book, more opportunities as a DemRevver open up for them.

Connecting Political Issues Scripts

That syllogism above pretty much works for any issue. So you can comment on almost any issue on Facebook, Twitter, TikTok, YouTube, et cetera, or in letters to the editors in newspapers using that argument chain. Examples:

Let's try racism: Mobilizing the army to suppress protestors angry over the systemic problems of racism is another failed Republican policy response. The real solution is to have a democracy revival so we can have leaders pass effective policies that most Americans want. First, we need to throw Republicans out in November. Then we force Democrats to focus on reviving our democracy by passing the #DemRevPlan. This enables us to address racism effectively, not with heavily armed soldiers or police.

Let's try pandemics: The Republican approach to COVID-19 was a disaster. To get out of this mess, we need a democracy revival so that GOP re-election concerns aren't driving our policy responses. First, we throw out Republicans in November. Then we force Democrats to focus on reviving our democracy by passing the #DemRevPlan. This enables us to heal this current pandemic, prepare us for the next one, and help rebuild an economy for all of us, not just the super-rich.

Let's try climate change: The Republican approach of doing nothing to reverse climate change will lead to the unnecessary deaths of millions of people each year. In order to get a better approach, we need a democracy revival so that big oil can't stop reform. First, we throw out Republicans in November. Then we force Democrats to focus on reviving our democracy by passing the #DemRevPlan. This enables us to actually focus on problems and not let profit motives of big corporations tie up Congress and doom the Earth.

Holidays

Heck, we even have a message for holidays:

- Thanksgiving: Give thanks that we live in a democracy and then work to save it.
- Christmas: The Christmas spirit is about giving back, and it's time we give back to our democracy. (BTW, I've heard this book makes a meaningful Christmas gift, much better than pajamas.)
- New Year: Want to start the new year off right? Volunteer to revive democracy; be a hero.

Letters to the Editor

If you're unable to get the local newspaper to do an editorial or opinion piece supporting #DemRevPlan, then try a letter to the editor. Most newspapers allow online or email submissions but will have a maximum word count. Make sure you mention the member(s) of Congress for your area and the #DemRevPlan. A sample 125-word letter might look a little like this:

> Once Trump is out of office, Congressperson _____ will have many fires to put out. But the first thing our new Congress and president must fix is our democracy. I would like to know whether Congressperson ___ will prioritize democracy and cosponsor the #DemRevPlan legislation from the book *Last Chance to Save American Democracy*. Anything less than a democracy revival will be extremely disappointing for those of us who have suffered ten years of GOP control of Congress or the White House. We need an end to gerrymandering, voter suppression, unlimited dark money, and diversionary propaganda. We sent Congressperson _____ to DC to fix this. We look forward to hearing from them on what they are planning to do.

If you are more than just your average bear, you might be able to get an op-ed published. You usually need to have some expertise in the subject, standing in the community, or unique angle. If you think you do, then go for it! You can write a much longer piece (typically 500–800 words) as an op-ed. Again, feel free to copy *anything* you see in this book in line with the Creative Commons license—just mention the book title, mention #DemRevPlan, and tag your congressperson.

Podcasters et al.

Focus on political podcasters, Facebook groups, or YouTube channels (or Instagram, TikTok, etc.) with which you are familiar. Here are the three levels of approaches you can use when contacting them. My recommendation is to start at level 1 and a few days later move to level 2, then level 3 a week after that.

- Level 1: Find an episode, video, or post that is somehow connected to the topic of this book or the #DemRevPlan. Your message to the creator/sharer of that content would go something like this:

  Thank you for the episode/video/post on _____. Have you read the new book *Last Chance to Save American Democracy*? I think you should try to cover this book as soon as possible. It lays out a very convincing argument that Democrats will need a set of specific solutions called the #DemRevPlan to revive our democracy. Until that is passed, there will not be meaningful progress on any other issue.

- Level 2: "Have you thought about interviewing the author on his new book *Last Chance to Save American Democracy*? I think we listeners would love to hear you guys talk about what the most important policies are that should be passed in the first hundred days of the next administration in order to revive our democracy."

- Level 3: "Would you consider doing a podcast/video/Facebook live with Common Sense Democracy during their Democracy Revival Camp in mid-January 2021? They are trying to rally prodemocracy citizens to pressure Democrats to save our democracy in the first hundred days of the next administration. Their #DemRevPlan is in the new book *Last Chance to Save American Democracy*."

APPENDIX 4

Meeting Congressional Democrats Tips

Updated each week at CommonSenseDem.org/organize
To be used during Phases 1, 3, and 5

Finding Your Democratic Congressional Representative in the Wild

E ven with COVID-19 in our midst, most house members and senators hold public events, whether virtual or in person: town halls, speaking engagements, meetings, and panels. They want you there! Democracy wants you there! Most Democratic congressional representatives post events or calendars with the details of their upcoming events on their .gov website. To stay updated and receive reminders about the events, take these three steps:

- Find out who your member of Congress is: govtrack.us.
- Sign up for their email newsletter.
- Follow them on social media.

If all else fails, call the local campaign office to ask about upcoming events. Then attend them. Bonus points for sending in your questions ahead of the events. Our advice on how to approach those public meetings is found in the "For the Meeting..." sections.

How to Score a Meeting with Your Democratic Congressional Representative

For most of us, it is much easier to go to the local office of our congressperson than to travel to the Douglass Commonwealth. Here's the first step you can take before a meeting in order to get the meeting. If you have not previously supported this Democrat with a campaign contribution, do so now. Donate one dollar to the congressperson's campaign. If you can't find it online, then just donate to DCCC.org (for the House) or DSCC.org (for the Senate). This makes you a "donor."

Sad but true: It is 6.5 times more likely that you will score a meeting with a member of congress if you self-identify as a donor instead of just a constituent.

If you don't want to donate to Democrats, then donate to us. If you donate twenty dollars, you are part of our "Major" category. Then you can call yourself a major political donor when you call the congressional office. Donate one dollar per day for a few days to them—or to Common Sense Democracy—and then you can say you are a frequent political donor.

The second step—as mentioned previously—is to recruit five or more friends to agree to go to the meeting with you. Now have them donate that one dollar as outlined above. If you are able to say you represent a group of six donors, the congressperson might even agree to have the meeting at your house and have their staff wash your car or babysit your kids as well.

Okay, that's unfair. I'm going to call myself on that one. It's all true, but I really do sympathize with elected officials—of all parties. They are forced to cater to donors just to survive. That's what we are trying to change. Believe me when I say that their lives will be meaningfully transformed if the #DemRevPlan is passed and they no longer have to spend all their time begging for money from nice-smelling rich people.

I recommend sending a letter or email first, then following up with a call two days later. If there is a staff directory, look for a scheduler or someone similar so you can have a direct email and/or phone number.

Sample Email or Letter:

SUBJECT: Meeting with **local campaign donors** about cosponsoring the #DemRevPlan

Dear [SCHEDULER or CHIEF OF STAFF NAME],

My name is ___. I work with a group of local political donors in your district. We would like to meet (or Zoom with) the congressperson as soon as possible. We are extremely concerned that the GOP's attacks on our democracy this past decade are not being addressed sufficiently. We want the congressperson to hear why we expect them to cosponsor the #DemRevPlan as found in the *Last Chance to Save American Democracy* book. This legislation reviving our democracy is needed if we are to recover from this pandemic, to heal racism, to reverse climate change, and more. Could we arrange such a meeting during the week of ___? Our members are looking for just twenty-five minutes to have their concerns and ideas heard. We are looking forward to hearing from you on what time might work well and who our members can expect to meet with. Thanking you in advance.

Signed,
J. Hancock

For the Meeting Online or by Phone

After telling the staff person that you and a group of frequent donors want to meet with the congressperson, refer to the email or letter you sent. When the staffer asks what you want to meet about, tell them you want to know what the congressperson is doing to revive our democracy and if they will cosponsor the #DemRevPlan. This is a key moment. If they do not know what the #DemRevPlan is, ask them if they have not yet read the book *Last Chance to Save American Democracy*. If they haven't, what the heck are they doing in a political job? Mercy. Don't ask that out loud. Or, I don't know, maybe a little shaming might work on them. Regardless, ask them if they need us to send it to them and ask them to promise that they will share it with the congressmember. Make sure you have their name and address. Feel free to share that with us—as well as the date and time of the meeting—by emailing us at moc@CommonSenseDem.org, and we will send them a copy of the book.

For the Meeting at Their Office

Oh, boy. I wish I could be at each and every meeting DemRevvers have with congressional folk. By now, you have a team recruited. If not, go back to the Teams and Assets Tips in appendix 1. Your volunteer group of DemRevvers might fall nicely into different roles: question askers, video recorders, media mouths, googlers, sign and T-shirt makers, et cetera. Regardless, the idea is that you want your member of Congress to make sure legislation on these matters is drafted, and if it already is, to cosponsor it. Easy-peasy.

First ask them: What do you think is the most important thing Congress should address in the first hundred days of the new president? Boo-yah. Want to see a politician sweat? That's the question to ask.

We know the correct answer: revive democracy! If they give you that answer, then you have found an ally! I would take the one-pagers at appendices 7 and 8 or our more directed "Congressional Cheat Sheet on the #DemRevPlan" from our website CommonSenseDem.org/organize to help you.

Can't Score a Meeting with Your Democratic Congressional Representative?

That's not acceptable. But fortunately, there's a way to turn that frown upside down. It's called the First Amendment. It tells us that in order to preserve democracy, we must exercise the power to peaceably assemble and petition our representatives to solve our grievances. That's a fancy way of saying: protest! With signs! (That's the petition part.) My recommendation: have fun, get creative. Literally google "creative protests" and look at the snazzy ideas waiting for DemRevvers. If you have any Dreamers, Occupy, antifa, or BLM members in your group, they will bring in plenty of mind-blowing ideas. Remind them that they will never make any progress on their issues unless the #DemRevPlan is implemented, so this is as much their battle as anyone else's. Reach out to them!

Here's what I am going to do. I will find a big Amazon box, a cut-up sheet, or other material at least three feet wide and two feet tall. Then, with some red, white, and blue paints or markers, I will vaguely (that's an appropriate word considering my Pictionary skill level) re-create the US flag. I will then write two things in black across it: "Pass #DemRevPlan So We Can…" and then I will add another #1 issue ("…Stop Racism," "…Save Mother Earth," etc.). So I might say "Pass #DemRevPlan So We Can Reverse Climate Change."

So you think you are more creative than me? I look forward to your posting the visuals you create on our Facebook page. You could even find a local artist, studio, or guitarist and see if they would be interested in joining the protest for democracy. They can bring the art, you can bring the snacks.

Give the media at least seventy-two hours' notice and send a few reminder follow-ups. If you have any local YouTube or podcast hosts, invite them as well. TV, radio, and newspapers are all likely to cover this, considering they are protests aimed at Democrats by Democrats. Inviting other groups to join in is always a great idea, but remember, your actual goal is to pressure this member of Congress into talking to you about the #DemRevPlan. There's really no other issue we can solve until the #DemRevPlan is implemented.

For the Meeting at a Town Hall or Zoom Public Forum

Definitely bring your lozenges and a smaller sign. On one side of the sign, write, "We Demand Better," in red, on the other side, "Thank You," in blue. You will use these based on whether you like—or don't—what is being said. This works for Zoom, too, in that you can put the sign up to the camera and have it fill your thumbnail on the congressperson's screen. This also makes a great visual for the media to take a picture of or screenshot.

So here's the #1 DemRevver rule for forums, town halls, and Zoom calls. They belong to you, not to the politicians. *They* may not know that. It is our one chance to really make politicians listen to us and to hold them accountable. Do not let them dominate the conversation. They should speak for two or three minutes, and then it's time for us to get antsy. I recommend shouting out, "We have questions," "Let us speak," and "Time's up." The more powerful the person is, the more you need to insist. Remember, their power is all derivative and borrowed. It's actually our power; we are just temporarily entrusting it to them.

A few more quick tips for online or in-person forums:

- Tell everyone you can that you want support at the event.
- Hold a prep meeting with your Volunteer Team.
- Go over the Congressional Cheat Sheet on the #DemRevPlan (at CommonSenseDem.org.organize) to decide which questions to ask and who will ask them.
- Let the media know you will be there. Tell them you are hoping to speak to them at the event and let them know how they will find you.

At the forum, the best strategy is to immediately stand at the microphone when the meeting begins. They may tell you, "We will let you know when to stand for questions. You can sit down now." You get to say: "Thanks, but I sit a lot anyway. I prefer to stand so I can ask my question." Now, if five or so friends join you at the microphone, you will see even the most seasoned politician start to get nervous and hurry up their remarks. That's a win for everyone!

Meanwhile, everyone should be flashing their red "We Demand Better" and blue "Thank You" signs, depending on what is being said.

Finally, get that cell phone out of your pocket, make sure you have it on record (don't be like me and always think I am recording but then realize I only started recording once I tried to stop the recording). Afterward, upload those videos and pictures to the "Last Chance" Facebook group for that member of Congress, as well as to the CommonSenseDem one and your own social feed, while tagging us.

What are the questions you should ask the congressperson? Find these on our website, commonsesnsedem.org/organize. These questions center mostly on how the member of Congress plans to fix anything if the Republicans can filibuster it, if the super-rich can target them with millions of dollars, and if the Supreme Court can swat it down like a fly. We also have a lot of suggestions on how to push the #DemRevPlan as the only reasonable answer to those questions. Other questions may be pretty direct, like, "Why haven't you publicly announced support for statehood for DC, Puerto Rico, and a state for all of the Native tribes?"

Regardless of how the congressperson may answer, the key is to ask the follow-up question. If they agree with our reforms, ask them what they are going to do to get them enacted. If you feel like they did not give you a direct answer, don't doubt yourself. You are probably correct. They are slippery like that. Pin them down for an answer. If they claim to not know of an issue or solution, ask if they will meet with you and other concerned citizens in this next week so they can become more educated. And ask them who on their staff you should contact.

APPENDIX 5

Democracy Revival Camp January 18-22, 2021, Tips

Updated each week at CommonSenseDem.org/organize
To be used during Phase 4

C ome to camp! It's free! Singing, dancing, eating, staying in a tent. Just note, it's bring-your-own songs/dance/food/tent.

Location: Washington, DC—maybe Upper Senate Park—and simultaneously in 285 or so of your local Democratic congress members' home offices.

This is where we really show our Democrats that we want democracy revived. And when do we want it? Now—or at least in the next one hundred days.

Camping out by Capitol Hill should be fun—and a tad cold. Wait, you don't camp? Most colonists did not make a practice of revolting against the British Empire—until they did. Most soldiers who fought against the fascists in World War II were not soldiers until they volunteered for the war. Most suffragists who got women the vote were not marchers until they first marched. But you may sponsor a hardier person if camping out is not your thing. Or you might consider staying with your favorite DC-based college friend or shacking up at a unionized hotel.

Yes, I've got three daughters at home with whom I would much rather spend time (oh, and my wife as well!). But the spirit of '76 has taken control of my fingers and—with each keystroke—is irrevocably committing me to this path. Great, now I've just booked the flight (under $100—amazing!). Well, it's only five days or so, I know I'll make some friends, and boy will I have some stories to tell! Will you join me? Please. I'll be the one wrapped in four giant parkas wondering why I didn't just camp out in the great state of sunny Southern California.

Check CommonSenseDem.com/Camp for the latest information on camp.

Watch for: Obviously Trump is never going to admit he lost the election. He wouldn't even admit he lost the popular vote by three million voters. If it's a landslide, then it mostly won't matter. Yes, there will be a group of voters who never accept Biden as their legitimate president. Those are people who will never, ever care about their fellow Americans, so fuggedaboutit. But if it is a close election, it's going to be a little crazy as we explored in Weapon 4, chapter 4. What are you ready to commit to if Trump and Republicans are that brazen in their attempts to steal the presidency? If that happens, I will not be using my return ticket from DC until Congress (or the military) rejects the coup. If you are in one of those states where Republicans are fooling around with the elector slates, get your protest boots on and start marching in your capital.

But it would be much easier to just win in a landslide so that not even Republicans answer Trump's tweets for a coup.

APPENDIX 6

Hosting DemRev Parties Tips

Updated each week at CommonSenseDem.org/organize
To be used during Phases 1, 3, and 5

I will keep this section short. For more information, please go to our website at CommonSenseDem.org/organize. A few party tips:

- Have copies of the #DemRevPlan one-pager and *Last Chance to Save American Democracy* one-pager, which can be found later in this appendix.
- Have a few books out for a $20 donation. Keep the extra money for future salsa and chips or other costs. If you need multiple books, contact us, and we will get them to you at cost.
- Have copies of an agenda available.
- Gotta have a singalong. Why? Because it will either go well and be great bonding, or it will be truly cringeworthy and be great bonding. Embrace the cheesiness. Just know your audience. Some folks prefer Joan Baez, others Kendrick Lamar, others Andy Grammer.

Sample Agenda

See Phase 3's secondary goals

1. Discussion—Let everyone know this takes twenty minutes *max*.
    a. Introductions—name, where from, what they do, what issue is most concerning them right now. Let everyone know: two minutes max each.

    b.   Host (or other selected person) reads a favorite or relevant passage from *Last Chance*.

    c.   Ask if anyone would like to discuss a current issue in the news this week and connect that issue with the #DemRevPlan solution(s).

    d.   Finally, go around the room and ask everyone to connect one of the issues they are most concerned about with the #DemRevPlan solution(s).

2.   Action—The actions depend on what phase we are in, which goes by dates (see chapter 11). Obviously, we always want to know who attendees have in their networks that can help push the #DemRevPlan. Here are some additional actions to take, depending on the phase:

    a.   Phase 1: Find the group of friends and voters who we each are tracking to make sure they obtain an absentee ballot and vote early; expand the Facebook group you have helped create for your member(s) of Congress.

    b.   Phase 2: Plan to be Democratic Party observers or poll worker.

    c.   Phase 3: Approach city council members to support #DemRevPlan; recruit for a meeting (or protest) at your local congressional office; recruit for DemRev Camp.

    d.   Phase 4: It's all about camp week, see appendix 5.

    e.   Phase 5: Plan to lobby members of Congress to cosponsor the #DemRevPlan and find more support for the #DemRevPlan.

APPENDIX 7

Last Chance to Save American Democracy One-Pager

1. The conflict in our society is between those who want to strengthen democracy versus those who want to accelerate the concentration of wealth and power into the hands of the elite.

2. After the Democrats' 2008 landslide, Republican elites feared they would become the permanent minority. In response, they implemented 4 Weapons Against Democracy: unlimited dark money, gerrymandering, voter suppression, and diversionary propaganda.

3. Through its 4 Weapons, the GOP has stayed in power in many states and even in the federal government despite consistently having fewer votes than Democrats.

4. Democratic leaders have failed to effectively sound the alarm against this Republican corruption and attacks on democracy.

5. Politicians treat our power to vote as a privilege they confer us instead of understanding they are the temporary caretakers of our power.

6. Trump's historic unpopularity will likely lead to Democrats regaining the White House and majorities in the Senate and House in the 2020 election. Democrats will then have a small window of opportunity to make the essential changes to save our democracy.

7. With the much-hated Trump no longer on the ballot after 2020, the GOP's 4 Weapons Against Democracy will reassert themselves, and they will become the permanent party in power beginning with the 2022–2024 election cycle unless Democrats pass the #DemRevPlan.

8. Democrats will not save our democracy unless we organize ourselves to force them to revive democracy in 2021 through the 12 Solutions of the #DemRevPlan. *Last Chance to Save American Democracy* lays out what each of us can do to save American democracy.

9. After the #DemRevPlan solutions are implemented in the first one hundred days of the new administration, we can then move our country forward on a whole host of important issues. But without these solutions, none of our issues will ever be addressed.

APPENDIX 8

#DemRevPlan One-Pager

1. **Fix the Filibuster** by implementing former Senator Harkin's proposed reform on Sunday, January 3, 2021.
2. **Fair Representation or No Taxation** for all Americans in the Senate and House to fairly apportion congressional representation.
3. **Court Reform, Not Court Packing** to undo McConnell's politicization of the court.
4. **Citizens United Vouchers** to counterbalance the narrow political speech currently limited to those with massive wealth.
5. **Instant Runoff+** and nonpartisan commissions to eliminate gerrymandering.
6. **Our Power, Our Vote** to stop our political servants' ability from suppressing our power to vote.
7. **A Representative Electoral College** that mandates the proportional election of electors.
8. **Citizen Dreamers** and Cooperating Victims of Crime welcomed into our citizen family.
9. **Clean Slate to Revitalize Unions**, our essential allies to revive democracy.
10. **Citizen-Run and Citizen-Owned Media** where Congress gives NPR/PBS a giant endowment and then transfers ownership to a nonprofit, member-owned co-op.
11. **Unmasking Trolls** to end the ability of bots, trolls, and Russia to attack our democracy by removing their anonymity.
12. **Pardons for Truth** creates a joint truth & reconciliation committee to publicly investigate corruption and crimes against democracy while recommending pardons and prosecutions.

APPENDIX 9

Republicans Will Fight a Democracy Revival in 2021 Using These Three Tactics

N ow that you have learned the 12 Solutions to the GOP's 4 Weapons Against Democracy, let's review how Republicans will attack these solutions.

Slapping a White Glove Across the Face, Republicans Accuse Democrats of Overreach

By accusing Democrats of "overreach," Republicans scare just enough Democrats to make passing legislation impossible. A recent example: Democrats tried to mandate hackerproof voting machines, Republicans cried "federal overreach," and Democrats backed off. "Lawmakers have, by and large, been hesitant to impose more restrictive standards on states out of fear that they'll be accused of federal overreach."[1] I can hear the Democrats now: "Not overreach, sir. Please, sir, accuse us of anything but that. Why, if my friends heard you say that, how could I go out into public? Indeed, I'd rather lose an election than be charged with overreach!" Okay, maybe that's not how Democrats in DC talk. But you have to admit, it is certainly how some act.

Perhaps Democrats think voters are somehow carefully keeping score. Or perhaps—to be fair—they are scared that conservative billionaires are keeping score. Fortunately, there's the only effective plan that can counterbalance the billions of those billionaires in part 3 of this book.

InfoWars' Alex Jones Finally Eats His Neighbors

If Democrats are serious about reform and reviving democracy, Fox News will howl that any reforms are a coup. Militias will march around in khakis,

the Ku Klux Klan will burn a few crosses and blame the Jews, Russian bots
will go into overdrive on Twitter and Facebook, your right-wing cousin
will repost memes of Biden as Hitler, and editorial boards of corporate-
controlled media will finger wag and maybe even utter mean, ominous
declarations in unison like some Sinclair Broadcasting version of *1984*.[2]
McConnell will denounce the next president for cheating, for not being
moderate, for having caved to Alexandra Ocasio-Cortez, representative from
New York, and her left-wing socialism. Hannity will have an on-air stroke.
The anchors of *Fox and Friends* will weep for the Constitution and claim
it is all a conspiracy to take away guns and increase abortions. InfoWars'
Alex Jones will finally eat his neighbors, as he has repeatedly threatened to
do whenever there are policies passed that he doesn't like.[3] They will use
words like "coup," "traitors," "communists," and "corrupt," and phrases like
"shredding the Constitution." They will cry for the days of bipartisanship
and cooperation and moderation. They may publicly wish the Democrats
would act more like Barack Obama and will definitely blame the She-VP.

Political pundits will issue dire predictions that Democrats will pay the
price in the next election; lobbyists will jump from their penthouse suites
onto the pavement below. And all the chicken heads in the political world
will go running for cover.

Republicans—once they are out of power—will say anything to stop
the expansion of actual democracy in our own democracy. That strategy
has proven effective against a large class of Democratic politicians. Those
politicians want so badly to be seen as levelheaded, reasonable, and moderate. They aspire to be called the grown-ups in the room. They especially do
not want to draw the ire of well-founded attack machines. Fortunately, the
#DemRevPlan will revive democracy and protect these would-be victims
of Fox News and the Koch network.

To sum this up, Republicans will just offer loud noise. Activists—and
you are now ready to be one if you have read this far!—can counter GOP
doublespeak by pressuring Democrats to follow their principles: fairness;
equal representation; one-person, one-vote; and democracy.

But really, Democrats just need to pass smart reforms. Quickly. If the
Democrats implement the #DemRevPlan in part 3 of this book, they will
actually, for the first time since the 1970s, be able to implement policy. Yes,
Democrats could govern instead of careening from one political fiasco to

the next. Once the Democratic Party actually does the job of governing, that changes the agenda. Fox News guests will now howl about pipelines being stopped, militias will focus on their weapon training when police reform is passed, and the corporate-controlled media can nitpick whatever health care plan is put forward.

In other words, once passed, the hullabaloo over the slate of reforms in this book called the #DemRevPlan will be short-lived. The media, the GOP, and the public will all move onto the next policy fight. And that's the point of the #DemRevPlan: to let parties pass the policies they think are good for a majority of America, not just good for their political benefactors.

Republicans Will Claim Democrats Are Shredding the Constitution

Full disclosure: I only got a B in Constitutional Law at the UCLA School of Law. It was my lowest grade during law school. I thought it was unfair. My grade suffered because of my final exam. The professor gave us ten important (but obscure) cases, and we had to predict the outcome of each and explain our rationale. I predicted all ten of the cases correctly but got a C- on the test. Prof didn't like my explanations; I simply counted the number of justices appointed by Democrats versus Republicans and showed that correlation had a 100% match to the case outcomes.

Twenty-six years later my predictive formula is truer than ever. When the Supreme Court picks which cases they want to accept, they have a motive to do so. That motive is 100% animated by their political philosophy even when they obscure it with legal terms like "originalism." There are almost zero important Supreme Court cases that are unanimous. Logically, that means our best legal minds in the country completely disagree about what the Constitution means, usually by a five to four count.

Get where I am going with this? Almost every single liberal policy is unconstitutional in the eyes of Republicans. The same is true for Democrats as well. Simply count which party has appointed the majority on the court, and that will tell you which party has the Constitution on their side—for now, at least. While Justice Roberts throws a bone to Democrats once in a while, it is simply to keep down the outrage that would animate the LGBTQ or Dreamers communities. Even Roberts understands that decisions against these groups so close to an election would boomerang back on Republican electoral chances.

Let's dig a little deeper. The conflict over almost any reform that would make our system more democratic is a conflict over the Tenth and Fourteenth Amendments to our Constitution. In sum, the Tenth Amendment gives the states the right to set policy over issues that are not specifically mentioned in the Constitution as being under federal jurisdiction. We often call this the States' Rights Amendment.

The Fourteenth Amendment, passed after the sin of slavery was ended, has in it (a) the blessed "Equal Protection of the Laws" language; (b) this doozy: "Representatives shall be apportioned among the several states according to their respective numbers;" and finally (c) this kick-ass bit: "Congress shall have power to enforce, by appropriate legislation, the provisions of this article."

Republicans often claim to love the Tenth Amendment (except when liberal states do things they don't like). Democrats—and our reforms in part 3—love the Fourteenth Amendment. Republicans will attack almost every solution presented here with Tenth Amendment arguments. Democrats will defend these reforms with Fourteenth Amendment arguments; i.e., Congress has the power to pass legislation to enforce the equal rights of all Americans and to make sure elected representatives are apportioned equitably by population.

Perhaps if I had mentioned that on my final exam, I would have gotten a higher grade. Please consider this my appeal.

How about precedent? Is that worth anything? Obviously, my C- analysis says no. Right-wing Supreme Court Justice Brett Kavanaugh agrees with me in a 2020 case: "Indeed, in just the last few terms, every current member of this court has voted to overrule multiple constitutional precedents."[4] The Supreme Court is just as political as Congress. Just ignore my ConLaw professor. He'd lose his job if everyone adopted my almost 100% accurate predictive formula for court decisions.

The Supreme Court Cannot Rule on Political Questions

Republican-appointed Supreme Court Chief Justice Roberts has held that issues like gerrymandering are political ones that the courts should avoid.[5]

If the people want things changed, they are to elect new representatives in Congress to make those changes, according to Roberts. He insists that political questions like voter suppression should not be left to the federal courts to be resolved. The #DemRevPlan pretty much fall under this political questions doctrine. Therefore, there should be no concern that the Supreme Court will overturn any of these reforms.

I wouldn't bet on that.

The Republicans on the Supreme Court will immediately reverse their reasoning once they are presented with policies that hurt their Republican team. Do not worry. As you now know, built into the reforms of the #DemRevPlan is a reform of the courts. It is most definitely not a court-packing scheme. But it will guarantee a Democratic majority for at least the period of 2021–2024. After 2024, the majority on the court will fluctuate basically based on which party controls the White House.

Notes

1.   Schulberg, Jessica. "Good News For Russia: 15 States Use Voting Machines That Have Been Easily Hackable For More Than A Decade." *HuffPost*, HuffPost, 17 July 2017, www.huffpost.com/entry/electronic-voting-machines-hack-russia_n_5967e1c2e4b03389bb162

2.   Fortin, Jacey, and Jonah Engel Bromwich. "Sinclair Made Dozens of Local News Anchors Recite the Same Script." The New York Times, The New York Times, 2 Apr. 2018, www.nytimes.com/2018/04/02/business/media/sinclair-news-anchors-script.html.

3.   Alex Jones Promises to Eat His Neighbors. Repeatedly. 1 May 2020, https://www.youtube.com/watch?v=rfZcKClcug8

4.   Greenhouse, Linda. "A Precedent Overturned Reveals a Supreme Court in Crisis." The New York Times, The New York Times, 23 Apr. 2020, www.nytimes.com/2020/04/23/opinion/supreme-court-precedent.html.

5.   Rucho v. Common Cause, No. 18-422, 588 U.S. (2019), Slip op. June 27, 2019, https://www.supremecourt.gov/opinions/18pdf/18-422_9ol1.pdf

APPENDIX 10

Republicans Brand Democrats Like a Cowboy Brands a Heifer; Democrats, Not So Much

Get ready. After the 2020 election, the Democrats may act like the horrors of Republican rule never even happened. We all saw that in 2008. It's up to you to keep the memory of this terrible 2010 decade alive. We do that by branding the Republicans. Democrats have never made a concerted effort to label Republican officials as dishonest, cruel, incompetent, antidemocratic or corrupt. Heck, Democrats never even mention the hypocrisy of Christian Republicans on such an obvious issue as immigration. According to the Gospel of Mathew (2:14–16), God made his only Son an illegal immigrant in Egypt when his family fled overnight to escape Herod's Massacre of the Innocents. So sayeth the scriptures. Time for Christians to read the entire New Testament, not just the passages supporting Fox News-thought.

Until they impeached the criminal Trump, Democrats—and the media—had done virtually nothing about the attacks on democracy outlined in this chapter. Other than waiting for Mueller, the Democrats have barely talked about these attacks until the very rushed impeachment hearings. Those hearings were rushed so as to not interfere with the 2020 elections. Democrats seem to think that slowly educating the public about Trump's misdeeds would have been *bad* for their party. That is, of course, the exact opposite strategy the Democrats successfully used during the impeachment of President Nixon.

No matter how much corruption the Republican Party is guilty of, how much hypocrisy, how many lies they are caught up in, Democrats have refused and failed to brand the GOP over the past fifty years.

I will resist the urge to go over the particulars of Watergate from the 1970s here. But some of you remember Iran-Contragate from the 1980s. That's when Republican President Reagan sold military weapons to the Ayatollah of Iran—our enemy who had held our embassy staff hostage for 444 days. He did this in exchange for Iran sending money to arm the Contras in Nicaragua to overthrow a democratically elected socialist Sandinista government. Reagan did this in violation of a law passed by Congress prohibiting the arming of the Contras, who were viewed as terrorists by the majority in Congress. The administration then covered it up, lied to Congress, and destroyed a mountain of evidence before it could be turned over to investigators. Eventually, the Secretary of Defense and thirteen other administration officials were indicted—and then pardoned by the Republican president. Then–attorney general William Barr (yes, Trump's attorney general was attorney general for Bush Sr.) supported the pardons. This scandal actually makes Trump's appear pretty tame. But the Democrats did not try to brand Republicans as dishonest during these lies and cover-ups.

Republican Newt Gingrich took over the House of Representatives in the 1990s. His new breed of Republicans passed the Contract with America (a.k.a. Contract on America), which slashed almost every social welfare program that existed. They then impeached Bill Clinton when he lied about that blow job. But the Democrats did not try to brand Republicans as the party of cruelty—or overreach.

Then, in the 2000s, Republicans Bush and Cheney lied to get us into the Iraq war after the 9/11 terror attack by Saudi Arabians, despite Iraq having nothing to do with that terrorist act. They claimed Saddam Hussein had weapons of mass destruction even though he did not. This contributed to the Great Recession of 2008 caused by George W. Bush's two wars and ridiculous tax cuts to the richest 1%. But the Democrats did not try to brand Republicans as the party of liars or incompetents.

In the 2010 decade, the Republicans were led by the Koch brothers, Mercer family, DeVos family, and Karl Rove's network. They flooded elections with unlimited campaign contributions. Gerrymandering. Voter suppression. You know the history now. But the Democrats did not try to brand Republicans as the party that worked to destroy democracy.

Now we've had three years of Trump and scandal after scandal, with Republicans protecting the president no matter what or getting fired if they refuse. But the Democrats do not try to brand Republicans as the party of corruption.

Despite the Republican's enduring playbook of corruption, Democrats have only sustained focus on Republican political corruption one time since Watergate. That was the impeachment of Trump due to his attempt to pressure the Ukrainian president to illegally help him in the 2020 election.

And what happened?

For the first time in three awful years of Trump, a majority of voters wanted him removed from office. Before impeachments started, that number stood under 30%. In just a few quick months, it went to over 50%. Do we need a political scientist to explain to Democratic leaders the basic formula? If a party sustains focus on an issue, the media covers it; if the media covers it, then the public becomes aware of it and will become concerned about it.

Democrats need to drive the messaging about Republican corruption and the need to fix democracy. We heard about Benghazi and Hillary's emails for four years and through six Republican investigations. Republican house leader Kevin McCarthy even admitted it was to hurt Clinton:

> Everybody thought Hillary Clinton was unbeatable, right? But we put together a Benghazi special committee, a select committee. What are her numbers today? Her numbers are dropping.
>
> —Kevin McCarthy[1]

In fact, an analysis after the election showed that the number-one issue covered during the entire campaign for president was Hillary's emails. Daaaaamn, why are Republicans so much better at this stuff than Democrats? Coverage of Trump focused on his stance on immigration and Mexico, among other items. There was comparatively less coverage about his sexual assaults. Trump drove his branding of Clinton and messaging forward. Democrats failed to do so against him.

Don't let them fail again.

Note

1.   Andrew Prokop, "A Top House Republican Was Accidentally Honest about the Benghazi Investigation," *Vox*, 30 Sep 2015, https://www.vox.com/2015/9/30/9423339/kevin-mccarthy-benghazi.

ABOUT THE AUTHOR

HAVEN SCOTT MCVARISH is a political strategist. This is his second book on building political movements. McVarish started his career as a community organizer, then worked as a union leader, including running a dozen political campaigns for the California Teachers Association and affiliates. He later worked as a small business owner, founding one of Los Angeles' most successful immigration law firms, the Immigration Law Office of Los Angeles as well as a worker-side employment non-profit Strong Advocate (StrongAdevocates.org). More recently, McVarish hosted the podcast "Your Daily Trump" and currently runs the nonprofit Common Sense Democracy (CommonSenseDem.org). He has a BA, JD, and master's degrees from UCLA and its School of Law and Department of Public Policy respectively. McVarish trained at a Liberation Theology Seminary in Central America for one year and has dabbled in stand-up comedy, though the two are unrelated. He lives in the great State of Southern California with his wife and three daughters, where he practices dad jokes and shooting TikTok videos.